ALSO BY ERNA FERGUSSON

◆

Dancing Gods

"The chief values of the book are its author's great knowledge of the dances and traditions of the Indians, and her wholly sympathetic feeling for them. . . . It is hard to imagine how her performance could be bettered, either as interpretation or as writing."

— *The Yale Review*

Fiesta in Mexico

"Miss Fergusson writes as entertainingly about her adventures in discovering the fiestas as she does about the fiestas themselves. These sketches have the true ring of Mexican travel. . . ."

— *The New York Times*

◆

THESE ARE BORZOI BOOKS, PUBLISHED BY

Alfred A. Knopf

Guatemala

Guatemala

by

ERNA FERGUSSON

New York · ALFRED · A · KNOPF · *London*

1938

I WISH TO ACKNOWLEDGE MY INDEBTEDNESS AND TO EX-
press my thanks to the friends who gave me the benefit of
their knowledge in certain fields touched upon in this book
and who read and criticized certain chapters. Aside from
those who are mentioned in the text I am grateful to Miss
Elizabeth Wallace, Professor Emeritus of the University of
Chicago, Chester Lloyd Jones, Professor of Economics of
the University of Wisconsin, Charles A. Thomson of the
Foreign Policy Association, Miss Mary Butler, archæologist of the University of Pennsylvania Museum, Karl Rup-
pert, archæologist of the Carnegie Institution, and Antonio
Goubaud Carrera of Guatemala.

For the use of their pictures I extend my thanks to Miss
Florence Dibbell Bartlett of Chicago, Miss Mary Butler of
Philadelphia, Morris E. Leeds of Philadelphia, and Webster McBryde of New Orleans, whose pictures were taken
under the auspices of the Social Science Research Council
of Tulane University, and of the Carnegie Institution.

Contents

Illustrations

Guatemala

I: Guatemala from Mexico

WHAT WOULD GUATEMALA BE LIKE — ESPECIALLY AFTER a couple of years in Mexico, traveling all over it, living in it, making such friends that it no longer seems a foreign country, but another home?

Tourists said that Guatemala was more fascinating than Mexico, more untouched and picturesque. Indians still wear native garb, markets are riotous with color every day and not only once a week.

" It is," a student said, " Mexico before the Revolution, still a dictatorship, still sharply divided into classes. Indian labor is mercilessly exploited. You should know it to understand Mexico better."

Understanding Mexico has come to be a real need. Somehow we of the north, the efficient, the mechanical and critical, must understand our southern neighbors better. We must get close enough to rub off, maybe, some of their instinctive knowledge of human relationships; of that adaptation to nature which gets a living out of land without destroying it; of how to know your pleasure when it is at hand. Above all, we must make them know us for friends and not dangerous imperialists. If only they knew how unimperialistic we feel, most of us!

3

There were warnings, too, about Guatemala. Mexicans said: " You won't find Guatemalans *simpáticos*. They are hard, and they hate Mexico. For them, we are the mighty grasping neighbor to the north. They fear Mexico as we fear the United States. And you, who are Mexican and Norte Americana too! "

I went to the Guatemalan consulate for a visa. Mindful of my Mexican manners, I rose when the gentleman was at liberty, extended my hand, murmured my name, " at his orders." He shook hands, but he was clearly not at my orders.

He fixed me with hard black eyes. " Why do you want to go to Guatemala? " I felt that he suspected me of designs on the portrait of Alvarado which hangs in the capital.

" To know it. I understand that your country is well worth a visit." But feeble joking was quite out of order.

" Come again," he said, " when you have four front-face pictures of yourself." And that was all. No parting handshake, no " to serve you."

But he had taken my name, and I was sure the Mexican police would be asked to scan their list of undesirables. Any writer is in a precarious position in Mexico. Write as enthusiastically as you will about the enchantments of that land, but if one word creeps in which might cast a shadow, you are considered to have blackened the fair name of Mexico. *Denigrante* is the word. We have no exact translation of its full implication. Probably we are so used to foreigners' criticism of our United States, even from Mexicans who lampoon, caricature, and defame us in word and picture, that we are too hardened to show resentment. But

I might have been guilty of the crime of blackening. It would be too bad, I thought, if the Mexican police could not in conscience recommend me to Guatemala. But when I went again, I found that Guatemala would admit me. It had been necessary to telegraph the capital for authorization: my first experience with that country's powerful centralization.

The minister dropped in as we finished the business: a cordial gentleman with a close-clipped white beard. He was glad I was going to Guatemala, made a courtly remark. Even the consul melted from his stern official manner.

Nobody advises going by train from Mexico to Guatemala, but it is an edifying approach, even in its vicissitudes. Overnight to the port of Veracruz it is, and a day and a night through that state and Oaxaca, getting warmer and more tropical every minute. Jungle grows always denser with mimosa, tamarinds, and palms. Big-leaved plants are tangled with ropy vines and orchideous plants. Parrots flying, blue and white herons in lagoons, and many queer plants that flower without leaves: casahuates, baganvia, and something with ash-rose flowers I could not learn the name of. It was pleasant to feel my skin slightly damp, to luxuriate in a temperature one did not have to fight against.

My train idled along, stopping at every flag station for another family with bundles. A Pullman is no place to travel, for all those families rode second class: the musically inclined were there; and venders offered their wares at day-coach windows, not at Pullman screens. While I was tendered eggs and ham on a white cloth, they could choose chicken in toothsome sauces, tamales in banana leaves, turnovers oozing richness, sugary cakes, melons and ices. What they could not eat, those travelers took along, piling baskets on crates and stringing to the racks their bunches of bananas, whole pineapples, jars of fresh cool drinks.

For a whole day we rode across the heavily timbered state of Chiapas, which has produced many a mahogany fortune. Life there looks easy from the train. As we waited on a bridge, I watched an old woman standing in the stream and rubbing clothes in a wooden tray. She ladled up water in a gourd, poured one over the clothes, the next over herself. The cool water must have felt good, splashing over her bare breasts and back. When someone came along, she squatted in the water, lit a cigar, and chatted awhile. Then she spread clothes on the grass, scooped, and treated herself to another douse from the gourd. I am told that these lives are meager and dreary, that Mexico must be industrialized. But compared with life in a factory town! I have read of machines equipped with a harness to snatch the hand back when the worker tires. Imagine the horror of a weary hand, jerked and jerked! As long as work must be done, I cannot grieve much over women washing, half-naked, in running streams, at their own time.

The Pan-American Highway, connecting Canada with Tierra del Fuego is to run through here, once they get the swamps drained and the terrain considerably remodeled. Pedro de Alvarado is credited with making the first road from Mexico to Guatemala in 1523 when he pushed his four hundred and fifty Spaniards through these miasmic bogs to the conquest of Guatemala. The Cakchiqueles, a Maya tribe, had offered to submit to Cortez in return for aid against their enemies, the Quichés; and Cortez sent his brilliant captain, Don Pedro, to bring them all under the ægis of Church and Crown. Alvarado was then just under forty, at the top of his powers, courageous, ruthless, an accomplished commander, and ambitious to achieve a conquest of his own. It would not be easy, for the Quichés, more mettlesome than the Cakchiqueles, were altogether opposed to foreign intervention. At Tonalá, Alvarado defeated his first Quichés and sent word to their kings — they always had two — that he would accept their submission to the King of Spain. Otherwise they would be treated as rebellious and disloyal. The Quichés were not yet ready to accept the Spanish assumption that all creation belonged, by right, to the Emperor Charles V and that all who denied it were to be suitably punished. Alvarado was to have his troubles with the Quichés.

At Tonalá I met difficulties too. We were too late to cross the border that night, but they told me so only after we had left Tonalá, and the last good hotel. The customs officer on the train described the hotel at Suchiate as *regular* — an ominous word that always means and is often followed by " *más malo que bueno* ": worse than better. The host, when he appeared, did not reassure me. Unkempt and taciturn, he stayed silent when the officer commended the Señorita to his best attention, calling on him to see and all the saints to witness that I should lack nothing. He was to be my last exuberantly friendly Mexican.

The hotel was an extensive board shack, open all around to catch the breeze, with chickens on the porches, pigs just outside, and a flock of Negroid girls shuffling around in pantofles and never getting anything done. The bath was a bamboo shed with wide cracks, a chair on a dais, and a big tank of water with a baby's pot floating in it. But the bath was refreshing, and a canvas cot is not bad in a hot country. One's standard comes to be solely that there shall be no bugs.

Suchiate is a sandy waste with no plaza; nothing but the railroad, the hotel, and an office where they gave me twenty-four quetzales for my eighty-eight Mexican pesos. I wondered how long I could survive in a country with currency on a par with ours. My host, who had consistently overcharged for everything, took me in his car to the river Suchiate, which divides Mexico and Guatemala.

There three men and one woman inspected my baggage. Guatemalans are delicate; a woman paws through a woman's things, but thoroughly! They all wished me well, exhibited an English phrase, and let me board the flat-boat. On the other bank a little fellow in blue dungarees nursed his rifle under a rustic arbor. He copied my name from the passport and said it was too late to pass. But we had a smoke together, agreed that it was pretty hot there in the sand, and he let me go on through a grove of fine almond trees to Ayutla, my first Guatemalan town.

"Now is not the hour. Too late."

"But may I not go to the hotel for lunch and come back?"

"Too late. Now is not the hour."

Then a man with a big stomach strolled up and ruled that the Señorita might go for lunch, leaving her baggage.

Ayutla looks like a barracks, with a wide shaded street

full of soldiers and police. At two, the hour, my bags were all opened again by a man and one woman, who was just as interested as the one on the other side. Seven men and two women, up to that point. But I was not through yet. The police still had to pass me, making a total of eight men and two women for getting a lone traveler across the frontier. Guatemalans say this border must be well guarded because all bad things come from Mexico, including grasshoppers and radical propaganda.

At five the next morning Ayutla was dark and sweet-smelling. As I dressed I heard palms scraping against a dull blue sky. Sand crinkled under the porter's cartwheels on the way to the station. Only a few people were stirring and I was the only passenger. As day came, the country showed itself. We ran close to the Pacific, which lies south of Guatemala. Honduras is east, and Mexico north. Guatemala touches the Caribbean only where it runs into a point at Puerto Barrios. Sometimes we could see the shoreline; sometimes only lagoons where waterfowl rested. Many clear streams cut the plain. We passed bamboo-walled villages tufted with coconut and date palms. Coffee plantations, shaded by bananas, shaded in turn by taller, white-barked trees, which bear a fruit also edible. I never saw so much food in any landscape. The cattle were stout, and the cheese they gave me at Ayutla was of the finest, flaky, delicate. Corn shows, but it is not the prevailing crop. An infinity of fruits whose names run like water: anona, chirimoya, mandarinas, limes and sweet limes, papaya, zapotes, big and little, yellow and green. At every house, turkeys and chickens; pigs for scavenging, and buzzards to help. No

wonder the dominant race says the Indian fares well on
ten cents a day or less. Everything that grows produces
food, it seems.

All small children were naked. One, fair as a magazine-
cover child, came running toward the train. She had long,
soft, golden hair, and her skin was lightly browned, with no
trace of Indian blood — no overlay of rich brown, no
straight coarse hair: a pure white baby running naked
among mahogany playmates. Near by was a frame house
with wooden lace trim, a shingled roof, and green shutters,
boarded up. I wish I knew what white woman bore that
pearly child and left her. Did she die? Did the man die too?
And what Indian woman keeps the little body and fair
hair so clean now?

Inland towered the volcanoes, a regular rampart of volcanoes, taller and taller. Tacaná and Tajumulco, and Santa
María, which have literally leapt and flamed twelve and
fourteen thousand feet into the air, making fabulously
fertile soil with their volcanic ash and providing every
sort of climate. There can be no generalizations about
Guatemala. The narrow fringe of sea level is sultry tropics
with monkeys, parrots, and alligators; iguanas served as a
delicacy; and endemic diseases like yellow fever, which has
been conquered; hookworm, which may be; and malaria,
which gets them all sooner or later. That is below two thousand feet. From four to six thousand is the perpetual spring
they advertise. It makes for marvelous days, and evenings
a bit chilly. Above that, it is frankly cold at night, though
the sun still does service by day. Little larger than the state
of New York, Guatemala must be thought of as extending

not lengthwise and across, but up and down. From Retalhuleu on the coast to Quetzaltenango in the highlands, the
road rises almost seven thousand feet in thirty-five miles.
Behind those volcanoes, I knew, lay the highland Guatemala I was so eager to see.

Alvarado knew that too, and that there he had to conquer
those intransigent Quiché kings, who had sent an army to
meet him at the river Somalá. The Spaniards, whose horses
and cannon were still news in Quiché, won that brush also
and entered upon a swift one-hundred-day campaign in
which they conquered the three kingdoms. Among those
dauntless invaders was Doña Luisa, whose father, the
Tlaxcalan chief, gave her to Alvarado: the fair-haired Son
of the Sun. She bore him several children. One, according
to the baptismal record, was born on March 22, 1524: the
lovely Leonor, whose life covered the whole period of the
Conquest.

As I rode along that day, I realized how complete was
Alvarado's conquest. He made Guatemala a white man's
country. Indians were on every side, but all the men in
charge were white: the conductor, the brakeman, and station officials. Men who boarded the train to ride only a
station or two looked like our Western ranchers in their
outdoor clothes and Stetson hats. Most of them were fair or
sandy: probably gringos, but the Guatemalans were of the
same type. This is stock country; maybe dealing with cattle
produces such men in any clime. They talked business and
parted casually, shaking hands at meeting and parting, but
more perfunctorily than in Mexico.

Even in the manner of wearing their hats the Guatemalans seem a different people. A Mexican, with his sombrero, points himself up. It is accolade, emphasis, plume in the helmet, pride of race. He may have lost everything else, including his shirt and most of his pants, but even as he goes down for the third time his hat rides triumphant, flaunting defiance to the end. In Guatemala there are few tall-crowned sombreros, and a hat is merely head-gear, set straight on the brow, forthright and simple. I never saw a Guatemalan who swaggered with his hat, except one little boy in Antigua, a very special little boy.

The eating-houses were most sanitary, screened and provided with modern toilets. Even Indian women offered food for sale in wire cages. We passed one hacienda — I had not learned to say *finca* — which had rows of stucco houses with iron roofs, screened porches, and chimneys! Could it be that they cooked with coal or wood instead of charcoal? It looked like a California development with its palms, straight streets, uniformity. Other signs of North American influence were frequent: distances are computed in miles, altitudes in feet. And many key words are in English: tickets, restaurant, toilet, all right, good-by, hello, dollar.

Guatemala likes the United States. A young Guatemalan, speaking of the depression, said: " It causes us much distress. Your country has always been a beacon to us, and we don't like to see our beacon flicker." No, to Guatemala the imperialistic colossus of the north is Mexico, not the United States. I am told that Salvador and Honduras distrust Guatemala as a dangerous power with ques-

VILLAGE OF TAHUESCO (PACIFIC SHORE), SALT-MAKING AND FISHING CENTER

ABOVE, *At sunset.* BELOW, *Palmetto-thatched houses, with coco palms and fenced fresh-water wells.*

[PHOTO, WEBSTER MCBRYDE, FELLOW, SOCIAL SCIENCE RESEARCH COUNCIL, 1935–6]

GUATEMALA

ABOVE, *The Cathedral.* BELOW, *Sixth Avenue*

[PHOTOS, EICHENBERGER]

tionable designs. A procession of countries, each looking apprehensively back at a feared and hated neighbor. To make it complete, we should work up a good hate for Canada.

I began to see the variety of costumes Guatemala is famous for. At Palín women came in numbers, for the train from the port of San José passes there too and they are tourist-wise. Their tight blue skirts fell to the heels; their huipiles were white, and each one had a big kerchief, which she folded on her head or used for carrying things, including babies. The Tabascan chief's gift to Cortez might have looked like that: those twenty slave girls of whom Malinche was one. Blue and white and red, and on every head a flat basket piled with golden oranges and granadillas. On every back, of course, a baby. Among Indians *woman* connotes *baby*.

Something more attractive must have happened at the other end of town, for suddenly they set off, not at the jogtrot of the Mexican Indian, but with a long-legged lope, loaded basket on head, heavy baby on back, and arms pistoning to balance the whole.

Then we reached Lake Amatitlán and scalloped a long and lovely course around it. We saw the volcanoes. Agua, trim and exquisitely coned, which washed out Alvarado's capital at Ciudad Vieja. Fuego, mis-shaped by the explosive bad temper which still throws snarls of smoke from its uneven sides. And its mate Acatenango. Volcanoes dominate Guatemala; not only by their grandeur, but because they have made so much of Guatemalan history that one cannot forget them. They loom in beauty, they brood, they are a constant menace, and excitement.

Long before I reached Guatemala — here, as in Mexico, the nation is La República; the capital has usurped the name — I knew that Guatemala is not a little Mexico, nor is it at all like Mexico. It has its own character, its own allure, and, as I was to learn, its own way of making a stranger feel at home and welcome. It is a less effusive way. In Mexico they say of an effervescent one that he is *lírico*. Guatemala does not grow lyrical. The back-slapping Mexican hug becomes there a restrained gesture. Fingertips may touch shoulders, but scarcely. Chambermaids in Mexico call one *niña*, weep at parting, bring the children bearing gifts, work up a dramatic frenzy. In Guatemala servants are quite accurately described by the terms most favored: respectful and humble. The younger ones fresh from the country even fold their arms and duck their heads for a blessing. Very embarrassing until you get used to it.

A Mexican, on his first visit to Guatemala, said: " Give a Mexican half a jigger of tequila and he pulls his pistols, dances and leaps, sings a song, makes love. It's cheap to fill a Mexican with dynamite. But I've seen five Guatemalans sit drinking for hours, completely wordless except when they say: ' Another bottle, if you please, señorita '! No, I am not rich enough to liven up a Guatemalteco."

Six months in Guatemala only confirmed my first impression that it is a white man's country. In spite of its sixty-five per cent native population, the white race dominates it, marks it. I became aware, too, that the white man's culture rides very lightly on that of the Indian, as foam on a profound dark sea. That sea still ebbs and flows a tranquil tide, but it has terrific power, yet unaroused. I wonder if it will ever wake to a realization of its own power, and if it does, what will happen. Many people in Guatemala wonder about that too. Few speak of it.

II: Guatemala, the Capital

GUATEMALA IS A CLEAN, FRESH LITTLE CITY OF A HUN-
dred and fifty thousand people. Streets and avenues cross
at right angles, and every one leads toward a blue-green
velvet mountain. In December, the middle of the dry season, the days were dazzling with that southern sunshine
which harmonizes colors — red and magenta, orange and
vermilion, bright blues, and vivid pinks and greens — that
go sour and discordant under any other light. The country-
side was burned bare of all light growth, but city parks
and gardens, artificially watered, were luxuriant.

The creamy stone Cathedral faces stern gray barracks
across the Plaza de Armas. Most of the other structures on
the plaza are government buildings, representing various
periods of architecture. The President's new mansion, set
at the back of an open square of garden, is up to date, and
all its windows are fitted with rolling steel shutters. On
the south pillared arcades shelter shops and booths —
the most Latin American and the liveliest spot in town.
The plaza itself is three blocks of park, as tidy as a flower
show, with shrubberies, lily pools, and a fountain which
sprays into electric rainbows on tourist nights. Indian

16

gardeners were forever setting out new plants in rich brown beds, and vines rioted in blossom over pergolas. Blond babies played there, watched by barefooted Indian nurses, and schoolchildren in uniform passed with satchels of books. Many older people strolled through or lingered to read a paper or get a shoe-shine. The Spanish custom of wearing mourning for even distant cousins keeps women much in black. Many men wear formal black or mourning bands. It is all very quiet and well ordered, and a little sad.

Guatemala is a new city. Founded in 1776, after the destruction of the older capital at Antigua, it was distinguished for its splendor even among the lordly cities of colonial Spain. But in 1917 it was practically demolished by an earthquake that left few buildings standing, and its aspect now is very modern. Happily, in the rebuilding the Spanish colonial style was kept. The houses, plastered in soft and pleasant tints, are mostly of one story, as more resistant to earthquakes. They stand flush with the streets, and their heavy doors open into patios full of flowers and birds. All the main thoroughfares are paved. Some cobbled side-streets must be very old, for they dip to the center as the Spaniards made them instead of into gutters. In rainy weather the police rush out little bridges to take pedestrians across the rivers that fill the streets.

There are two policemen on every corner: one on a box under an umbrella, another one at hand. They have uniforms for every day, feast days, rainy days. They are organized as a subsidiary army corps, in case an extra army is ever needed in a hurry, and they exercise their authority quite politely. Traffic is practically nil. At the

busiest hours — there are no busy hours — one can gaze
four ways from a corner on Sixth Avenue without seeing a
car. A boy on a bicycle may pass, or an ox-cart loaded
with charcoal. But traffic rules are numerous and well
observed. The speed limit is twenty kilometers an hour;
kilometers, not miles. At each intersection a driver slows
down, honks ever so gently, and waits until the policeman
signals him on with a whistle as dulcet as the motor's horn.
If he leaves town, an officer takes his number, telephones
it ahead; and if his spin has been a trifle too dizzy, the
speeder finds himself arrested at his destination. It would
be redundant to state that accidents are rare. There are
no street cars, and buses run even more slowly than private
cars. There are no street cries. One forgets what makes
hurly-burly in other metropolises. But it is not the silence
of death; a sense of expectancy, rather, as though the city
were swept and garnished and waiting. It may be obscurely
aware of some sublime destiny; maybe it is only ready for
the horde of tourists sure to arrive soon.

For tourists, Guatemala is the coming paradise. Official
Guatemala is clever enough to refuse larger tours than it
can handle, so it is still the delight of the few. On regular
days the streets come alive with modest motors bearing
travelers in what New York considers suitable costumes
for the tropics. An altitude of five thousand feet in the
torrid zone makes a most accommodating climate; cool
enough for winter suits if you live there, warm enough for
white linen if you are on a southern cruise. All comers
visit the Temple of Minerva and study the country's con-
tours from the relief map, where the volcanoes are peaked

up even beyond their natural exaggeration. At the other end of the city are the zoo, with a fair assortment of unfamiliar birds and beasts, and the archæological museum. The tourists drive through the Paseo de La Reforma, for Guatemala as well as Mexico had its reform President; past the Eiffel Tower, for why should not Guatemala be Latin America's little Paris? And the smartest modern residences. Widely spaced in lawns and gardens, they suggest a Los Angeles suburb. Architects, unfortunately, admire that bastard style which came about because California, to be Spanish, debased Mexican colonial into a jumble which Latin America is even farther debasing as Californian. The result is a dismaying hotchpotch of tiles too red, grilles too ornate, balconies too narrow, and doors too ponderous; of turrets, cupolas, pillars, and scrolls; of walls that inclose nothing, and gates that lead nowhere.

Guatemala's few sights would not bore the most sated tripper, and there is endless informal diversion in listening to the band in the park, or the marimba at the Palace, playing tennis or golf at the Country Club, or buying. Curio-shops are plethoric with textiles, and the market in the capital is the hub on which the whole Republic turns. Aside from what the Europeanized minority needs, everything that Guatemala produces or uses comes into the great market behind the Cathedral. Need I say that it is quiet and orderly, clean and pleasant?

All the Guatemalan tribes converge there, and its sights and sounds and smells together reflect a wavering and imperfect image; but still an image of the whole country. No Indian lives on too distant a mountain to make his way sooner or later to the capital, bringing the woolly blankets he wears at home; or in too trackless a jungle to turn up some day in El Mercado Central with an ocelot skin or a choice bit of alligator meat for sale. Most Indians come to town in typical dress, for every hamlet has its own: costumes so striking in color and style that they reduce the whole correct city and vapid white race to a paltry background for their display.

Most familiar are the San Juaneras in red and yellow huipiles, held under wide belts that define their hard-muscled haunches and flat backs. They tie their hair in black wool which cascades under wide basketfuls of live fowls, or flowers in fresh and fragrant sheaves. And they stride along at a rate which takes them easily twenty miles into town in the morning, and back again in the afternoon. The town's serving maids wear native dress, too, but they are not purists like the village Indians. They like huipiles of store stuff, full skirts, and sometimes, but not often, shoes. Upper-class babies have wet-nurses, preferably from Mixco, because Mixco women have a reputation for cleanliness and good milk.

Even the convicts are picturesque in Guatemala, in their clean pink and white striped pyjama suits. They grin cheerily as they are marched out to work or back to prison, attended each one by an armed soldier. They say that if a prisoner escapes, his guard must take his place. Very few escape.

The town is full of soldiers, well drilled, correct at salute, and smartly officered. The point of ecstasy is reached in the cadets of the national military academy, who realize

D. H. Lawrence's ideal of virile youths in tight scarlet trousers. The scarlet is very bright, and many of the cadets uncommonly fine examples of every type from almost pure Negro to very pure white.

Hotels are adequate, though quite without character, and nobody has thought of serving first-rate Guatemalan food. The best restaurants are Mexican, Italian, United States; and the usual hotel meal is that well-known international hotel meal. There is better living and closer contact with Guatemalan life in a pension (given the Spanish and not the French pronunciation).

In the Señorita Fernandez's house, day began before dawn with the maids giggling and splashing at the fountain. All day they ran, on silent bare feet, around the patio. They swept the rooms with soft grass brooms, hung towels out to sun, helped the Señorita with her birds, watered the plants. At intervals they went out on errands, always in pairs, coming back with big baskets on their heads, piled with groceries and flowers. The last thing at night I could hear them praying with the Señorita before she locked them in at ten. For a mistress guards her maids' morals and sees that they go to mass every Sunday.

One day a San Juanera came with turkeys. The front door was open, so she walked in and sat on her heels until the Señorita noticed her.

" How much? "

" Eighty pesos." About a dollar and thirty cents.

" Each one? Whoo-oo, very dear." The Señorita went about her affairs.

The Indian sat on, her wrinkled old face passive and her

flat-breasted body as straight as a young athlete's. Maids
passed, running to the door, carrying bowls and pitchers.
As each one went by, the San Juanera asked, always more
insistently:

" But what will she give me? What does she offer? "

" They are too dear, she says."

" Mary, the Most Holy! They are good birds. Only look,
buyer, child! "

" Too dear, she says."

At last the Señorita relented and the deal was closed.
They pegged out the turkeys in the kitchen patio, where
they could be heard for days gobbling their last hours away.

Guatemala, being a capital, is cosmopolitan. Upper-
class Guatemalans have for centuries been educated
abroad. Lately boys go more to professional and technical
schools in the United States than to European universities,
and girls are sent to convents in New York. Women's col-
leges are quite inconceivable. But all educated people have
lived abroad and speak several languages. Consequently
there is no sharp line between foreign colonies, and the
tone of society is Guatemalan, with an old-fashioned charm
as well as an international complexion. Entertaining is
done at home. There are no night clubs or road-houses.
A paradise for parents! Only the most formal affairs are
held at clubs or hotels.

Early evening is the young men's hour. After work they
appear. On Sixth Avenue no two or three are allowed to
gather together, but they go vacillating along, three or four
abreast, forcing swifter movers into the street. Or they post
themselves in cigar-stores or doorways to watch the girls

and make remarks. " *Qué chula!* " which might be interpreted as " Hey, deary! " and equally innocuous remarks,
toned to leerful meaning. This is called *throwing flowers.*
All over town the undetermined stand on corners in twos
or threes until all hours. Those with definite hormonic
urges add much to the romantic aspect of the place by playing bear. Girls, shiningly coifed, lean in the barred windows and receive their *pretendientes,* who stay for hours. I
understand that if one of them comes often, the family ex-
pects something explicit.

Aside from these spottings of gallantry, nights in Guatemala are devoid of life. At eight, heavy iron shutters hide
the shops' display windows, and the streets are practically
deserted. Though there is a proud new picture theater, the
movies are scatteringly attended. One evening, when I left
before a second show, I asked a policeman if there would
be a bus.

" Ah, señora," he grieved for me. "It is very unlikely
that buses should pass now that it is late. It must be nine
o'clock. Ah, no, señora, at this hour there will be no more
buses."

As I walked home through the cool impersonal streets,
I tried to analyze the sense of transitoriness that assailed
me in Guatemala. It was not only that I was transient; the
city itself seemed without footing, as though it had no tap-
root to plumb the country's subsoil. It perches on top; a
flower in the buttonhole, and an imported flower at that. It
is the capital, nothing more. To know Guatemala, one must
leave the capital.

III: Tourist View

TOURISTS TAKE GUATEMALA TIMIDLY. SURELY THE WORLD has never before produced as timorous, self-coddling, and jittery a specimen as the modern American tourist. Incredible that the grandchildren, even the children, of the hardy conquerors of a continent should be so scary. And what will come next? Of what earthly use will be these children who prattle of germs in their perambulators, who are trained to consider comfort above all gods, and who are so sheltered that they acquire no immunities, either to disease or to the least discomfort or inconvenience? Even this generation is afraid of everything: of food and water, of uncertainty, delay, boredom, the strange. Why this pampered soul ever leaves home is a puzzle to people who like what is unexpected, different, even difficult. But he does travel, and anyone who has ever served him knows that he must be handled as gingerly as a basket of baby chicks. Kept warm, but never hot; fed frequently, but nothing he is not used to; shown things of interest and told facts, but never too much or too many; and always and forever reassured. Nobody in any country understands this better than Alfred Clark of Guatemala, who conducts tours which give one a fine sense of adventure and a chance to see Indians in curious costumes; but through plate glass, at a safe distance, and in a sanitary nursery atmosphere. I decided to take one.

Our guide was Mr. Logan. Well-informed and courteous, he wore the official white cap and an invisible coat of impermeable patience, which I saw threatened only once. We stood on the hill of Carmen, above Guatemala, viewing the valley of the Virgin and the volcanoes. Mr. Logan told how the Volcán de Agua got its name, in 1541, when it erupted water in terrifying torrents which roared through " the old city " — Ciudad Vieja — and demolished it completely.

"And who," inquired a tourist, " was responsible for that? "

" God," said Mr. Logan, for once letting his natural wit rise above his tolerant understanding of how unaccountable a foreign country can seem. Then, abashed, he explained what geographers say about an inner lake's breaking loose.

He did not mention Hunahpú, the legendary King of the Cakchiqueles, who was buried in the volcano which bore his name. From his sepulcher he saw the enslavement of his people, the destruction of the archaic monuments; and one night he turned in his grave, tore out the side of the volcano, and loosed the catastrophe.

We drove south out of the capital between the hideous stiff museum on a hill and the animated market at its foot. Beyond we ran through Avenida Simón Bolivar, said to be the busiest thoroughfare in Central America. From before dawn until long after dark its four-car roadway and side paths stream ceaselessly with traffic. There are few beasts of burden; trucks carry produce and people with produce from all the provinces, both lowland and highland. But most of the commerce, even now, is borne by human carriers. Men and women, even children, expertly packed with crates, baskets, and bundles, lope along as though no mechanical conveyer had ever been. It is an ambulatory bazaar, chameleon-colored, of grotesque people with queer head-dresses and unfamiliar cut of coat and skirt, less human than some sur-realist's puppets, designed to express the oddities of a subconscious world. It is primordial Guatemala bringing food and service into the paved modern city.

When the road for Antigua turned off, we took the other to skirt Lake Amatitlán, where the President goes to rest and enjoy his motor-boat. Society has followed him with a notably ugly assortment of country houses.

In the village of Palín we stopped under its ceiba tree, generously outspread over the whole plaza. This was where those long-legged women had run away from the train. Tourists must have come in by motor. I left the others dickering for kerchiefs and went into the church, redolent of its carpet of drying pine needles.

At a side altar knelt three little girls, heads bowed under their Dresden-patterned coifs. Remembering all I had heard of the deeply devout Guatemalan Indian, I was careful not to disturb them as I slid into a seat. In a second they were upon me, worshipers transformed into traffickers for cash.

"Buy, señora! Four quetzales, four dólares! " offering the kerchiefs snatched off their pious heads. " Mine, señora, buy mine! Three fifty! Three! " The market broke and crashed. " Two! One! " One was a fair price, and by that time I had shooed them out into the open, where their commercial steam was less apt to result in a dangerous explosion.

From Palín we rose, rounding the shoulder of the Volcán de Agua, through oak forests with hanging moss and lianas and the air plants which are the orchid's poor relations. When Mr. Logan mentioned an altitude of sixty-five hundred feet, we ran into a village built of upright bamboo, roofed with grass, and sitting right in the lap of the volcano. Here intrepid souls take off to scale the peak at night, to suffer penetrating cold till dawn, and then, by the simple device of turning the head, to gaze upon two oceans and intervening views of inexpressible grandeur. Chill winds sucked through the lanes, even at midday.

Women in bright magenta kerchiefs, fading exquisitely, came to the fountain. They dipped their jars into the lower basin and took drinking-water through bamboo reeds from little jets at the top. We remarked that the government must be making headway with its health measures. Then a group of recruits, dismissed from drill, ran up to drink, all imbibing through the same sanitary reeds! Children broke out of school, the little girls in wrapped blue skirts and magenta kerchiefs like the women. We looked into a house where a weaver sat on the dirt floor, her loom tautened by a heavy hip-strap. On the edge of town, women were washing piles of clothes, with babies jouncing on their backs as they scrubbed.

As we swung toward the valley of Panchoy we could see

ruined Ciudad Vieja, which rested too trustingly on the slope of the Volcán de Agua. It was the original Most Loyal and Noble City of Saint James of the Gentlemen of Guatemala. After its destruction they built Antigua, known now as the ancient capital. Less than a hundred years ago this valley was a network of the cactus plants which fed the cochineal bug. Now gray-green gravilea trees make shadowy aisles between sprouting fences and the coffee's bright leaves. Round the chapel of the Calvario and through the Via Crucis with its empty stations of the cross, we entered the abandoned capital, still stately in its ruin. The most important Spanish city between Mexico and Lima, it endured two centuries of recurrent earthquakes before it was deserted in 1776. Residents of Antigua like to mention that since then they have had no serious shakes, while Guatemala has been wrecked and rebuilt so often that little of it is old. Almost none of Antigua is new.

The Palace of the Captains General preserves its perfect sixteenth-century façade, but inside is only a littered yard with broken walls around. Churches are topless cloisters or gaping domes. Of the pale stone Cathedral only one chapel is intact, and the padre's house, built around a patio reminiscent of Toledo. Weavers or pottery-makers have put up lean-to's in stately convents, and swine root around what is left of fine gardens. But nature has made up for man's neglect and hidden the worst with masses of flowers and ferns. Wild roses and anemones cling to fallen stones, little orange trees try to cover broken tombs, poinsettias sing a cheery note in gray corners. Many people find Antigua sad. Only one with great inner resources would

settle there for long. Fortunately one did. Dorothy Popenoe, the English wife of an American botanist, remodeled
a storied old house where she read about Antigua, looked
at it, and wrote its history in a charming little book: *Santiago de los Caballeros de Guatemala.*

At the Church of San Francisco, Juanito picked us up.
He could say " Chine, ten cents," and he wished to be
taught more English at once. Little boys are a great help.
They never let you miss anything, it is true, and must at
times be reminded that there are moments for eating, dressing, sleeping, or just sitting supinely still. But, that established, a retinue of youngsters is invaluable for carrying
things, finding places, running errands, and supplying that
misinformation which is more revealing than facts. Juanito, for instance, took me to see the stone cross in front of
the Church of La Merced, favorite of all Antigueños for its
confectioner's front of white arabesques on French gray.

" See, señora! " He was hoarse with eagerness, pointing
and fighting off other urchins who offered the bust of Fray
Bartolomé de las Casas in opposition. " That cross they
took, the padres, to the Volcán de Fuego, but it refused it.
The other volcanoes, look, señora, Agua and Acatenango,
they accepted their crosses and they never returned to
erupt, but Fuego refused the cross and threw it out and so
they brought it, the padres and all the people in procession,
señora, and they put it here by the Merced where you see
it, señora, right now."

Nobody will allow me to have that story, but I like it.
And I see no reason to doubt that priests who habitually
took the saints out in procession to intercede for them might

have tried to appeal to a volcano's better nature by planting a cross on it. Or why, really, a minor explosion in that tempestuous land should not have thrown it down.

At the hotel we ate only too well. To please a North American clientele, the original breakfast of frijoles, eggs, tamales, sweet breads, and coffee has been enhanced by orange juice, oatmeal, bacon, and hot cakes. With the addition of big pink slices of papaya with cut lime, brown zapotes with mellow insides, anonas like green bombs inclosing a white pulp delicate as a mousse, or hard-shelled granadillas full of seeds in slippery fiber; you have quite a meal. Essence of coffee was served in a flask accompanied by pitchers of hot water and milk. The other two meals were as overwhelming. Both include aguacate, for the vale of Panchoy is the home of that luscious oily fruit. You may slice it into the soup, the preferred Antigua way, fill its hollow with all the condiments on the table, and eat it as a separate course, or add it to your salad.

In the evening, replete, I sat in the patio under the pink linda vine while Juanito shined my shoes. Other boys came along. One begged a cigarette and soon all were smoking. Then the little doctor drifted by, looking for a shine and company. Slim and not tall, gray and frail, he had more interests at eighty than the combined youth movement of the United States. But he was appalled at my smoking company.

"Please tell those youngsters, but seriously, it's not a joke, that they are injuring their health by smoking when they are so young. It can really stunt their growth."

I translated, and the boys crushed out their smokes respectfully. When the doctor's shine was done and he rambled away, Juanito, squatting against the pillar, grinned at me. " El Señor Doctor didn't grow very big, did he? " he asked.

Antigua is warmer than the capital. From there on, and up, we were rising into the temperate zone, with layers of woollies recommended. At noon, even in Chichicastenango, one is glad to shed. At night it is cozy to snuggle into them all again. At Chimaltenango we stopped to admire their fountain exactly on the continental divide, and to learn that the name means Place of Shields. *Tenango,* in Aztec, is *place of.* Alvarado's Mexican allies are responsible for all such names in Guatemala.

The roads are wide enough for two cars and so well graded that they are passable even in the wettest weather. As many tourists notice, they do go up and down and round curves — a tendency almost unavoidable in a mountainous country. Many Spanish bridges are still in use, squat stone arches, solid as the day they were built. We met people constantly. Merchants harnessed like beasts with the heavy head-strap to hold the burden on the back. Family parties with small children staggering under loads, little hands on the tumpline to ease the weight, young faces too strained to respond to a greeting. A woman in a striped red skirt had laid down her bundle while she knelt in prayer before a roadside shrine. Then she kissed the cross, resumed her burden, and ran on.

Costumes changed as we left each village behind. At Patzúm and Patzicía the women's skirts were blue. Those huipiles with wide rose tops came from Comalapa. Men in checked woolen skirts were from Sololá, or Nahualá, depending upon how they fastened them behind. It seemed impossible ever to learn to which village each costume belonged, but Mr. Logan could locate every one at a glance.

In Patzúm an old spinner sat against a wall twirling her spindle in a shallow bowl and pulling off a smooth and even thread. Her face was gentle, amused, and she posed willingly for a picture, only straightening her white chef's cap. Sanitary legislation requires caps for all who handle food, and it has, apparently, become the thing for general wear.

The church in Patzúm, like all old Spanish churches, has its share of wonders: paintings and statues brought from Spain and badly rubbed now, silver lamps, and a silver altar rail. For those Spaniards nothing was too much trouble, no distance too great. What could be moved was imported; what could not, was made; by Indians, of course, but under the direction of the padres. And anyone who has tried to get anything made — a pair of shoes or a piece of pottery — according to his taste, knows that the padres' job was not inconsiderable. They got hundreds of churches built, enormous structures embodying the principle of the arch, formerly unknown to the Indians, finished with carved hard woods, decorated with sculpture, paintings, enamels, hand-wrought metals, fabrics — everything that was known in Europe. Salvation lay that way. Every temple meant so many souls saved from damnation, so much more glory for God. So sixteenth-century civilization expressed itself.

" Our civilization," I remarked to the old doctor, " can

boast of no force comparable to that until we get a hospital and a social center in as many inaccessible places as they put churches."

He bristled up at once. " We have hospitals," said he. " In New York State there is not a town of five thousand without a decent hospital and a man capable of making a creditable appendectomy." As though a sixteenth-century Spaniard had boasted that every village within a day's journey of Madrid had its church. The church at Patzúm was many months' journey from Madrid.

Going on, we passed many road-workers. Every man in the Republic owes two quetzales annually for road-work. Most natives prefer to work it out, and the government prefers that too, as a day's work is valued at eight and a half cents. We passed a gargantuan machine, labeled: " Chicago, Illinois: made in Green Bay, Wisconsin." The doctor was too busy getting a picture to make me the deserved retort; but there was our civilization, digging out a hillside, connecting all the world with Chicago. Ours is a civilization of roads, after all, and machines; not of individual health or well-being.

Lake Atitlán is lapis-lazuli; too deep to sparkle, too deep even to plumb. Two volcanoes, Peter and Luke, come right down to it: sheer rock-blue mountain into gem-blue lake. They hold it really for rock slides have blocked all the exits and the lake is mountain-bound now. Another volcano, James, stands back a little way. James and Luke have Indian names as well: San Lucas Tolimán, Santiago Atitlán. These are the names of villages too, and all the other apostles have sponsored pueblos near the lake. Beyond the look-out where we saw all that, the road kept the lake in view almost all the way to lunch at Tzanjuyú: Nose of the Mountain.

The lake, when you reach it, is friendly, intimate. Water lilies and water hyacinths bloom where streams fan out to enter it. In some coves grow the rushes they weave into mats. Indians in dug-out canoes paddle back and forth to market. And every village gives that sense of remoteness in time and space that makes Indian life so soothing. San Pedro houses are thatched to a peak, and men wear embroidered drawers. Santiago Atitlán has ridge-poles, and the women's hips are slim in tightly drawn red skirts — the red of roses fading into a purple death. Where they wash along the shore they look like flowers thrown away. Even schoolgirls have learned to knot that strip of red skirt so it never slips.

Beyond Tzanjuyú we rose steadily into colder country. Wheat grows there. Corn, the omnipresent, clings to the most impossible slopes. Sheep appear; so many black ones that I worried about the state of morals in Guatemala. Houses, except in the towns, are of wattled poles roofed with grass; sometimes very shaggy, sometimes nicely barbered. Fences are of corn-stalks bound together, much stronger than they look. No chimneys. The native has never thought of making himself comfortable. We had many glimpses of the lake as we mounted, curving always higher until we touched an altitude of almost nine thousand feet at Los Encuentros, where a road veers off for Totonicapán and Quetzaltenango. We were for Chichicastenango and we were meeting hundreds of people bound there for the feast of Santo Tomás.

Many were *Maxeños:* people of Santo Tomás. Generally they wear ordinary clothes on the roads, but as this was fiesta we saw them in their best: men in short black serge jackets and smallclothes, women in heavily decorated huipiles. A big fiesta lasts eight days, and the crowd was going both ways or resting in dry leaf shelters by the road. A few mules rustled along under corn-husk fodder, but most of the loads were carried by men or children. Animals were going to market or to new owners. Cattle have sense, but pigs! Any pig is a cantankerous traveler, but getting along a populous road with a dozen little porkers, each on his separate line, each shrilling his individual plaint, takes a lot of doing.

Just at dusk we began bumping over cobblestones — sure sign of a town. Chichicastenango! A few electric lights in the streets; many in stores no wider than their doors. Many people, but little noise. Bare feet go so quietly. We passed the market: the whole plaza under canvas, with pitch flares held high on sticks, ruddy faces, black heads, opéra-bouffe costumes. We whirled round a corner and there were the two churches, paper-white, facing each other along the side of the plaza. Another corner and the Mayan Inn.

Hieroglyphics painted on the walls, boys in the village costume, pottery from Quetzaltenango, Momostenango blankets, napkins woven specially for tourists, and many pieces of furniture from good old houses. But the real thrills are for wood fires on those chill evenings, for rooms with baths, and, final luxury, a hot water bottle in every bed. Menus are such as Mother would plan back home, with hot cakes for breakfast. Nothing — not the shifting spectacle of native life, not the towering volcanoes, the emerald green nor azure blue of the lakes, not the breathtaking amazement of unfolding mountains, ridge after ridge under a brilliant sky — nothing calls forth such enthusiasm as hot cakes for breakfast. Yes, Mr. Clark knows his tourists well.

IV: Fiesta of Santo Tomás

GUATEMALAN MARKETS START LATE, BUT BY TEN O'CLOCK the plaza was abustle with ordered confusion. The store at the corner was full of drinkers, even so early. Every canvas shade in the square lured one to see what it hid. But the way to the church was most enticing. Meat-stalls and eating-booths outlined the swarming passage to the parish church, where Saint Thomas would be venerated all day, from the Chapel of the Calvary, which we were warned no white person dare enter or even approach. On its steps men wreathed themselves in copal fumes from clay censers, and a few devout Indians went in and out. But the circular white steps of the larger temple teemed with worshipers. Men in those black suits like court pages lit their incense at big glowing braziers and swung a blue haze through which candles inside the church punctured little holes of flame. People knelt or mounted step by step on their knees. Often groups made the hard ascent together, men praying, women meek and silent, humped with baby on back, their upturned bare soles pitifully exposed.

These Maxeñas are the uncomeliest Indian women I have seen anywhere. Short, almost dwarfish, their legs and feet are often mis-shapen and much too prominent under tight scanty skirts. Their huipiles — white or brown, with wide yoke patterned in red — are handsome. Bound under thick belts, they make the little figures look like clumsy toppling dolls, precariously balanced on spindly legs. I remarked that their protruding stomachs looked to me like a biological miscalculation.

" Ah, no," said the sentimental spinster, agasp with the wonder of everything. " I find them beautiful. To me these women typify the glory of motherhood."

In such case, one spinster's guess is as good as another's, but I did not think that even the most glorious motherhood would bulge so high. Later I learned that maternity, even in Chichicastenango, follows the usual lines and curves. Those bulges were not motherhood, but hookworm, contracted in the fincas on the coast.

The rare Maxeña is pretty, with a well-cut nose in a flat face and a curving mouth. Thick hair, well brushed for fiesta and braided with black wool, is a real adornment, and every one wore a mass of shiny silver glass beads at ten cents a string.

The men are better favored in knee-pants with pocket flaps like wings and bolero jackets. All is made by the man himself, who finishes it off with braid and embroidery. Some were strikingly Oriental in the tasseled *sute*, the red or purple turban. A tradition persists that these Indians, being originally from the Quiché royal city of Utatlán, wear Spanish court costume and embroidered symbols of the sun, as evidence of their nobility. If so, it is an aristocracy that has fallen off a good deal.

Always mindful not to distract the suppliants, we entered the church through Padre Rossbach's patio. The entrance was full of parishioners waiting to see the priest, who was receiving guests at every moment that he was not in the church. Bustling and friendly in English and German, Spanish or Quiché, he was discussing archæology with Mr. Diesseldorf of Cobán, the fiesta with village headmen, flowers with his Indian gardener, a baptism with a grandmother, the church with ladies from Guatemala, and ushering tourists in to see his jade collection, said to be unequaled in the Americas.

As a lad, Ildefonso Rossbach was sent out from Germany to work on a coffee finca. He learned Spanish and an Indian tongue, and as he became acquainted with Indians, he knew that his life must be dedicated to helping them. A Protestant, he thought the way to do that was to become a Catholic priest. So he went to New York with very little money and no English, only a great conviction that he must prepare for his chosen work. His struggles were epic. Unprepared, unknown, and poor, he found it hard to get even a hearing. Finally, of course, he did and returned to Guatemala as an ordained priest. Traveling about later, I learned that Padre Rossbach has served in many highland towns, is known and loved everywhere. His parish now extends over a wide region and includes many chapels which are opened only when he rides in on horseback for the monthly or less frequent mass.

On the padre's hint, I slipped through a side door into the church, dusky after the daylight. Underfoot were pine needles. Clean, aromatic, soft to the tread, and deterrent to fleas, no better carpet could be imagined. Indians had set up bunches of flowers on the floor, scattered torn petals, and stuck candles among them. Guttering and smoking, they added the smell of burning tallow to the aroma of pine, copal scent from outside, and the unforgettable effluvium of unwashed Maya. The devout knelt or prostrated themselves beside their offerings or crawled to where the padre sat for long hours with holy water and hyssop, praying and sprinkling benison. A man prayed aloud, seeming to talk companionably with God as one who had dropped in for a chat. His woman, kneeling behind him, let her eyes take in everything, nursed or patted her baby. Another man made supplication for a whole group. The general piety seemed to swirl into pockets of prayer quite unconnected with the high altar or the pictures and statues of saints along the walls. Only when they left, each worshiper crept from saint to saint, noisily kissing the railing or the floor or holding children up to smear the glass with kisses.

Outdoors again, I discovered that all the religion was not Catholic. At the foot of the steps eight men of decorous mien and advanced age were making ceremony in their way. The table where they sat was backed by other men holding silver-topped maces. The business of the meeting seemed to be risings and sittings, slow speeches in Quiché, and the measured imbibing of aguardiente; for that potent liquor, aside from being a comfort to the body, figures in every religious affair in Guatemala. Younger men were rigging a rope from the belfry to the ground, and I decided that life there was too interesting to leave even for the market. Casting about, I saw my appointed place. In an

CHICHICASTENANGO

ABOVE, *The church.* BELOW, *A street.*

[PHOTOS, EICHENBERGER]

OCTAVIO (*at right*)

[PHOTO, MARY BUTLER]

CHICHICASTENANGO

ABOVE, *The men pray, the women look around.* BELOW, *Masked dancers.*

[PHOTOS, EICHENBERGER]

LEFT, *The Church of Santo Tomás.*

[PHOTO, FLORENCE DIBBELL BARTLETT]

angle of the padre's house, steps led to a platform. On the lower level a barber was lathering, scraping, clipping, and brushing hairs into the air. But a masonry bench above invited me, and in a moment I was settled: high enough to get the whole sweep of the kaleidoscopic plaza and with the principal acts right at my feet.

At that point Octavio came into my life. Several youngsters squirmed in beside me, but it was Octavio who possessed himself of my bag, took definite charge of me and my affairs. Octavio looks like Tom Sawyer. He is thirteen, with round serious eyes, crooked teeth in an occasional smile, and hair that grows a lot of ways. He is always clean. Fresh collar turned down over his round jacket, white trousers, and scrubbed bare feet. It suggests Simple Simon, but there is nothing simple about Octavio, unless a desire to serve and to do everything just right is simple. If everybody were as straight and honest as that boy, as eager to do his best and to give full value, all our problems would be solved. The world can do something terrible to boys like Octavio.

As we sat in our angle, the boys helped me jot down descriptions of costumes in my note-book. Wrapped striped skirts, blue and green, with drooping wraps, Totonicapán. That particular woman, with four pigs tied together, three children running free, and one on her back, lives in Chichicastenango, but keeps her native dress. Men in red frogged jackets, like a band-master, had walked all the way from San Juan Zacatepéquez. The family camped on the steps below us was from Santa María Chiquimula. The mother's skirt was long, her huipil heavily flowered around the top, and her hair braided with colored ribbons. Her little girl, surely not more than three, was her perfect replica. She leaned at ease against her mother, who alternately picked at her rumpled hair and watched the show. When the baby fretted, she pulled it round in front and poked a hard brown nipple at it, as impersonally as though it were rubber from the drug-store. When the sucking stopped, she let her breast hang exposed until the huipil fell over it again.

Octavio spoke in the tone of one bound to see that a visitor misses nothing. " Do you go to the cine tonight, señorita? You must not fail to see it. It talks, and for the first time a cine that talks comes to Santo Tomás." His solemn eyes contemplated me for a moment with no shade or gleam of self-seeking. But Eduardo was not so subtle.

" We've never seen a cine that talked," he submitted, and then choked on the bitter look Octavio gave him.

Later we strolled around among the booths. Vegetables and fruits were near the fountain. Raw foodstuffs and woven stuffs were piled and hung in porches and temporary shelters. Furniture stood exposed and blankets carpeted one whole side of the square. Food sizzled and steamed. People haggled, standing or squatting, interminably over their selections. Octavio seemed to have an objective and at last we brought up at his mother's sweet-drink stand. She greeted me with the gesture of feeling in the dark, her finger-tips touching my shoulder. I treated the boys to a saccharine watery drink, and the Señora pressed another on me as a compliment to her son's *patrona*. Octavio thought we had better go on, and manifested it by working one set of toes over the other. We lost a lot of coppers playing a game with a bouncing ball. I bought one of the flat white bags the men carry; and Octavio has never forgiven me for paying too much. He could have acquired it for much less.

Passing the city hall, where barefooted soldiers in blue dungarees lounged in a passageway, Octavio stopped, struck by the movie posters.

" If you should care to go to the cine tonight, señorita, I could buy your ticket," he said. But I was mean enough to let it ride, waiting to see what Tom Sawyer would do with his Huck Finn.

Huck was weary of delay. It was almost time for the show. "The cine is only fifteen cents . . ." but Octavio held him back, hissing at him. As I dickered for a leather purse, I heard the words *ill-bred, the correct manner*. Whatever was done must be done properly. No crudities would be tolerated.

It was really time for the movie, so I headed for the hotel. Octavio, encumbered with my bag and purchases, asked if he should come in the evening. " It might please you to see the plaza with the lights." The perfect gentleman could do no more, so I offered to finance the cine party, which would be so kind as to excuse me, as I wished to visit the zarabandas. Octavio left me with bows, hat in hand, feet close together.

" Señorita, until tomorrow. May you rest well."

A zarabanda is a dance, with liquor. Indeed, the potations outrank the ball for both buyer and dancer. Every storekeeper puts in beer, aguardiente, and a marimba, and clears a room for dancing. It is not an Indian dance, not even a folk-dance, but a drunken orgy, leading to empty purses, tortured heads, and jail. All day, every day, for the week of fiesta, those rooms reverberated to the tinny thumping of marimbas and were jammed with a swaying crush of Indians, pressed by spectators into the smallest possible dancing-space. Aguardiente was the preferred drink, and treats seemed to be the rule. Women drank as much as men. Each danced alone, heavily, stupidly, jigging a sort of one-step, around and around. Intervals with the bottle, lurching against the bar, and then the dance again. Very drunk, they danced together, more for mutual support than from conviviality. It is all so voiceless, so without joy, such a sullen determination to drink and dance until one falls wholly obfuscated and is carried out. Women were especially pathetic in their sodden helpless bobbing, bound perhaps to forget all life meant for them, to forget even the baby jolting loosely on the back. It seemed that they must fall, that tipsy mothers must stumble and crush them. But I saw no fatalities in several days and nights of intermittent watching. Here, too, the gods guard children and fools. Too sottish to stand, dancers were rolled by friends into a corner and left to sleep. Only the hapless ones found drunk in the streets were marched off to jail.

The fine was one quetzal, and by the end of the fiesta the town was richer by over eight hundred dollars. Besides that the Ladino (or white) merchants had a large share of cash recently paid to the Indians for labor, and numberless liens on future earnings, which would be faithfully paid. A profit of from two to five hundred quetzales during fiesta week is not unusual, I was told. The storekeeper's reply to criticism is that liquor is a government monopoly and that each town is required to sell a certain amount yearly.

When I came out from breakfast the next morning, Octavio was waiting, sitting on his heels by the gate. It was December 22, the very day of Santo Tomás; the dance of the *Toritos* was promised and a procession. We walked about the village to see the cofradía houses, distinguished by pine boughs at the door and officious cofrades, brothers, in ceremonial dress. Octavio even found a wall from which we could look into a patio where the performers were trying out their steps.

Close views of the streets were dismal. Both men and women showed black eyes or were still staggering from the night's debauch. Babies, forlornly dirty, hung whimpering from indifferent maternal backs. Older children were pinched with weariness. The eating-places were mussy, with the general aspect of a too long bazaar. But distant views were to be recommended. The church's white set off perfectly the color on the steps, black, red, and purple predominating; with curling incense smoke, clusters of tall sky-rockets, and down in front the agitated plumes of the silly-faced dancers.

In cheap court costumes — shorts, long-tailed coats, cocked hats, velvets and puffed satins — they were prancing to the tune of a violin, a flute, and two drums. All wore masks: black with gold beards, or red faces with long brown curls. The bull wore a sort of ecclesiastical cope, and his horns were tied on by a handkerchief. He made sorties at small boys, who squealed and ran, only to come back and dare him again.

A toy horse and horseman were jumping up and down the rope we had seen strung from the belfry yesterday. Xocolá, Octavio said, but he did not know what it meant. I suspected Santiago, Spain's patron saint, who appears in so many Indian rites. Later Señor Don Flavio Rodas, who is a deep student of these things, explained that the Mayas worshiped a divinity who ran as messenger between man and the sun. When the Spaniards brought horses, so much swifter than men, they elevated that animal to the post of messenger.

Mass over, the church door framed one saint after another, tilting tipsily as it was borne over the threshold and down the steps. Women hovered about, white huipiles hanging loose, as is correct for formal occasions. " *Las capitanas*," whispered Octavio. The most esteemed saints rode in huge cloth frames which exactly fitted the door's arch, and were decked with mirrors, Kewpie dolls, paper flowers, and plumes of peacocks, ostriches, even the rare quetzal. The last image was that of God in person, swathed in yellow calico and holding a bleeding little Christ on His knee. Four marimbas tried to outdo four orchestras of drum and chirimilla. Fireworks popped and boomed as men ignited tubes of powder or set the tall reeds soaring into the sky while people gazed breathily enraptured at smoke smudges against the blue.

Fireworks are not only noise to the Indian. The slender reeds, rising skyward, symbolize the soul going up to the sun. To understand it, according to Don Flavio Rodas again, one must go back to the grandmother of the Toltecs. Those valiant youths wished to go to Guatemala to play basket ball with the Mayas, but the old lady advised against it. She was afraid they would be defeated and utterly destroyed. The Toltecs, being very brave, insisted, but they told their grandmother how she might get news of them. She was to plant a certain reed, which dies down in the dry season. They assured her that if it grew again, it would be a sign of their success. So the grandmother waited many anxious months, but was finally comforted to see the reeds burgeon fresh and green. After that they could be only the emblem of life eternally renewed and so they stand to this day.

Late in the afternoon Octavio and I sat in our niche by the padre's house, watching the day soften into twilight and be shot full of garish electricity. That chromatic, diversified plaza held the answers to all the questions that boiled within me, and I could not read them! What I needed was a private archæologist, a resident folklorist, a handy historian, an interpreter in constant attendance, a court ethnologist, an expert in assorted handicraft, a botanist. I needed to know. And I wanted to understand. But I never should. White men do not understand Indians; least of all, I felt, in Guatemala, where the underlying Indian sea is still so undisturbed, so silent, and so deep.

V: The Shrine of the Black Christ

In January, Guatemala goes on pilgrimage to the little town of Esquipulas, where a black image of Christ Crucified is reputed to work miracles. Indians walk incredible distances on this pilgrimage. Special buses run out from the capital. The society columns announce that Señora This and That, with her daughters, is making her annual peregrination to the fabulous shrine.

As Esquipulas is on the way to Copán, one of the most magnificent Maya ruins, it seemed the time to visit them both. Such a journey would touch Guatemala's past at two high points: a regal city of the Old Empire and a mediæval holy place. However overlaid it may be by modern life and ways of thought, these two still shape the character of Guatemala. Fully a third of the people speak a dialect of ancient Maya and practice some form, however distorted, of Maya religion. An even greater percentage is Catholic.

Mary B. said she would go with me, so my wish to travel with a private archæologist was to be fulfilled. An authority in the field described her as " a sound archæologist." Certainly she is a charming girl and one of the few satisfactory traveling companions in the world. So few can run off and

amuse themselves alone! So few can accept a country and
a people as they are without drawing invidious comparisons
with their own flawless homeland and their own superior
compatriots. The third test is to know that the way to see
what Indians do is to sit still and watch. Mary B. was all
of that; and she could, besides, bring a cool fresh humor
to every situation.

We went by train from Guatemala to Chiquimula, over
toward Honduras. Everyone had commiserated with us
over the torrid heat we should encounter; to say nothing of
malaria and assorted venomous insects, including the tick
that bores in and never comes out. Upon advice we took
powders and sprays against the biting bugs; quinine and
whisky for malaria; tea and cheese and raisins, and even
cots and mosquito nets, because imagine us stuck somewhere
with no house to harbor us and nothing to eat. I had little
hope that anything so exciting would happen, but after
those icy days in *Los Altos,* I was ready to revel in hot
tropics. I took a top coat, having traveled in hot countries
before.

At Chiquimula we waited in a pension for a car going to
Esquipulas. As it was early morning, we were privy to all
the goings-on. Men shaved at the fountain, where maids
were filling water-jars, and a Ladina woman scrubbed her
baby, unmoved by the child's screams as she rubbed soap
into its eyes and poured cold water over its little body. Her
Indian maid took the child into her shawl as soon as she
could, warmed and comforted it in the sun. A group of
men breakfasted together. One, in high buttoned shoes, a
black coat, and tweed trousers, should have been the town

undertaker. They bowed as they passed our table and courteously paid no more attention until they finished. Then each one noisily rinsed his mouth, spat into the flower-beds, said: " *Buen provecho*," politely, and left.

We shared our car with three: a couple and a mother-in-law. The man was alert and well-informed, mother-in-law fervently told her beads, and the wife sat helplessly among the mounds of fat that submerge so many women of her race after marriage.

We crossed mountains, making long curves and descents and passing drowsy villages. The people moved more slowly than those of the Heights. Many women wore dark blue skirts with white huipiles: that always cool combination. Almost every man was smoking a cigar, for tobacco grows there and they all make their own. Every village was dressed up with arches of cypress and cedar, with flowers and curtains and flags, and the main street and often the road were strewn with pine needles. For the President was expected any day now. He would certainly get as far as Chiquimula and maybe to Esquipulas. The country was green with both pine and palm. Bare-branched *madre de cacao* bore flowers as pink as almond blossoms. Murul was flowering with yellow. And close to the road was the large purple shrub which seasons tamales for Sunday breakfast. We saw birds all the way, but our driver was too interested in his own ideas to tell us the names of things.

" People say the United States is imperialistic, but I say no! If the United States wanted these countries she could take them without firing a shot. Just let her send a hundred thousand men to pay gold for everything they used, and every country would be hers. That's all, gold. But the United States doesn't want these countries. All she wants is a market. She paid a lot of money for the Philippines and what did she get? Nothing but trouble. No, they don't want any more uncivilized people."

At a shady place, where a rill cascaded over rocks, we stopped for water. A group of young men came along. One after another sank down, resting his load against the bank, shook his head free of the tumpline, smiled at us, and settled to rest. Pilgrims, certainly. Such peaceful faces, and their hats were wreathed with the gray moss and yellow gourds that mean Esquipulas. They were Kekchi from Cobán, and their *cacaxtes* held seeds which they had taken to be blessed. They wore ordinary shirts and blue jeans, but their tranquil faces were the justification for all pilgrimages.

The driver still had a lot to say. " I like Norte Americanos. They say they are all for business, but I say no. They are more full of sentiment and idealism than we are. To know that, you have only to listen to the radio and read their magazines. I don't read English, but I read translations, and I hear American songs over the radio every day. That country is for progress and we must have progress. Abyssinia should be conquered by Italy. Italy means progress for those people."

" But," said the gentleman from the back seat, " Italy might conquer Abyssinia as you say the United States could overcome us, with gold."

The driver laughed and let it go.

From a hilltop we could look down on Esquipulas: a

chalk and brown village, with square church towers as
white as a paper cut-out. Along here the pilgrims stop to
make their first obeisance and prayers. As he swung his
car along the looping road, the driver told us about the
" Rock of the Compadres." *Compadres* are the parents and
god-parents of the same child.

" It is," he elucidated, " a spiritual relationship established by our Holy Church, and for them it is a mortal sin
to unite, to procreate." The Spanish language has a pellucid
clarity. " Once a man came here with his *comadre,* and as
they came down this hill, quickly with the descent, they
fell in love with each other. And right there in the road they
made that mortal sin. So our Lord, for punishment, turned
them into two rocks, one on top of the other, as you will
see. And there they stand as a warning."

Sure enough, there they stood, a large rock and a small
one. And where the larger overhung, there were pine
needles, scattered ashes, and withered flowers, suggesting
that other compadres had thought it well to seek protection,
or forgiveness, there. A troop of pilgrims were just leaving
as we arrived.

The Black Christ of Esquipulas was made, in 1595, by
Quirio Cataño, Guatemala's outstanding sculptor then and
one of the most famous in any day. The artist made the
figure black not, according to the Church, as an Indian
Christ, but because a dead body, blood-covered, would look
very dark. Nor does any legend attribute the color to the
accumulated sins of the world, as is the case in other places.
In fact, legend and miracle were lacking until the shrine
was long established. In 1735 the newly elected Bishop of

Guatemala arrived from his home in Lima, Peru, very ill. Hearing of Esquipulas, he went there, was cured, and ordered the construction of the magnificent church that now houses the sacred statue. Esquipulas became a place of pilgrimage. After the Bishop's cure innumerable miracles are cited. The best, as a story, is that of Señor Don Juan Palomeque y Vargas, a wealthy shipper of merchandise between the colony and Spain. His story is dated 1629, and I paraphrase it from a pamphlet written in 1914.

" Whether as a result of his excesses or because God wished it, Palomeque had begun to suffer from a sharp discharge of the eyes which went on aggravating itself until it took on the character of a true ophthalmy. . . . He consulted the most able doctors of the capital, and not finding relief, he finally decided to offer a visit to Our Lord of Esquipulas, to whom alone he trusted his healing. Such was, then, the object of that devoted pilgrimage which Don Juan should have undertaken in a more humble and Christian spirit. But the case is that Palomeque had added to the offering of his visit that of a chain of gold, and thinking of this gift, that puny soul considered the matter of his recovery a simple business deal between our Lord of Esquipulas and himself. Consequently he judged that if he obtained his cure he would be obligated to the Lord as he would be to a merchant.

" He arrived finally on his knees to place himself before the altar where the sacred image was located. He made a brief prayer and deposited the chain at the foot of the crucifix. Instantly the opaque veil which covered his eyes disappeared and he felt at the same time as if a soft breath had tempered the burning fire that inflamed his pupils. But the unfortunate one kept the worst of his blindness, that of the soul.

" Palomeque left the church full of joy and went to the house which was prepared for him. His journey had no other object than to fulfill the vow made to our Lord, and so he disposed himself to rest that morning and to leave after dinner on his return to Guatemala.

" ' What a joke, Gonzalo! ' said Don Juan, laughing with good humor. ' What a joke on the doctors to see me completely cured! '

" ' Señor,' answered his attendant, ' the important thing is your cure. For the rest, it cannot be denied that human wisdom cannot understand why it is reserved for the power of God. So, my master, give infinite thanks to our Lord of Esquipulas, and be forever his devotee.'

" ' Thanks to the Lord of Esquipulas,' replied the hidalgo with an ironic chuckle; ' rather you mean to say to my gold chain.'

" The attendant was horrified to hear these expressions in which ingratitude was aggravated by blasphemy, and he did not answer a single word. As he pronounced the impious sentence, Don Juan put his right hand in his pocket and found there the gold chain which the day before he had left at the feet of the image of Jesus Christ, and, having recognized it, a dense cloud covered his eyes.

" Palomeque gave a cry of horror and exclaimed: ' Blind! Completely blind! O unfortunate one! ' "

Not having a house prepared for us, like Señor Don Juan de Palomeque, we sought out Concha, who was gratifying a lifelong desire to visit Esquipulas. She advised Doña Carmela, Widow of Rodriguez. The widow's house was full, but when she learned that we had our beds, she offered a room, a wash-bowl and pitcher, and meals. The widow's meals were palatable: savory black beans, tortillas, hot and crisp, well-cooked meat, and coffee. For sanitary arrangements there was a banana grove behind the high adobe wall with a latch-string which read occupied or not according as it hung in or out. Flies were kept down by a long-legged, long-necked species of heron in the patio. His voice was that of a piece of machinery needing grease badly, and it never ran down. The widow said that he squawked like that only when a car passed, jealous of a sound even more exacerbating than his own. If so, he heard more motors than the human ear is attuned to. Still we were comfortable at the widow's.

High noon was blue and sparkling, and the village crowded. We pushed through people between booths lining the narrow street to the temple. It is fair as well as pilgrimage, and traders had come from all over Guatemala, bringing hand-woven goods and pottery from the highlands, manufactured trinkets from the capital, and food in every stage from cattle on the hoof to cooked meals served on table-cloths. Baskets had come from Salvador, painted gourds from Chiapas in Mexico, and hats from Honduras. Mary wanted a hat, but they were too small. Hat after hat perched unsteadily and too high. Merchants in other booths began to offer other things. A shawl. A string of beads. No, Mary wanted only a hat. *Solamente un sombrero.*

" Only a hot? " said a voice from the next booth. " My

God! A *hot!* " Somebody from Livingston, where they know
how to deal with tourists.

The atrium was packed so tight with people that we were
plastered up against the railing. A procession was pushing
through from one church door to the other. Over a sea of
jet-black heads floated the silken canopy that shaded the
image and the priests. And above that slowly moving mass
of heads a multitude of candle flames flickered redly in the
sun. The priests were chanting; there was that low murmur
of a crowd at prayer.

In a room young student priests were selling pictures,
frames, rosaries, medals. I bought rosaries for the maids
in my pension. Inside the church these things were blessed.
A young priest with a fair, uplifted face paced between the
people on the floor, each with his little packet of purchases
spread out. The priest murmured benediction and scattered
holy water on the gifts and the people. He must have been
fresh from the seminary: uplifted, consecrated, pitifully
sensitive, doomed to be terribly hurt by life, even a life
inside stone walls.

Afterwards we rested on the stone balustrade around the
atrium. Sitting quiet and motionless among Indians, you
soon merge with the scene, and the people, absorbed in their
own affairs, forget you. So the ideal is achieved of knowing
what would transpire if no stranger were there. An outsider,
especially a white person among brown-skinned folk, creates a palpable disturbance. He fills the air with bustle and
strange speech; but, even worse, the natives react to him.
The better of them withdraw, postpone whatever is important until the annoyance is removed. A few play up cheaply.

On the church steps men were singing religious songs from books they had to sell, and pilgrims went up and down on their knees, kissing the stones, throwing kisses as they backed away. Beggars whined: " For the love of God," and " May God reward you! " Men in white with peaked sombreros looked like Mexicans, and, sure enough, they had come from Oaxaca.

" What grace will these people win," they wanted to know scornfully, " coming at ease in automobiles? We have walked twenty-one days to honor our Lord, singing hymns and making prayers night and morning."

Below us on the slope was an interesting camp. From their costumes, they were people from Los Altos, a journey much shorter than the Mexicans had made. Women were picking nits out of each other's hair, suckling their babies, brewing coffee, or modestly rewrapping their skirts, with equal indifference. Men moved about, sat and ate, got up and went away. It was dirty, but friendly dirty, like a gypsy camp. One girl, when her hair had been well picked over, combed, and braided, was very pretty to look at.

Concha found us there. She plainly had us on her mind, having been told by her mistress in the city to look after the strangers. She found most of the food pretty questionable, but she had a friend who was selling coffee. In short, Concha had come to do her duty by inviting us to take coffee with her. The friend was equipped with a low charcoal fire, a couple of chairs, and a few cups on a plank laid across trestles. She fanned up a glow and set a jar of water in the coals. When it bubbled well, she dashed a handful of coffee in, without measuring it, and set it aside. Then she called her daughter and, with great to-do, they wiped off the table, poured sugar into the settling coffee, called across to a neighbor for sweet breads. In no time we were served. We tried to learn what miracles were reported this time, but our hostesses agreed that the time of miracles seemed to have passed. They had heard of none this year.

Concha offered to prepare us each a garland for our hats. She said that otherwise nobody in the capital would know we had been to Esquipulas. Mary, who had at last found a hat to fit, chose the colored paper flowers which are replacing the traditional adornment. After I had carried those heavy yellow gourds around for a few hours, I was ready to agree that paper flowers mark an advance in comfort, if not in religious zeal.

Just before dusk, going to sit again in the church, I found in the nave a huge catafalque under a black velvet pall, flanked by tall candles in silver candelabra. I asked a woman near me.

" Oh," she said, " that is for tomorrow, when there is a mass for the souls of all the dead who ever came here on pilgrimage. That's why it is so lovely to visit our Lord of Esquipulas! "

We missed the mass next morning, but we sat a long time watching the farewells. Loaded for the trail, people came to say good-by as to a human host. A woman tacked to the wall a crude painting illustrating her miraculous escape from an accident. Resplendent in the upper corner was our Lord of Esquipulas, black in a burst of yellow paint glory.

The smooth-haired woman from Los Altos came in with

several others. They knelt in a row, each backed by his crate or bundle. A boy rang a small ordinary bell, unremittingly. When his right hand tired, he transferred it to the left, but never stopped. A man swung a pottery censer and the fumes of pagan copal came drifting up against the Catholic incense. They all watched him and we took him for the leader, though he drooped against his cacaxte as though fastened there. His head-kerchief slipped and was pushed up again and again by a woman next to him. He chanted steadily. Was he the Indian shaman, we wondered. Why did that woman bother him so? He swung the censer more and more slowly, would have let it drop if the woman had not caught it. Others came in. Women with bundles, men bent under heavy crates. The little boy kept ringing.

Cleaners were sweeping their way down the tessellated floor, scraping up spilled wax and pushing the litter before them with soft brooms. If worshipers did not move at once, they shoved them roughly. We, too, moved, and that brought us closer to the Indians kneeling just inside the door. The copal fumes were stronger. The officious woman had taken the censer away from the old man. Then, as she pushed up his kerchief and wiped his face, we saw that he was not an old man, but very young, and sick; wavering and weak, but not with age. His chanting choked and ended. A man beside him took up the prayer. His words were neither Spanish nor Latin. Were they all, perhaps, invoking a pagan deity, with the child's bell, the copal smoke, the combined appeal of now it was eleven people kneeling there, all intent upon the prayer; except the woman beside the invalid, who was only concerned to see he did not fall? She arranged a roll of rags to support his pitiful head, wiped his face again and again. Tuberculosis might make a man look like that.

The young priest with the consecrated look strolled by. Off duty now, he walked slowly with hands in pockets through his cassock, observing. The scent of copal struck his nostrils. Without altering his steady pace he turned his head, gazing from the aerie of his seminary training, his intellectual Catholicism, his youthful intolerance, upon that outlandish, unchristian, intolerable performance. All wrong, he knew it to be. But he knew, too, that a Church much wiser than he would ever be, tolerated just that. If the Indian must express his faith so, then he may. His youthful reverence was scandalized, clearly, but he went slowly by, at even tread, his eyes turning as he passed to assure themselves again that such things could be in a Christian temple. Only his nostrils and his mobile mouth expressed his perturbation. It will be many years, I thought, before he will know the tolerance of such men as Padre Rossbach at Chichicastenango, of the Padres Knittel at Momostenango and San Francisco El Alto.

The Indians were ready to go. Several were busy with the patient. A net supported his feet. The woman wrapped him warmly in torn blankets, and he laid his head wearily on the bundle of rags she had tied there. When he raised his hands they were gaunt, shadowy. Every man knelt, harnessed himself to his burden, and rose, staggering with the weight. One knelt behind the sick man. Thin as he was, he made a heavy load. When the bearer stood, they all rested a moment, still. Even the little boy had stopped ringing. The patient moved his hand feebly in the sign of the cross, and on his face was such a look as only God and the angels should see. Faith, pitiful, tragic faith. It did not seem that he could possibly live until night. They carried him out then, slowly, backing reverently to the door and moving steadily down the steps. Twelve or fourteen days at least to their home in the Heights.

VI: The Ruins of Copán

Leaving Esquipulas, we found places in a seven-passenger touring car. As two people always ride with the driver, we begged that honor. In the back seat were a man, two women, and two children, and in the middle two men, another woman, and a baby. Complete, we thought. But at the city hall we picked up a soldier and his friend. The friend's bundle was tied on somewhere; a bath-towel around his neck was the soldier's only impedimenta. Our protest that no car should be expected to climb mountains under such a load pained the driver deeply. It was a good car, and besides, the last two were a promise, an obligation! There is no reasoning with a man of such sterling honor, so we subsided. The supernumeraries stood on the running board in some danger of being scraped off, but handy when a push was needed. With their aid the car did make the grade. All advertisers of motors should observe their performance in Latin America. With parts missing, the engine exposed to the weather, a starter that does not function, dangling wires, tires worn to the fabric, and loaded to double capacity, they thump over the most taxing grades, steaming and rattling, stopping often for water, for punctures, for minor repairs; but they never fail to arrive. Any manufacturer would be amazed at how often they arrive; dismayed at how long they last.

At Chiquimula we had to secure a visa, as Copán is in Honduras. Hot and dusty, we made no speed about cooling baths and drinks, and it was half past five when we crossed the plaza to the government building. Soldiers in well-washed blue snapped to the salute, and one directed us up wide stone stairs. The *corredor* was full of men: peons in white, sitting with that almost inhuman patience of the Indian. With the equally inhuman insistence of the *Yanqui* we pushed through and were greeted by Colonel Montenegro, in crisp white and varnished boots. He must, he said, wire to the capital, but he anticipated a reply within a couple of hours. We might get off for Copán in the morning. Convinced that no Latin American government could do anything in a couple of hours, we resigned ourselves to a whole day's delay and tried to match the Colonel's suavity as he saw us to the stairs. As the officer passed along the *corredor*, all those waiting men rose, with the rustle of sandals on stone, and stood at attention, humbly. He heeded them no more than as if they had been corn agitated by the wind. I thought of a mayor at home, greeting his constituents.

Knowing Latin America, we knew not Guatemala. Before eight that evening our visa had arrived. We might start as early as we liked.

It was another drive of mountain ridge after ridge, with the same sinuosities, up and down; all negotiated easily by a powerful car and a skillful driver. No village was too small to have a uniformed policeman to stop us and ask all the questions. Every hamlet was fragrant with lime and orange blossoms, swept and adorned for the President, rumored to be coming here too. We crossed a divide where hundreds of men swarmed, widening the road, shoveling, sweating, heaving, bossed by a flat-nosed Irish boss. More than fifty years ago Guatemala was invaded by hundreds of Yankees, mostly Southerners, who built her railroads. So the strain of the North American adventurer may show itself anywhere. We rode under magnificent ceiba trees, interspersed with cedar. Orioles and woodpeckers were familiar. A curassow, yellow-crested, black and stately, crossed the path. Blue and gray jays chattered, and humming-birds whirred in iridescence through the mimosas. We even saw the yellow-breasted trogón, a cousin of the quetzal and probably as close to that mythical bird of freedom as I shall ever get. Beyond the road-gang we followed the old track, narrow and addicted to hanging itself out over precipices. Every lift opened up vaster extents of valley and peak. There seems to be no flat or uninteresting inch in the whole Republic.

From the Vado Lelá we had five hours at least on the mules sent from Copán to meet us. One for each of us and one for baggage on which Manuel treated himself to an occasional lift. Afoot he made better time than we did. In Guatemala, which does not know the Rocky Mountain pony, the belief prevails that a mule is something to ride on, but five hours is adequate proof of the error. A mule does dig his hoofs in so at every step, and with a jerk to jar the very marrow in the bones!

At the border a dark congeries of huts emitted men. An

old one in spectacles took our papers and burrowed back into the unlighted house, where he must have performed magic over them; he certainly could not have read them in that gloom. There remained with us a malarial individual, lean, yellow, and sardonic; and two soldiers, one black as jet, the other leather-colored. They asked the invariable questions: Where were our men? Had we no men? We risked a joke. Even the malarial one was betrayed into a grin. The old man poked out again with our papers and his ideas all in a muddle. Captivated by the archæologist's slim prettiness, her flying fair hair, and her facile Spanish, he put all his queries to her. "And the other woman? What's her name? How old is she? What does she want to go to Honduras for?" The malarial one finally wearied of the game and suggested that we probably had no contraband anyhow.

So we were in Honduras, and hungry. Manuel knew a family. They apologized because they had only tortillas and coffee. But with our cheese and chocolate, and the pineapple they remembered at last, it made a fine meal. Father and grandmother smoked while the daughters served us and a young matron suckled her baby. The children offered slipping little hands and then sat very still. This family, like the men at the border, wanted to talk about that most capable engineer, Don Gustavo, who had just driven a truck over these trails to Copán — the first automobile many people had ever seen. The children remembered. They had seen it; it made much noise. This ride we were making in five hours had cost the intrepid Don Gustavo eight days, largely occupied in road-building.

Don Gustavo is Gustav Stromsvik, one of those happy beings who have found their level and their work by force of personality and ability. A Norwegian sailor, he appeared at Chichen-Itza at a moment when a man who could handle ropes was much needed. In moving tons of irreplaceable stone, knots must hold. After several years with ropes and cement in Yucatan, learning constantly, Mr. Stromsvik advanced to setting the stelæ at Quiriguá in permanent bases. He planted each one firmly in cement, bored a hole through its length, inserted a backbone of wire, and protected it with heavy fencing. Earthquake-proof, even tourist-proof. Quiriguá had suffered from a visitor who whacked off a nose for a souvenir. Dr. Morley faced that vandal in his New York home and recovered the nose, which after many vicissitudes is back where it belongs. Mr. Stromsvik is now in charge at Copán. Modest about what he knows, aglow with the joy of what he is doing, his enthusiasm would infect anyone with the urge to dig. It is a human manifestation that would be well worth the trip even if it offered no wonders in stone.

The end of the ride was dragging, long. Any Indian wishes to be kind; so Manuel assured us, for hours, that Copán lay just over the next hill. " *Tras lomita, tras lomita.*" But at last we rode into the cobbled village and up to the long porch of Don Juan Ramón Cuevas's house. We were greeted by three young men in white linen. The Carnegie Institution takes a bit of formality into the jungle, as well as the odor of sanitation. Years of exploring have taught it that in the wilds dressing for dinner is quite as important as iodine in the water or nets over the beds.

In the morning when Don Gustavo took us to the ruins, we realized that the renowned truck had not lost its novelty. Dozens of inhabitants rushed out to see the fabled monster pass; we might have been riding a dinosaur. In a few minutes we reached the little museum the Honduran government has put up and the heavy wire fence that protects the ruins. The whole valley, about twenty miles square, was occupied by the prehistoric Mayas, but this was its heart, pulsating with government and business and with ceremonies in the idol houses, as the Spaniards called the temples. John L. Stephens first mapped it in 1839 when he bought the site from a finquero for fifty dollars. By what right the finquero sold it and who owned it afterwards nobody seems to know, but since the settlement of a border dispute with Guatemala, Copán belongs to Honduras.

The valley is prolific of a rich and varied living. The zapote tree gives the ironwood the ancients used for door lintels and beams; its fruit is edible, its sap is chewing-gum. Tropical fruits and vegetables: cacao for money and for drink; palm for food as well as hats, raincoats, and roofs; gourds, and rubber. The jungle was cut down in 1860 and only a few noble ceiba and cedar trees remain. But in the time of the ancients deer and peccary abounded, anteater (which the natives still relish), monkeys, and certain dogs for food; jaguar and ocelot for furs. The storax gives copal, the pungent gum whose aroma is as evocative of Indian rites as Catholic or Chinese incense is of theirs. In 1840 Colonel Galindo discovered the quarries of that volcanic tuff which was so readily carved into feathery designs. Mr. Stromsvik showed us how a penknife will cut it.

Exposed to air, it hardens into a durability that will last for centuries.

As we drove through the gate, the Acropolis towered ahead of us and to the east, forty meters high and veiled with jungle growth in many tones of green. It was named fifty years ago when archæologists thought in terms of Greece and Egypt. They called all such Maya mounds pyramids, though they are not truly pyramidal, but flat-topped; and they were not temples, but bases on which the temples stood. We left the truck beside an incongruous chugging engine which was boring a hole into the center of the mound, and went to see the stelæ first.

West of the Acropolis lies an extensive quadrangle surrounded by stepped walls like an amphitheater. It has been planted with Bermuda grass, which forms a mat too thick for the jungle to push through. At last they have found a way to avoid the old necessity of chopping down the bush every year before work could begin. More than twenty stelæ stand there, erect now, colorless in the sun-glare like ghosts of their own past.

A stela is a monolith, twelve to thirty feet tall, in the shape of a human figure compressed into a rectangular form. Standing with heels together and arms flexed, it generally holds a bar across the breast; and it is topped by a head-dress of great elaboration. To an eye trained by European art, Maya sculpture seems at first deliriously confused as a whole and hideous if not gruesome in detail. Dr. Herbert J. Spinden, in his *Maya Art*, published by the Peabody Museum of Archæology and Ethnology, explains that the Mayas, unlike the Greeks, did not aim to express an ideal human form. Their gods were represented by ophidian or animal forms or by composites. What human features they used were incidental, though faces are often so individual as to suggest portraiture. Legs and arms were sculptured almost in the round and too realistically, and in poses too difficult for any but a finished artist. Every stela is worth close study for the delicacy of its carving and for the fine and balanced dignity of the whole. The color which originally covered the sculpture must have clarified the design and lessened the confusion by bringing out certain lines and subduing others.

Set up at twenty-, ten-, and rarely at five-year intervals, the stelæ were time-markers. That they stand erect now is due to Mr. Stromsvik's work, using the technique he perfected at Quiriguá. Under many of them, in cruciform offertories, were discovered pottery vessels, sea-shells, and coral. Under Stela H, to be technical, they found the oldest wrought gold known in the Americas. It is impure gold, but it forms a couple of miniature but unmistakable human legs. A handful of jadeite beads was with them, all crumbled, maybe broken with intent. Together with these, but more shallowly buried, was a crouching figurine with a typical modern Mexican sombrero perched on an ornate head-dress. No explanation is vouchsafed of how he got so far ahead of the mode.

Walking back toward the Acropolis, we could see that only part of the stairway has been uncovered. On its slopes and sides enormous trees have been left, giving more impressively than anything I ever saw a sense of antiquity and of mystery. For hundreds of years those trees grew, burying in humus and loam masterly work which is only now coming to light, cracked by roots and discolored by soil. Men made those steps, carved the Hieroglyphic Stairway, placed the stelæ and carved the symbols so significant then, so meaningless now. The dates can be read; nobody knows what events they marked. Of a powerful people and their history nothing is left but dates, and we don't know what they mean.

In front of the Hieroglyphic Stairway is a pile of debris, monument to bad work. Pieces have been snatched out, pawed over, thrown out of all arrangement, and left with no record of where they were found. " If only," groaned Mr. Stromsvik, " if only they had told us where they found what they took! " For in archæology, as in society, position is everything. Finding this under or over that may upset a whole theory or confirm it. As the work progresses, it is hoped that some of those fragments may be replaced, but to the amateur it looks a hopeless task. There are seventy structures within a radius of a square kilometer. Five years' work, at least, just to clean it up, show what was there, repair what may be of the havoc of bungling digging.

On our hands and knees we crept into the tunnel the engine was working at. The motor was for light; the actual digging was done by Indians. These diggers are an important part of any archæological staff; they handle every bit of bone or pottery with care, understanding that it is important, and they seem to enjoy their kinship with the great people who made the idols and walls that hold such strange interest for the foreign gentlemen. A shaft into the center of a pyramid often serves to establish a sequence. The

Mayas made a practice of building one pyramid over another by erecting a larger shell and filling it in with rubble: an onion-like construction which leaves no doubt about the order in which things were done.

On top — and stepping up those high and narrow treads is an athletic feat — we saw work on a temple. Maya temples were rectangular buildings with very thick walls and, originally, two parallel rooms. The inner gradually became the enclosed shrine; the outer was modified into a portico. On this theme many variations were played. But the Maya architects were always limited by the fact that they did not understand the principle of the true arch, and their rooms could never be more than twelve feet wide, the limit of the corbeled arch they did understand. Intent and excited, a young archæologist was watching Indians scratch the dirt away from a piece of carving — his own discovery. It was in a narrow chamber which might have been of ceremonial importance, though certain out-jutting stones were unaccountable. It is always so; nothing definite is ever asserted in such a case.

Copán is one of the oldest sites so far studied; and its history covers practically the whole period of the Old Empire. In both architecture and sculpture the whole story can be read there. Dr. Spinden based much of his study of Maya art on Copán carvings because they illustrate the development from clumsy fumblings of primitives, unsure of their technique, to the work of the best period, comparable with the art of any people limited to similar tools, and superior to that of both Assyrians and Egyptians in knowledge of foreshortening. Maya decoration, as Dr. Spinden shows, began with flat figures, realistic but badly done. It developed through more and more elaborate stylization into what the layman sees as a nonsensical jumble of tails and skulls, claws and backbones, human noses and birds' tails. Only a student can pick out the ear-plug, the quetzal feather, the course of the spine. Many of the greater figures, like those of the stelæ, represent single beings, gods or priests or rulers, with an infinity of detail, showing lushness of imagination and riotous prolificness in the use of form, but always disciplined by the requirements of space and of the highest principles of art. Dr. Spinden remarks, arrestingly, that if we could once accept the Maya serpent symbolism as we accept the halo of the Christian saint, we should be able to appreciate their art.

We crossed the flat top of the pyramid and slid down the other side into the East Court. Archæologists take this to be the holiest spot because the most ornate temple stands there. Its doorway is formed of monstrous figures, rearing from skulls at the base to join their tails at the top of the arch. A supreme example of the combination that comes to seem typically Maya: grisly symbols of death with odious reptilian and grotesque human forms built up into a total effect of nobility and magnificence. The famous Jaguar Stairway is in the East Court. A burial chamber has been opened there and altars repaired. The oldest altars were drum-shaped, with scant decoration, but altars of a later period are in the shape of beasts and solidly carved with glyphs. Two-headed dragons, turtles, and jaguars appear at Copán, and at Quiriguá, colonized from Copán, they become complicated to the point of degeneracy.

These things are indescribable. As my archæologist truly said, " You can only tell people to go and look. If they can't see, it's impossible to tell them anyhow."

The main structure, centering in the Acropolis, was a gradual growth over possibly two centuries. This can be well understood by a view of the most interesting excavation at Copán: a piece of nature's handiwork. We rode out to the Copán River from where we could see how the stream has made a perfect cross-section of the pyramid. It must have changed its course, as tropical rivers do, after the Mayas abandoned the city. Relentlessly it cut through the mound, leaving exposed a bluff thirty meters high and a hundred long. It shows how the Mayas built, on a rubble center faced with cut stone and lime plaster. Various plaza levels are discernible, with pavements and drains. It is a superb profile, but enough has been done. The problem now is to make the river let well enough alone. So a crew of modern Mayas were digging the river a new channel a hundred meters away from the old. With the first rains, floods would rush through that man-made ditch, deepen it into a real river, and save the famous cross-section as it is.

Late that afternoon, while the archæologists talked technicalities, I sat on a stone bench facing the Hieroglyphic Stairway and tried to picture what an Old Empire chieftain might have witnessed from that seat. Today's ghostly gray stone was blazing with color then. The pyramid, shadowed now with heavy forest growth, stood clear then in the sun and aswarm with life. Even on an ordinary day the people must have been brightly dressed as the modern Mayas, and imagination hesitates before the gorgeousness of a festal day. That ruler could have seen a procession zigzagging down those steep steps, garbed as the figures on the stelæ are with skins and plumes and jeweled ornaments. They would have shimmered in robes of feathers, prismatic as tropical birds, set in patterns with mosaic-like precision. Priests carrying ceremonial bars most finely wrought by the best artists would have performed ceremonial magic, uttering oracular prophecies or portents of disaster. And surely the great court of the stelæ must have held such dances as exist no more, with animal, serpent, bird, and flower forms in bewildering splendor.

My mind went back from that to the cripple at Esquipulas. What a contrast! The faith of the mediæval Church, the glory of Maya art. Both achievements of the human spirit incomprehensible to the modern mind, but equally significant, possibly, if we could only understand.

VII: Maya Archæology in Guatemala

ARCHÆOLOGY IS ONE OF THE KEENEST SPORTS IN THE world: a healthy, outdoor sport, with all the suspense and challenge of a mystery story. First a crime is discovered. A splendid culture has been destroyed, apparently at the acme of its development. The corpus delicti is found in ruined edifices, and there is a mass of detail — potsherds, carvings, jewels, writings in code, and skeletons — that would baffle the most up-to-date detective. Clues have been confused, misread, and lost by blundering amateurs mussing around before the scientific sleuths arrived. The reconstruction of the crime needs the patience of a jigsaw addict who also likes cross-word puzzles. He should be young enough to stand wearing trips into insalubrious jungles and adventurous enough to take chances where game is plentiful but other food scarce, water lacking, and himself sure to be rated as a suspicious if not dangerous lunatic. If he is all that, he will have an exciting time and go home to be hailed as a scientist of the first rank. Which he undeniably is.

Modern archæology is a science in that men devote their lives to the painstaking accumulation of facts and the working out of conclusions, honestly founded upon facts. It and its related study, ethnology, are human sciences of the broadest possible application. When we know, for instance, where the Mayas came from, whether their development was autochthonous or depended from some old-world culture, and why it broke down, we shall know much more than we do about our own civilization. Dr. Kidder said: " If the world has produced another culture as high as the Maya quite independently of ours, we may conclude that the human animal is bound to produce culture. Ours is not just chance. And when we know why Maya civilization disintegrated, we may get light on what is happening to us, on whether we are on the way up or down. All quite aside," he added, " from the fun of digging."

Men so inspired will not accept anything as true until it has been established beyond the peradventure of a doubt. One who hopes for a few glittering generalities to put into a book confronts an unbreachable wall of caution. No archæologist admits anything without reservations. Very scientific and commanding much admiration, but it does hamper the reporter. After toiling to extract information from my private archæologist and others, I can explain why archæologists so generally marry one another. No girl untrained in scientific doubt could possibly realize that the hesitant young man qualifying every statement, hedging on every declaration, casting doubt on his own thesis, was proposing marriage.

Our race first heard of the great Maya temples when Alvarado, pushing his conquests into Salvador, was told of a stone city to the east, which must have been Copán. He did not visit it, but later travelers did and left accounts much more florid than anything a modern archæologist can be betrayed into.

In a letter to King Philip II, Diego García de Palacio describes Copán's " superb edifices." He saw a statue which " resembles a bishop in his pontifical robes with a well-wrought miter and rings on his fingers," and a baptismal font. Fuentes y Guzmán, writing his history in 1700, was even more romantic. He relates that the circus of Copán was surrounded by stone monuments about six yards high representing men and women in garments " wholly Spanish in style." He found this odd, " although the Demon could have shown the Spaniards thus arrayed to the Indians, even before the coming of the former to these shores." He also reports a stone couple, in Indian garb, dallying in a stone hammock, so delicately swung that the " lightest touch of the hand " could set it swinging. These astonishing master-pieces were unhappily never seen again. Colonel Galindo, in 1836, does not mention them. End of fairy-tales, begin-ning of science.

Science was picturesque enough in the person of John L. Stephens, a young American sent by President Van Buren in search of the government of Guatemala. As the govern-ment might have been anywhere in 1840, Mr. Stephens was free to roam as he liked. He liked to visit ruins, climb volcanoes, and frivol in the capital. Nothing dashed him except smoking ladies, but he tolerantly admits that they were good women in spite of it. He was one to listen to warnings against disease, danger, and difficulty and then to do what he intended from the start. He was knocked out, once or twice, by fever; " moschitoes " bothered him continually; but he rose from more than one bed of pain for an arduous trip, and when there were no nets against the mosquitoes he suffered through as best he could. Mr. Stephens was the first to write in English about the Maya ruins, and he put all later archæologists in his debt by taking along Frederick Catherwood to make drawings. They recorded for study several monuments since destroyed, and Mr. Catherwood's copies of hieroglyphics he could not decipher are so accurate that they are easily read by later students who can. But Mr. Stephens and Mr. Catherwood supposed all wrong. (One must speak of them with the formality they used. Two young men off on adventure in a foreign land, who literally fought, bled, and all but died together seem to have addressed each other always as Mister.) Having studied in Egypt, they saw kings in all the statues and took the carvings for records of regal doings. They did notice the few signs of war and marveled at a history with nothing bellicose in it. These two formal rascals covered nearly the whole of Central America on mules, saw and mapped the most important ruins, and produced a book, *Travels in Guatemala and Central America*, which is the most enjoyable of them all.

In the eighties and nineties an Englishman, Alfred Maudslay, made three visits. His photographs are supplemented by the drawings of Miss Annie Hunter. Dr. Morley considers her work a little too pretty — an English gentlewoman, making drawings in the eighties! — but reliable as to glyphs. Mrs. Maudslay accompanied her husband once, riding a side-saddle over the most precipitous mountains with umbrella, note-book, and camera. She wrote *A Glimpse at Guatemala,* while the doctor prepared scientific studies. Mrs. Maudslay set up housekeeping wherever she was, cooked and cleaned, and directed servants. She never seemed to feel put upon, but she did remark at Copán that she saw more of her kitchen than of the obelisks.

All comers assumed that they could best serve science by removing as much as possible to Europe or the United States. Thanks to Dr. Maudslay's expert packing, the Kensington Museum has one of the best Maya collections in the world. In that day it was incredible that Europeans could ever see Guatemala. The only way to show the world was to take the stuff out, and they did. That Dr. Maudslay was a most honorable man is manifested by the tale of his encounter with Désiré Charnay, a young Frenchman who thought the ruin at Menche Yaxchilan was his discovery. He named it Lorillard City after one of his backers, Pierre Lorillard, of the tobacco family. When he arrived, all set to dig, there was Maudslay, hard at it. Overcome with disappointment, Charnay offered to withdraw. But British courtesy proved quite equal to French. Dr. Maudslay bowed himself out, and Gallic chivalry evened the score by telling the story in the book Charnay wrote. It is a gentleman's sport, archæology!

Other French notables were M. and Mme Le Plongeon, who spaded up some invaluable treasures, thanks, they say, to Madame's gift for dreaming.

All these investigators were puzzled by the stelæ. Though most of them lay prone, they had obviously once stood erect. They were taken for gods or kings, and the telegraphic marks for incidental decoration. Only Maudslay had a glimmer that they might be numbers. They are a code, of which less than a third has ever been deciphered. Its reading began with students poking about among musty manuscripts in European museums.

In 1863 the Abbé Brasseur de Bourbourg in Madrid found the *Relación de las Cosas de Yucatan* (*Account of the Affairs of Yucatan*), written in the sixteenth century by Fray Diego de Landa. It was all the friar could learn about Maya life and customs from educated Indians who remembered the days before the Conquest. Brother Diego, later Bishop of Yucatan, owed civilization that account because his religious fervor had led him to burn all the Maya books he could find. To a sixteenth-century priest they were the Devil's own work, but what an irreplaceable record went up in that holocaust, and how many years have been spent trying to restore what fanaticism destroyed! Among other things, the Bishop describes the calendar, giving glyphs for the twenty days of the Maya month and for eighteen of the nineteen divisions of their year. He also gives an alphabet, but that breaks down in the light of later knowledge. What the Mayas said when they were not lisping in numbers is still enigma, but the cryptic dots and dashes took on meaning. They recorded not wars but the movements of stars and planets and the passage of time. Twenty years after the publication of Landa's *Relación*, Dr. Förstemann, studying a Maya manuscript in Dresden, discovered that the Mayas understood and used the zero centuries before it was known to our culture. By curious chance, J. T. Goodman of California, working with Maudslay's records and unaware of the German's report, made the same discovery.

Until well along in the twentieth century there was little consistent advance. Each investigator cleared the bush, gazed enraptured at the marvels revealed, removed what he could, and sailed home to write a book about it. Then the jungle stealthily overgrew the ruin, which showed only as a slight eminence in the verdant sea of the forest.

Beginning with the Peabody Museum of Harvard, various North American institutions have worked in the Guatemala field, building up, stone by stone, clue by clue, the case for a Maya civilization worthy to rank with ancient cultures of Europe and Asia. For the amateur the best book on that subject is Herbert J. Spinden's *Handbook of Central American Archæology.*

In the first decade of this century Dr. Edgar L. Hewett, Director of the American School of Archæology, headed a couple of expeditions to Quiriguá and Copán. Their greatest contribution was Sylvanus G. Morley, then on his first trip to Guatemala. His eagerness, his infectious enthusiasm, have fired all later students, and his scholarly presentation of the importance of the field interested the Carnegie Institution of Washington. In 1915 that organization authorized Dr. Morley to study the Maya area. Followed ten years of exploration: a thrilling decade when every turn opened up something more wonderful than the last. Already it has become a legend. Dr. Morley visited all the known ruins and discovered many new ones. In the Petén they offered twenty-five dollars a ruin to the chicle-gatherers, those semiaquatic creatures of no particular race and of the worst reputation, who tap zapote trees for the sap which makes our chewing-gum. They knew, of course, where carved stones stood. One enterprising one offered to show ruins at so much per day and expenses, but that method produced more expenses than worked stones and was abandoned. In densest jungles the temples and palaces of a very advanced culture appeared. The density of that population, their proficiency and fertility exceeded all expectations.

The most extensive and intensive work in the Petén has been done at Uaxactun, whose history, from A. D. 68 to 638, covers practically the entire period of the Old Empire. Dr. Morley named it Eight Stones in Maya, but the natives are sure he was honoring his national hero, Wash-in-tun. Uaxactun is the northernmost Old Empire site in Guatemala, but Palenque and Piedras Negras in Mexico were important centers too. Dr. J. Alden Mason and Mr. L. Satterthwaite of the University of Pennsylvania have found there exquisite figurines and the finest carvings in stone — work so artistic that it bears comparison with that of Egypt and of Greece.

Not all the known ruins have been worked; certainly many have not yet been discovered. Almost half the Republic of Guatemala runs away into the impenetrable jungle of the Petén, where the unconquered Lacandón Indians live out of reach of white men. It is country that white men have never seen except from the air when a group of archæologists flew over it with Colonel Lindbergh. As their eyes became trained to spotting ruins from the air, they could see evidences of more than one city probably quite as dazzling in magnificence and in interest as the greatest now known. That sort of thing they call orchid-hunting. The real job of piling up fact on fact into certainty is " dirt archæology " — a term rendered with the same intonation as " dirt farmer " — meaning, I assume, that all will be learned eventually by a slow and meticulous sifting of the sand and of the findings. But it is the carvings and the temples that attract us mere gazers from afar.

This second period of intensive study has taken Dr. Morley to Yucatan, and work in Guatemala is directed by Dr. Oliver G. Ricketson, Jr. And, to complete the picture, Dr. Alfred V. Kidder heads the Department of Historical Investigation under which all the Carnegie archæological work is done.

In 1936 Dr. Kidder and Dr. Ricketson, as plain and simple diggers of dirt, opened up a ruin within three miles of Guatemala. Finds indicate that it was occupied from earliest times almost to the Conquest. As it was on the main trade route, it may at any minute reveal a connection with Aztecs, Incas, anybody. Archæologists are forever breathlessly seeking that missing link! Several years ago Señor Lic. J. Antonio Villacorta C., Minister of Education, began excavations there. Reporters jeered that it was just an old brickkiln and that nothing good could be found so near home anyway. Señor Villacorta showed his mound to Dr. Ricketson, who is charmed to have a job that involves no mulerides through waterless jungles.

I went out there one day. A round hill had been cut in half to show a stone stairway mounting a pyramid. An audience of Ladino neighbors, Indians from the market, and the latest ship-load of tourists gazed into a hole in the ground. And at its bottom sat the cream of the archæological fraternity, rubbing soil in their fingers and poking around with spatulas to be sure no single precious jade bead was lost. With soft brushes they were cleaning carved jade ornaments and brilliant green ear-plugs. This was the tomb of a rich man, if not a king, whose fate seems to refute the theory that jewels are vanity. Of this gentleman only his jewels endure, and a few belongings buried to help him on his way. A slave among them. In his honor they have named the site Kaminaljuyú — Hills of the Dead.

They have found many vases of varying fineness, all of the Old Empire. One is in the form of a man with a wise old tortured face and the curling feet of a baby. Some are almost as thin as porcelain, others very crude. They are painted in fresco in dull green, red, black, turquoise, and soft blue with the delicate lines, balanced design, and harmony of color that only an artist is capable of. Every pot is pasted together — the jigsaw-puzzle department — copied by an artist, and maps, charts, drawings, and photographs made to show where every bit was found.

Modern archæology not only handles material in a studious and doubting frame of mind. It involves dealing with governments. The earlier way of shipping out as much as possible resulted in stringent prohibitive laws. Each country naturally wanted its own treasures. The Carnegie Institution, in full accord with that desire, agrees to turn over to the government every piece it finds. In consequence the Middle American countries have profited by North American diggings. It is one answer to the Colossus of the North phobia and has done incalculable good in promoting real understanding between our countries. In Guatemala this is enhanced by the interest of Antonio Villacorta and the Society of Geography and History of Guatemala, which is doing first-rate work, especially with old manuscripts. The *Popol Buj* was published by them. Discovered in Chichicastenango at the end of the seventeenth century, it had appeared in French, but the first Spanish translation was made by Don Flavio Rodas and Antonio Villacorta. This and the *Annals* of the Cakchiqueles, translated by Dr. Daniel G. Brinton in 1885, are invaluable for checking what the monuments show. When the monuments and the ancient manuscripts agree, a good case has been made out. Then there remain only the beliefs and customs of the modern descendants of the old Mayas to study.

Of late, archæology in the Maya area has entered a new phase. Ethnologists have been set to studying the modern Guatemalan Indians in the hope that what they do, and especially what they believe, may help to solve the problem of what gave their ancestors strength to build so splendidly and what weakness made them unable to maintain what they had built.

VIII: Maya Old Empire

THE QUESTION: WHERE DID THE MAYAS COME FROM? HAS elicited some highly imaginative answers. They are called the lost tribes of Israel; Negroes from Africa, a bit faded; survivors of the Lost Atlantis, who paddled over in canoes when their continent sank, bringing a knowledge of astronomy and the occult; or an unknown tribe who rode across a land bridge, since disappeared, on elephants. The elephant comes in because a creature with what might be an elephant's trunk is depicted on a stela at Copán. Not long ago an archæological congress in Berlin listened to two lengthy and abstruse dissertations: one to prove that the elephant's trunk was a parrot's beak, the other that it is from the toucan.

The approved theory is that the Mayas, like all American tribes, did come from Asia, but from the north; that they drifted south, discovered the teosinte, developed corn, and, being well fed, spread out and developed. If you wish to believe that they evolved right there, from their own monkeys, nobody can prove you wrong.

What is known about them my archæologist permits me to summarize as follows. The Maya culture was fully developed by the time of Christ. The Old Empire covers roughly the first six centuries of our era. Dr. Kidder believes it was at that time the highest culture on the globe, as Rome was in decline and northern Europe still in barbarism. The Old Empire must be studied from the monuments and the artifacts and deductions from what is known of the New Empire in Yucatan. It is the detective job at its most baffling.

The oldest cities as yet investigated were Uaxactun and Tikal in the Petén. Maya cities were religious and civic centers with handsome houses for rulers and priests, temples and government buildings, and ample courts for games and ceremonies. The lower classes lived in grass-thatched huts in the country, as they still do. Dr. Ricketson estimates the scattered population of Uaxactun at as high as fifty thousand people. It is notable that the great ruins are found in the lowlands while the descendants of the ancient Mayas prefer to live in the highlands today. Dr. Kidder says that the culture originated in the highlands, as indicated by such remains as Kaminaljuyú — Hills of the Dead. Corn, the basis of that culture, is a highland plant, but in the lowlands it gives a tremendous yield; so as culture developed and probably slavery with it, the wealthiest cities were built in the most fertile areas.

Besides corn the Mayas had a variety of fruits and vegetables, which any traveler may try. Beans and squash, sweet and Irish potatoes, chile, heart of palm, anona, zapote, jocote, papaya, pineapple. The exceptions are significant. No oranges. Bernal Díaz planted the first orange seeds near Tonalá. No bananas and no coffee, but cocoa. For meat they had turkey and other birds, rabbits, deer, wild pigs, monkeys, and a special dog they bred for food.

Farming was the most important industry. The Mayas knew, as some more advanced societies do not seem to know, that however remarkable your machine may be, man to eat must farm. So the center of Maya culture was the calendar and its interpreters who could advise the farmer when to clear, when to plant. In a monsoonal climate it is vital for the corn to catch the first rains. In Guatemala, fields are burned off in April, corn is put in when rain is due, and if moisture does not fall just after the first sprouts show, it means disaster. The ancients planted corn in a hole bored with a stick. They did not fertilize, and when a field was exhausted, they burned off a new tract and began again. So they destroyed the protective cover of the forests, needlessly, and moved constantly farther from the center.

The Mayas wrote on deerskin or on a tough paper of maguey fiber, folded screenwise into books, which are called codices. Only three remain, priceless fragments, but only fragments, of a great body of knowledge. In those selvas everything rots except stone, shells, and pottery. They dyed and wove cotton; made sandals and palm-leaf hats, doubtless with the same manual skill we so admire in their descendants. On the monuments are depicted garments of ocelot skins and feathered robes. Macaw, toucan, and parrot feathers are identifiable in head-dresses. Only priests might wear the plumage of the sacred quetzal. Jadeite and shell ornaments with a few of gold and emeralds from Peru have been found. From internal and external evidence it appears that the Maya ideal of beauty was a person whose head had been forced in infancy into a peak; whose teeth were filed and inlaid with precious stones; and whose eyes were crossed as the result of an amulet dangling on the brow. Plugs adorned and stretched nose and ears, and a coat of red paint seems to have been part of the dress of nobles and priests, probably on gala days.

They sang and played musical instruments — at least the drum and the flute — and they danced ceremonially under a leader to whom they paid reverence. They used the bow and arrow and spear, and they could fight as well as hunt. The tradition that the Mayas were a peaceful people breaks down as more data are collected. Old Empire carvings show warriors, even prisoners. It is likely that they were in a pretty constant state of civil war, but no battle scene has been found, no glorification of slaughter. Dr. Morley suggests that they concealed their wars as a well-bred family forbears to mention family spats.

Mayas were travelers and traders. Articles unquestionably Peruvian appear in Old Empire sites; doubtless they had been traded from hand to hand up the coast. Father Rossbach in Chichicastenango has a gold plaque which students identify as Peruvian. And they were in touch with the Toltec peoples on the Mexican plateau. There was no conquest either way; just peaceful infiltration by travel and trade. For money they used cacao seeds, sea-shells, gold in figurines or in dust, obsidian or jade beads. Toltecs brought copper bells for cash. They traded honey, wax, textiles, salt, pottery, and slaves. Before the Spaniards introduced civilization there were no contracts, no debts denied, no interest on loans. There were religious pilgrimages which, then as now, were also important for trade. They went in boats along the shores. Columbus, on one of his attempts toward the mainland, met a canoe full of men and women and children, gayly dressed. One, doubtless the chief, was sheltered by an awning. Mayas making their first bow to Europe. They strode across the mountains as they do today. Their only beasts of burden were men. And their men must have been strong and plentiful to account for the building they did.

To erect those huge stone edifices required mathematical knowledge of a high order, and real engineering. They certainly moved heavy stones on log rollers, but the axle was unknown. No wheels. The stone most generally used is limestone or sandstone, both readily cut with basalt, diorite, or flint and susceptible of fine carving. They had no useful metal. With these stone tools and maguey ropes they erected buildings which are true marvels of skill and beauty.

The Maya Old Empire comprised eastern Guatemala and reached out into Mexico, Honduras, and British Honduras. It was merely a group of city states bound by common language, art, religion, and science. Government was centralized as the buildings were. The king was a priest, and he may have been advised by councils of elders. Priests were learned in medicine, strongly infused with magic; in astronomy, heavily tinctured with astrology; doubtless in history and legend. Their complex pantheon can be quite fully reconstructed from the monuments, and something of their forms of worship is known from modern ethnological studies.

Dr. Spinden, in his *Maya Art,* full of fascinating pictures, shows clearly how " the trail of the serpent was over all." The serpent typified Kulkulcan, the Maya god who is identified with the Mexican Quetzalcoatl. Besides plumes, the snake sometimes is shown with clawed feet, and there is a serpent bird. Dr. Spinden recognizes certain other gods and goddesses, well defined and widely known: the Long-Nosed God, the Roman-Nosed God, the jaguar, second only to the serpent in importance; many lesser ones. From their symbols it is often possible to deduce their attributes. In fact, the higher gifts of the detective are never more active than in this matter of deducing what a lost people thought from what they did.

Blood-letting was used as an act of worship, taking drops of blood from ear-lobes, for instance. Human sacrifice is shown on the monuments, and at Uaxactun beheaded skeletons of young girls were found, obvious victims for the temples. Dr. Kidder says the Mayas were always reasonable about human sacrifice. He seems a kindly man; he must have been drawing comparisons with the idolatrous butcheries of the Aztecs.

The pinnacle of Maya culture is their calendar. Dr. Morley calls their hieroglyphics (really ideographs, like Chinese characters) the foremost intellectual achievement of ancient America. The calendar is one of the great achievements of the human mind of any age. It proves that as astronomers the Mayas were unexcelled. Their observations were so accurate that they could foretell eclipses far in the future, and plot exactly the variations of Venus from morning to evening star. The official year, which sufficed for all ordinary purposes, had eighteen months of twenty days each, with five extra days at the end. It was corrected at intervals from the more accurate priestly computations. The three-hundred-and-sixty-five-day year was almost entirely astrological and used for determining the right and lucky day for anything from planting corn to naming the baby. But the sacerdotal calculations, based on the movements of Venus, were more accurate than our calendar. No date thus calculated can recur for three hundred and seventy-four thousand four hundred and forty years! A virtual eternity. Maya astronomers also established a fixed beginning date — very steadying. If you date from the beginning of a reign, as the Egyptians did, a few centuries are readily lost here and there. To the Mayas, who exalted nothing human, it was heavenly bodies that mattered and their tremendous swinging through space; and accuracy was essential.

For the amateur the best expounding of the Maya calendar is in Dr. Morley's *Guide Book to the Ruins of Quiriguá*. There anyone with the patience can learn to read Maya dates, besides acquiring a fund of other knowledge.

As arithmeticians these extraordinary Mayas were the first people in history to understand numeration by position and to use the zero. The Hindus, who gave it to the Arabs, who took it to Spain and so to all Europe, did not get the idea until about A. D. 500. The Mayas used it before Christ; maybe five hundred years before.

Scholars can now read the Maya calendar with ease, but the correlation of their calendar with ours is still in dispute. Between two theories there is a difference of about two hundred and fifty years, almost a third of the duration of the Old Empire. This leaves great doubt of the rate of acceleration of Maya development, and adds to the difficulties of placing other American cultures. Laymen can only wait until doctors agree at last.

The other persistently intriguing query is why the Old Empire ended. Why did the Mayas abandon their well-constructed cities, representing such investment of time, energy, and wealth? Did the Mayas set up a mechanical civilization that so out-distanced their human development that they could not manage the machine they had built? The exodus was not due to war or to any natural calamity like earthquake or flood, because the ruins show only the deterioration of time. Nor is there any overlay of foreign culture on the later monuments to indicate conquest. The idea of pestilence has been advanced, or of increased rainfall making the jungle grow so fast that man could not combat it. Dr. Morley believes that so general a human movement was due to many causes, but he considers the greatest of these the continuing decrease of arable lands resulting from bad farming methods. The evacuation was gradual over a period of about a hundred years; but city by city it was abrupt. At least the dates end suddenly. The last stela was set up, the last date recorded, and the place abandoned. Prophecies of evil might have been the actuating cause if not the fundamental one. The modern Maya does not start a journey, close a deal, take a wife against the shaman's advice. His ancestors might well have left all they had at the behest of their priests. At any rate, Maya culture moved north and out of this book. But many stayed, simple folk who moved into the highlands where they liked the climate better and where they still cling to what their untutored minds can remember of their ancient ways, and brood, perhaps, on their ancient glories.

IX: The Heights and Cool Tropics

As THE PLANE LIFTS ITSELF ABOVE THE CAPITAL, THE country flattens into a plaid of tilled fields, torn with ragged canyons, dominated by mountain ranges and clouded volcanoes. At once it is apparent that Guatemala is suffering from erosion. Forests have been felled, leaving unprotected hillsides to be cut into strips by the hard rains. Cornfields show raveled edges which will soon tumble into the gullies and be lost. Cautious motor roads cling to the valley walls, but Indian trails boldly climb the craggy ridges, linking the rectangular white towns with their brown streets and one green spot for the plaza. Lake Atitlán, cerulean blue even from the sky, holds two long bays to the south, and its villages retreat each into its own cove. Beyond that the hills are better protected by timber, pines now; and many farmhouses stand in wide fields with yellow threshing-floors like gold buttons on the plaid. At last the broad valley of Quetzaltenango, Guatemala's temperate zone and granary. I understood why an economist said that Guatemala will never be industrialized. It has no land flat enough for machine cultivation. And those hills produce neither coal nor oil nor gas to make the machinery go. Guatemala's strength lies in her man-power. To the stranger it is a recurrent sur-

95

prise to see what can be done *by pure arm,* as the Spanish says it.

Quetzaltenango is an unattractive town in a setting of startling beauty. Its jagged sky-line intensifies in color as clouds surge up the valleys. The capricious Volcán de Santa María unveils itself from time to time: a cone so clear-cut that its precision is a joy. But all that is lost in the morning fog, hidden again in the evening haze, apt to be marred at any hour by spiteful winds spitting dust. Citizens insist that the cold is salutary. But surely only one avid for punishment in a world that seems to offer enough in any case could honestly enjoy such a disciplinary climate. Quetzaltenango, in the unhappy position of second in size, lacks the glamour of the capital, the friendliness of a smaller town. It used to be lively, but the electric railroad that connected it with Retalhuleu washed out several years ago, and a government given to motor roads does not rebuild it. So Quetzaltenango is a dull town without enough Indians, except in the market, which is polychromatic and diverting; and with too many Germans of the class that bellows at servants in a way to shatter the quiet courtesy so engaging in any Indian-Spanish land. Many have fortunately married Guatemalans, and their children reflect the grace of their motherland.

Even at eight thousand feet houses are built on the assumption that this is tropics. Wide entrances, shaded patios, open corridors, everything invites the air. No German hotel man has retained enough love of his national *Gemütlichkeit* to bar out the breezes, or to warm them once in. My hotel advertised hot water at all hours, which, being interpreted, meant that one could get a hot bath between five and six if all the water had not been used in the kitchen, or if a sprier tourist had not got it first.

The best bet is to journey to the baths at Almalonga; or to Las Aguas Amargas, which doctors say will some day be more famous than any European spa. I did not go there, having no illness worthy of a cure more remarkable than a European spa. Instead I drove on past Almalonga, round the mountain's curve, and into a narrow gorge completely blocked by Santa María. In the hamlet of Zunil, women in red huipiles and head-dresses were carrying water from a terracotta fountain; and just beyond loomed that incredible volcano, swathed in white mists, swirling, never still. The most flirtatious volcano I ever dealt with.

This is the canyon Alvarado marched up from the coast, over a trail so narrow the horses could hardly pass. The poor beasts must have suffered agonies on that seven-thousand-foot climb, from the coast, where they floundered in swamps, to these frigid rocky peaks. At Santa María they found an old woman and a dog dead in the trail: sacrifices which the interpreters explained as a sign of war. Why Tecum-Umán, the Quiché, did not attack the Spaniards there is inexplicable. Even if his army was much less than the thirty thousand claimed for it, the invaders were fewer than a thousand; he could have demolished them to a man. Instead the Indians retreated after a scuffle with the Mexican allies, and the Spaniards gained the plain. Where they could maneuver cavalry they were invincible. That was the end of Indian rule in Guatemala. Right there the white race took possession for all time.

Alfredo Morescier, in *El Ultimo Maya,* describes the

Quiché as praying during those days in their capital at
Utatlán. Señor Morescier writes imaginatively, but from
such sound knowledge that it might have been as he says.
A priest in a white robe adorned with silver and opals
swung the censer of copal. An aigrette was fastened to his
head with rubies and diamonds. A Prince in a feather robe
as green as his emerald coronet knelt by the altar. The King,
even more sparkling in a jewel-encrusted cloak, carried the
sacred quetzal, so cleverly wrought of metals and gems that
its head turned, its eyes flashed, its wings rose as if to soar.

This fabulous bird had led the people across mountains
and deserts, dividing the waters of the sea, calming rivers,
opening a way through impenetrable forests to their appointed home. It typified freedom, for in captivity it dies.
Emerald green, its iridescent crown flashes into ruby and
azure tints; and it is so proud of its yard-long elegant tail
that its nest has an exit as well as an entrance, in order not
to muss the feathers. The quetzal is still Guatemala's national emblem. Surely no other nation has one so indomitable and so fastidious.

Before it, in Utatlán, the people prayed for strength to
resist the invader. Music of drum and conch-shell began
like distant sobbing and grew in volume until it roared
accompaniment to the battle-song chanted by all the warriors. Flags waved, arms clashed, and the kneeling people
were bowed as by a hurricane. Priests showed the god's
image, never exposed before. And the idol's eyes were full
of tears, weeping for the fate of his people. Not very heart-
ening to an army about to meet a foe armed with thunder
and lightning and mounted on beasts never seen before in

all creation. The Indians advanced in detachments uniformed in different colors and led by officers garbed like eagles, lions, or tigers, brave with feathers and ablaze with gems. Conch-shells clamored, drums reverberated, fifteen thousand warriors shouted defiance. Brass trumpets answered them, and the battle-cry of " Spain and Santiago! " The Indians fought bravely, but arrows tipped with obsidian fell harmless from coats of mail. They tried to pull down the horses, who, infuriated, plunged, dealing fearful death. Mounted lancers thrust mercilessly down on men armed in quilted cotton, and to the horror of steel was added the terror of arquebuses and cannon, vomiting fire, making thunder. No courage could stand against it. And when they loosed fierce dogs, trained to hunt and pull down Indians, the brilliant ranks broke. The river Olintepeque ran scarlet with their blood.

So the Spaniards took possession of Xelahú, Padre Godines said mass, and I hope Doña Luisa found a comfortable place for the birth of little Leonor. The Tlaxcalan soldiers changed the name to Quetzaltenango: Place of the Quetzal. Leaving a garrison there, Alvarado marched across the plain to meet Tecum-Umán and a considerable force, which stood again valiantly in a battle best remembered for its legend.

Tecum-Umán, to prevent further slaughter, challenged the Son of the Sun to single combat, and Alvarado as a knight could not refuse. The white captain rode a magnificent horse, armor clothed him, and he wielded a sword that could cut a man in two. The brown King was afoot, with paint on his face, a tiger skin across his bare shoulders;

and his weapons were obsidian and flint. But above his head hovered the flashing quetzal, his *nahual,* his mystical familiar, as well as symbol of his people's freedom. He fought well, he managed to kill the horse, and his followers trusted in his victory until something struck the sacred bird, and it fell dead. At that moment, the King fell too, pierced by Alvarado's sword, and the victory was to Spain and Santiago. That was how the Spaniards came to Quetzaltenango, how the town got its name.

I read these tales in José Milla's *History of Guatemala* in the mornings when it was too cold to get up, and at night when it was too cold for anything but bed and lots of blankets. When the day warmed up, I strolled out to look at Indians. Quetzaltecos wear no distinctive dress, but the women's costume is the most graceful in the Republic. Full blue and white skirts ripple over bare feet as they sail along, swift and busy. Their huipiles are many-colored, and their wraps are striped with cherry red, warm and grateful in the chill. Many Quetzaltecas are truly beautiful and all are conspicuously clean. Two sisters let me sit for hours in their market booth, watching and learning to identify new costumes. I bought their bread, fresh and fragrant, and coffee from a woman near by. Then my friends returned the treat with a thick sweetish drink of ripe corn. It would have been filling at any time, but after breakfast and the sweet rolls it reduced me to a lethargy in which the medley of the market wheeled dizzily around a plashing fountain where a rainbow of people dipped and shook wet vegetables and gabbled in half a dozen incomprehensible tongues.

Quetzaltenango is the hub of the west, with the coastal

Stela and altar at Copán

[PHOTO, EICHENBERGER]

The heights

[PHOTO, MORRIS E. LEEDS]

BELOW, *An altar at Copán*

[PHOTO, EICHENBERGER]

ABOVE, *San Francisco el Alto market; blanket-venders, of Momostenango and local, in foreground.*

BELOW, *House-thatching party, San Martín Chile Verde (Sacatepeqnez), Department of Quetzaltenango.*

[PHOTOS, WEBSTER M^CBRYDE, FELLOW, SOCIAL SCIENCE RESEARCH COUNCIL, 1935–6]

RIGHT, *Volcano of San Pedro.*

[PHOTO, LEGRAND]

plain below it, and above the highlands, mounting to the Cuchumatanes, highest ridge of the cordillera. Much of that region is accessible over excellent motor roads, well graded, solidly constructed, able to resist even the winter cloud-bursts. The volcanoes aside, the terrain is rather like New England. Tidy little farms with house and barn and granary are walled into one whitewashed unit, with well-tended fields around. In January, midsummer, crops were in, watermelons ripe, and the country dry and dun-colored, with only the conifers green. Peach trees were in bloom, but that was all right, I learned, because after summer comes in Guatemala, spring is not far behind, and winter begins in June with the rains. When you consider it, there is no reason why Central America, standing between hemispheres, should not name the seasons as it likes.

Beyond the river Olintepeque the road climbs to San Francisco El Alto, which gets all the valley view and all the sweeping winds as well. There Father Knittel and his sister have made comfort in the old convent. In a dining-room gay with paint and native cloth, they served me hot soup with noodles, kalter Aufschnitt with Schwarzbrot, coffee with thick cream, coffee cake, and other German dishes.

The Fräulein is like any woman who tries to keep house in a foreign place with strange foods and an unfamiliar tongue, and to take care of two feckless men. Her younger brother has the church at Momostenango and she often travels there to see how things go. They can go very badly. Padre Francisco is dickering for a horse he by no means needs, the maid has been neglecting the corners, or the Indian boys are failing to water the plants properly. Both priests must ride to cover their parishes. Father Carlos came in in khaki riding-clothes with only the clerical collar to mark his office. I should call his placid face saintly, with its halo of silver hair, if I did not feel the amused scorn with which he would repudiate the idea. Completely without pose he comes close to the ideal of the Franciscans of old who taught a religion of love to Indians and befriended them against rapacious masters. Cleaning up the sacristy, Padre Carlos uncovered a fine old fresco of Saint Francis. So far he has not had money to remove more plaster and see what other treasures are hidden there.

In Momostenango I was domiciled in the Hotel Escobedo, where Doña Marta trotted all day, worried with having a foreign guest. She scolded the dwarfish Indian maid, who ran so fast her tight skirt popped; but she could not understand the strange Spanish nor get the orders right. She yearned out the window to see the cofrades go by until Doña Marta yanked her in again, complaining: " So are these Inditas, always doing their customs and not their work! " I was very comfortable with Doña Marta. The room was clean, there was an extra cover when I asked for it: a store blanket. Even in the village noted for its blankets, an upper-class lady would not condescend to an Indian article, however warm and fluffy. And there was really hot water at all hours. The great thrill of travel is that you never know where your luck will overtake you.

Don Ernesto Lang entertained at dinner. In the cramped store his handsome half-Quiché children served customers in that idiom; they greeted the Fräulein in German and me in Spanish. Highballs were served in the room where Don

Ernesto receives foreign visitors. Everybody calls on him.
A Momostenango boy is painting Maya gods on the walls,
and native fabrics cover the tables and chairs. Dinner was
a lavish feast, with savory dish after dish and cool beer and
good talk. That Fräulein Knittel spoke no Spanish, Don
Ernesto no English, and I no German did not inhibit the
party at all. The two priests spoke all three and could have
run on in a couple of Indian tongues as well.

Don Ernesto is a brisk, bright-faced German with a red
cap over one of his clear blue eyes, and a wide, deep, sympathetic knowledge of Indians, who give him their complete
confidence. Every recent writer on Guatemala has sought
him for assistance. I can bear witness to how generously he
gives it.

On the way back we passed many gangs of Indians widening the roads, handling huge pines, rolling massive stones,
doing by man-power work that would call for machines at
home. They were so droll in their long serge gowns and
loose pantaloons that they suggested gnomes rather than
citizens of a modern state working off a road-tax. The driver
dwelt on their hardships. Each man, he said, had to feed
himself, even if he was away from home for weeks. And
often men were pressed into service even if they could show
receipts for the tax. So that was why they worked under
armed guard. At that point an affable old gentleman on the
front seat took over the conversation.

" You must understand, señorita, that no Indian works
without prodding, and these road-gangs are very apt to get
tired and go home."

The gentleman, I found, had studied medicine at the

Johns Hopkins and in Germany. But he preferred to devote himself to his fincas instead of to his profession.

Going on about Indians, he said: " Of course people have told you that the Indian is too lazy to work, will not better himself. But I tell you it is true of all of us. We are all lazy. For centuries we made the Indian do all our work, and now we are letting the Germans take our fincas away from us because they do attend to business. When the Indian gets a little money, he gets drunk. And when we get a little, do we save it or improve our fincas? No, we run off to Europe and spend it."

For days I rode in and out of Quetzaltenango. I visited the weaving villages, saw queer ceremonies, rode in every sort of conveyance. I spent a long day wedged in between two women on the front seat of a truck going to San Marcos. They worried because I was alone, were curious about the customs in my country. When I offered cigarettes after lunch, they each took one, but did not smoke. The older said: " You see, it is the custom in her country to smoke after lunch." To say that something is the custom is to justify it fully. They thought it odd that I wore a jacket made of Sololá skirts, but were glad I liked Guatemalan things.

In Huehuetenango the hotel proprietor announced with pride that he had arranged for me to share a car with one other. More expensive than the bus, but quicker and easier. And if the driver should find a third, even cheaper! When the car appeared, I thought we had acquired two thirds, but they did not count. The driver's family would accompany us, it seemed. One was a pretty girl, solicitous about a figure reclining in the corner, shrouded in a long black veil.

Mother, I supposed, had been bereaved and could not bear to face strangers. Later she coughed, and I thought: " How deep your voice has grown, Grandma! " But when we stopped on the divide to drain the boiling motor and slosh it full of cold, muddy water, the enigma turned out to be brother, who had been shot.

" Just drunks, señorita," the driver said. " A month ago. They operated, but not very well. Now I improve the opportunity to take him to Quetzaltenango to another doctor, who will, with God, get out the bullet which stays in his lungs."

Brother, unveiled, was a pale handsome youth with a light mustache and hot eyes. He coughed more and more. Sister had to hold him up, hold him in. I held my bags so they would not disturb him. The other paying passenger sat on the jump seat and we drove so slowly that the bus passed us half-way. I thought the poor young invalid would die at every jolt, but we got him to town, and his brother told me next day that he would live.

Los Altos is the exhilaration of high places, of roads that mount through scented forests of pine and cedar, and gusty skies cut by imperious volcanoes. It is expansive views where clouds roll up like curtains over upside-down mountains plunging deep into inverted blue peaks. And lost in that grandeur of nature are the bare plaster villages where Ladino burghers lead meager lives between house and church and store. Stark villages which burst into bloom on market day with bizarre Indian dress. In Los Altos one feels close to the threshold the Indians cross into their other life where everything is sentient and witch doctors pray to stone idols for bedevilment or cure.

X: Modern Maya

THESE INDIANS OF LOS ALTOS ARE ALL THAT IS LEFT OF the Old Empire Mayas, as the temple ruins and the stelæ, the broken pots and scattered beads are all that remains of their arts and sciences. And the Maya beliefs and customs are as deeply buried in ignorance and superstition, as heavily overgrown with foreign culture, as the deserted cities with jungle. Only by meticulous piecing together, bit by bit, of vestiges of the old life can anything be restored for study. This accounts for sundry young men in the villages counting market women and their wares, listing words and phrases, poking in wherever they are allowed, asking as many questions as they dare, and so piling up a mass of data which may shake down at last into a picture of ancient Maya life.

Many unbroken threads run back to the old culture. The idioms spoken in Guatemala stem from ancient Maya. More than a million people use them in preference to Spanish. The Maya calendar is used by modern witch doctors, who often preside at marriages and deaths instead of the Catholic priest. Idols and divination are commonplace. Incalculable difficulties beset the student of these things.

Young Indians, the readiest to talk for hire, often don't know; sometimes they try to see how much a foreigner will believe. The best-informed old men are hardest to reach. I follow Leonard Schultz Jena's report on Chichicastenango, which I have been generously allowed to see in an unpublished Spanish translation by Antonio Goubaud C. and Herbert D. Sapper. Chichicastenango serves very well as a type, however striking the differences between villages may seem to the uninformed.

The modern Maya lives as his forebears did, in thatched huts away from the center, coming into town for worship or trade. The district of which Chichicastenango is the center has a population of about thirty thousand. For administrative purposes it is divided into sixty-four cantones. What we think of as the town, the native calls the plaza or Santo Tomás after its patron saint. Whole streets of empty houses fill up on market or feast days. Then the Indians go home, drunk or sober, well provided or broke, and the town is Ladino again.

Ladino is a word heard every day in Guatemala and often misunderstood. It is not the equivalent of *mestizo,* which means a mixture of Indian and white. It derives from *Latino* and meant originally the Spaniard, but it was gradually extended to apply to all who spoke Spanish, mixed-bloods, town-dwellers. Indians live in the cantones. Ladinos live in town and are privileged persons. They do no manual labor such as field work or carrying loads; they owe no manual municipal service. They may be rich or poor; two cars in the patio or nothing to eat. They own the stores and cantinas, hold the offices, and are quick to exploit the Indian. The rest of Chichicastenango's permanent population is made up of foreign Indians from Totonicapán, Quiché, and Chiquimula, who keep their own costumes, ply their own crafts, and often work as servants.

Anybody can see this. The real life of the Indian, back in his ranchito, which in Guatemala applies to the house, is the elusive problem. Dr. Schultz Jena's method of checking modern custom with the ancient beliefs as set down in the *Popol Buj* has produced a very comprehensive sketch of the world the Indian lives in. Everything is symbolic there. The earth is prayed to as the giver of corn and of life: Dios Mundo, God World. Mountains with their flying mists and life-bringing clouds are appealed to for rain. A man's ancestors are invoked as gods, and his fate is mystically linked with that of some animal: his nahual. If a man's nahual is hit on the head, that man has a headache. If an old man loses his appetite, the buzzard who shares his destiny cannot eat either. A brave man's familiar is assumed to be a tiger. Blair Niles works out the idea very prettily in her *María Paluna* whose name and nahual were the butterfly. Such a life inevitably calls for supernatural guidance: the *brujo*. The Spanish word means *witch*, but as witchery may be good or bad, *shaman* seems a better word. The shaman, who may be a man or a woman, is most sought for divination. Nobody would dream of undertaking anything without consulting the shaman. He lays out his red beans from the pito tree, burns a bit of copal, says a prayer, and pronounces the day lucky or not.

The modern Maya, like his ancestor, depends on the priest to tell him when he should plant to catch the first rains at the right time. Beyond that, his farming methods are altogether destructive. He exhausts the soil, burns off valuable timber to clear new fields; he even sacrifices full-grown oaks to make charcoal. But in spite of bad farming, the Indian manages to raise enough corn and beans to feed his family. He is often a hunter, but in a manner very close to the ways of the ancients. The shaman is called in to propitiate the mountain divinity with offerings and prayers; virtually a purchase of the game and an apology for taking wild life. The hunter, thus sanctified, never takes more than he needs. In general, the man's work is outside the house, though in many villages men knit, sew, and embroider parts of their own dress.

Women do field work in planting-time, covering the dropped seed with a twist of the foot; and they help to bring in the harvest. But most of the time they work indoors. Corn must be boiled in lye, and ground: that endless, back-breaking grinding on the metate from which the Indian woman has never rested in all recorded time. Over a low charcoal glow she keeps a pot of beans simmering; she has onions and tomatoes for seasoning and a few other vegetables and fruits. At meal-times she shapes tortillas with soft deft spanks and browns them lightly on an earthern griddle. This diet is enriched on feast days with meat or fowl or game. Lake and seaside Indians eat fish. And whatever surplus there is is taken to town on market day. Life is so simple and the country so prolific that the Indian asks little of the industrial world besides the steel needle and the machete. That weighty, vicious-looking knife is indispensable. Made in Connecticut, it has invaded the remotest selvas of Latin America, where it serves all purposes, from peeling a fig to chopping down a tree, or an enemy.

Home life is patriarchal. A girl is considered marriageable when she matures. Though youthful preferences are considered, the affair is conducted by the parents, who first consult a shaman. He ascertains by occult means that the ancestors favor the match and establishes the propitious time for the proposal. The boy's parents inform themselves that the girl is handy about the house and not apt to disturb the peace. The girl's family, still officially uninformed, makes similar investigations. Then late one night, when the souls of ancestors are abroad, the boy's parents call at the girl's home, taking cacao and aguardiente. This formal asking is often attended by *testigos:* literally witnesses, but each one is also responsible for the behavior of his party to the marriage, whom he advises and, in case of infidelity, chastises.

The suit may be refused, but as this tale is to end happily, the girl asks to see where she is to live and there and then the marriage is consummated. Among Indians generally, the match is called off if the girl does not conceive. In San Juan Sacatepéquez the suitor lives with the girl's family until her pregnancy is assured, when he is morally obligated to marry her. In Chichicastenango the girl stays with her family for the betrothal period, during which the boy's parents call at intervals with gifts. They also furnish the wedding feast. At the final ceremony a hen and a rooster are exchanged, a necklace binds the two, and the bride goes to her husband's home. Sometimes the Catholic service follows, but it is easy to see why that would seem excessive

after so much to-do. The priests say there are not more
church weddings because of the government tax. Unbe-
lievers, because of the church fee. Indians don't say. If the
girl has been sought before, the shaman makes special
magic so the dismissed suitor will put no hex on the union.
Often they offer sacrifice to the idol on the hill.

Marriages are dissoluble if the girl is sterile or lax in
household work or if either party is unfaithful. The wife
and her children go to her family. If the man is blame-
worthy, he may be haled before a judge. Testigos and parents assist, and the whole effort is to effect a reconciliation.
Six children are considered right; there is even a prayer:
" six sons, six skulls, six bones." The child is named by
the shaman, who considers how long past the new moon he
was born. The child has god-parents in the Catholic manner
and the relationship between parents and god-parents is
taken seriously. Schultz Jena finds a similar relationship
in the older Mayan beliefs, often without any connection
with a child. The newborn is solemnly presented to the
community by the godfather, usually the day before the
church baptism. In a long and pompous speech he outlines
all that may be asked of the child in the way of public
service, all the honors he may receive, including member-
ship in a cofradía.

Some days later the god-parents take the babies to
church, where they are baptized, in bunches, by the priest.
The ceremony is well worth watching. Serious Indians:
women with their dress-up huipiles hanging loose and the
babies under them; men in their cofradía hats. As many
as twenty or thirty surround the font, where the padre re-

cites the prayers and then goes around the circle with salt and oil, poking his finger into every squalling little mouth, passing along whatever germs there are. Finally each infant is held, face down, over the font, and water poured on its head. The grave Indians, the babies squealing like piglets, the benign padre, innocent of germs and thinking only of souls brought to salvation, and the assistants who make jokes as the job is quickly done!

Indians love their children, pray for them as little flowers and rays of sunshine, treat them kindly, give them all they can. A mother will pull a tiny nursling around from her back to share her candy, a piece of pig's fat, even aguardiente. And against childhood's greatest evil she protects its head in a sack. As to what that evil may be, my own researches have disclosed answers to suit all temperaments. For those who like voodoo, it is said to be the evil eye; infants are so bagged only among strangers. Those who fear the tropical sun may believe the mother is shielding her baby's eyes. Advocates of beauty culture at an early age may follow the waiter at Tzanjuyú who says that the cap is to make the hair grow down instead of up. For the believer in pure science I quote a young ethnologist who maintains, in spite of the filth the babies habitually roll in, that the mothers have some notion of germs and are warding off infection! As the child grows he is supposed to go to school nowadays. Certainly he learns much by working. Tiny boys are taught to carry loads with the tumpline. Small girls have bundles slung on their backs as babies will be later, and they learn to balance weights on their heads. Both help about the farm and the house.

These Indians, living in one-room huts scattered in the woods and hills, come together when ceremonies are afoot or at market in the center. Each canton elects an officer who is responsible for keeping the peace there and for public work. This is not a very onerous service, as only one man in a family may be called on at a time. One who refuses to serve may be jailed, and the alcalde is liable for punishment if he fails to supply the laborers ordered. But such cases are unusual. Indians in Guatemala, as elsewhere, have a fine sense of civic obligation and each one willingly does his share of public work. Indian officials maintain order, oversee the market, and keep the town clean, as well as supplying laborers and porters for hire. They sit as judges in minor offenses and may impose prison sentences, fines, or forced labor such as street-cleaning. They are answerable, always, to the Ladino mayor, the *Intendente Municipal,* a federal appointee and as a rule an outsider. All the officers are chosen annually and are installed with portentous solemnity at New Year's.

The primitive love of secret rite and public procession is further gratified by the cofradías: fraternities which may consist of as few as six men and six women, but which commonly run above twenty. There are fourteen cofradías in Chichicastenango. Each one is the honored custodian of a saint, kept in the leader's house. Six of them own silver standards which heighten the grandeur as the cofrades march around in their best suits and turbans. Besides well-known saints like Santo Tomás, San Martín and San José, there appears one referred to as *Padre Eterno,* who may be identified with Dios Mundo; and *El Señor Sacramento,* Our

Lord the Sacrament, which proves how vague is the Indian's comprehension of what he hears in church. The cofradías owe public service too, connected in general with the church. Boys are appointed to serve as acolytes and to wait on the padre by bringing his wood, feeding his horse, watering his garden. The cofrades stand high in church. They helped Father Rossbach wash the image of Christ Crucified on Holy Friday. And in Momostenango the cofrades removed a holy statue from the church without mentioning their intention to Father Knittel.

The Indians pray much in church, but often in ways far from Catholic. Every visitor to Chichicastenango has seen them kneeling beside their flower petals and praying over the candles in Quiché. Often the man who prays is the shaman, invoking ancestors and not saints. If this is corruption of the Catholic form, it is also corruption of the Indian cult. Priest and shaman courteously allow each other's invocation. God, to the tolerant, is God, however you approach Him. It would be interesting to know which of the two has more power. Old residents and well-informed people seem to think the shaman has. The shaman's only insignia is his equipment: a little bag holding his pito beans, an idol, and quartz crystals. His principal office is divination. For the Indian everything works all right if it is done on the right day. He will postpone anything, give himself any amount of trouble, to get his dates right.

Each day is ruled over by a god, actually personified as divinity. Schultz Jena cites a prayer for a sick man: " Does his sickness come from the day of his birth? or from the moon? or from the stars? We offer candles and flowers

begging a favor of the god of the day Seven Ix, of the day
of the regeneration of the divinity of the earth. We pray
also to the god of the day Eight Cane, to the god of the day
Nine Bird, and especially we pray to the god of the day Ten
Deer." The day lord of a man's birth is most significant. A
man born on a Dog Day, for instance, is thought to be prone
to sexual excesses, and also safe from their consequences.
" Maybe Dog Day is my fate," says the Don Juan, shrug-
ging off his philanderings. It does not altogether clear him.
He should by right invoke his ancestors' help in overcoming
his lord day.

In case of illness the shaman begins with divination. If
the beans fall to indicate sorcery, he makes counter magic.
He may visit an altar: that of a Catholic saint or of a stone
idol in the mountains. Certain shrines, including the saints',
have efficacy in certain cases. In either place he burns copal
and candles and utters invocations naming the patient, Dios
Mundo, and Jesus. An Indian, asked if he thought the idol
could really hear and see what they did, said: " You have
only to see to believe it."

Shamans may make a very good thing of their profession. I heard of one who took in as much as fifteen dollars
a day during a ceremonial week. The regular fee on work
days is one cent for each incantation, though if a shaman
has to journey to see his patient, his food and lodging are
provided. There are tales of wiles and extortions through
fright, but shamans are generally considered honest and
sincere.

Aguardiente is an important feature of every rite. Alco-
hol, according to Don Flavio Rodas of Chichicastenango,

carries the prayers aloft by its volatility. And getting drunk with religious intent has no bad after-effects. Potations are followed by a brew of ground tortillas steeped in boiling water. Schultz Jena says that aguardiente assists divination because the well-known relaxation of tension creates the illusion of nearness to the divine. A finquera who had lent her house for an Indian wedding complained because all the guests approached the family shrine in a state of complete intoxication. The mayordomo, an Indian, explained to her that the drunker they got, the more religious they felt.

In case of death in Chichicastenango, the body is carried to the church, but not taken in. The coffin is whirled around four times while copal smokes, drum and chirimilla sound, and the shaman prays. Then they proceed to the cemetery. The body is dressed in its best. Old clothes are buried with it, coins, tobacco, and aguardiente. Schultz Jena says that Quiché has no word for *soul*. As the morning star is to him a supernatural transfiguration of the heart of Kulkulcan, so he thinks of his own heart when the priest says " spirit." Of the day they say: " Only the heart goes floating with all our ancestors who have died before. He no longer has his bones; only the heart has remained. He died, and now he floats. We do not see him. Only like flies they float through the air."

XI: Markets and Merchants

In spite of air mail from New York in two days, of the export of coffee to all the world, special banana steamers to the States, and buses on all the roads, a great part of the business by which men live still goes afoot in Guatemala. Merchants of today cover the same trails their Maya ancestors did when those tireless traders trotted from tribe to tribe, threading the ancient civilizations together. They were capitalists, followed by trains of bearers, loaded as these are now, and with similar wares. The Spaniards introduced beasts of burden and wheels, but Guatemalan Indians seldom use even the humble burro, and wheels enter their economy only for spinning and ceramics. Despite the all-weather highways which are Guatemala's pride, to the ordinary Indian an airplane is a whine in the sky, and an automobile a snorting menace from which he scrambles up the embankment, huddling his children and his dogs into safety. When it passes, leaving them smothered deeper in dust, they all grin cheerfully, as though it were a game. Maybe they figure that if they are not actually killed they have won.

Who are these people and why do they go forever along the roads?

They are, first, people coming into their center from their canton homes — probably more than half of any market. They bring their surplus to sell and so gain a coin or two for other necessaries. Nothing is wasted; what cannot be used must be sold. An extra rooster, a handful of peanuts, half a dozen peaches or tomatoes, a basket of corn, or a back-load of fodder is worth a walk of miles and hours of waiting. Each one seeks the same place every weekly or bi-weekly plaza day, and they rent the space according to their wares. Similar goods are grouped together, department-store style. Webster McBryde, who is studying markets for the Social Science Research Council, tells me that in Chicacao, where everything is dear, a man with a hundred dollars' worth of cloth may pay as high as twenty cents a day. The woman with ten or twelve soap balls pays only two or three centavos. They bargain even over the tax.

" What, you charge me four cents for these few cinches? "

" But you've almost sold out. I come late."

" No, this is all I had. By all the saints and Mary and Jesus! I've just come."

The few coppers they gain go for coffee, thread, a machete, a basket. The soap woman, selling at five cents a ball, may make twenty or twenty-five cents a day. As skilled labor earns twenty-five, her profit is not despicable. Mr. McBryde estimates, from a study of many markets, that eight cents a day will feed one person well, even if all food is bought, and that seldom happens. Barter is uncommon anywhere. Indians buy and sell. And though they use to-day's quetzal, they quote prices in pesos, to the stranger's utter bewilderment. Five pesos for a bean-pot seems out-rageous until one learns that sixty pesos equal one dollar. Currency was debased to that point early in this century, and the Indians have not caught up yet. All bulk goods are sold by weight. The price agreed upon after lengthy dicker-ing, the seller adjusts his two baskets or tin pans balanced on a stick, picks out the right weights, and cautiously pours in the lime or corn, spice or cochineal as the case may be. The buyer watches every move, indicates with a gesture that a little bit more would be just. A few spice- or dye-venders use old brass scales, family heirlooms and quite unpur-chasable. Every deal is in miniature; what is not weighed is sold by the pennyworth.

Every Guatemalan village offers something that other villages need; and in big markets or on feast days people from all parts of the Republic are found with their goods on the ground, hung on trestles, or piled in the arcades. Baskets come from Chimaltenango, Amatitlán, and Santa Catarina Aguacatán, near Huehuetenango. Few attract the tourist; they are unadorned cane or reed and made for use. Chimaltenango also produces the carrying nets and bags of maguey fiber which so many traders use to pack their goods on the trail. Butter comes from San Martín Jilotepeque, but it goes only to towns where rich folk live. Indian budgeting does not allow for butter.

No market is too poor or unimportant to display racks full of woven goods: striped blue and green *cortes*, strips for skirts which come off the looms in Totonicapán. Merino shawls from Quetzaltenango, striped in bright warm colors and tied into fringes at the ends, are an extravagance that every Indian woman aspires to. The wool that goes into them comes from up around Huehuetenango and Momostenango, where the climate would stimulate any sheep to productivity. It appears in the markets in fluffy piles of white and brown-black. There are piles also of unspun cotton, both white and brown, as soft as silk. In the halcyon days of Kulkulcan, cotton grew in all colors, according to the legend; but of them all only brown is left. They use it in Chichicastenango to weave huipiles. Finished blankets come from Chichicastenango, where they make a thick black one with a band of red and white checks at the ends, and long fringes. But Momostenango is the blanket center for a couple of republics.

Glazed pottery, the most ornate and brittle, is made in an old convent in Antigua. It is wholly Spanish in character; the Guatemalan's imagination does not take liberties with what his betters have taught him. Lowly cooking-pots and the wide *comales* for baking tortillas are the work of Mixco and Chinautla women. It is fun to watch a woman go stooping from pile to pile of the terracotta griddles, ringing each one with a finger-nail, hefting it, consulting other women, frowning in uncertainty. After all, one does not buy many in a life-time. Chinautla also specializes in the water-jar everybody must have: heart-shaped, narrow-necked *tinajas* with lids. Women are choosy too about their metates, which are made in Nahualá. As that village permits no sale of liquor within its purlieus, nor any white man for overnight, the art of making grinding-stones seems a suitable expression of their flinty nature. Two or three crafts per pueblo are the rule. Only Totonicapán artisans

RIGHT, *Maya type.*

LEFT, *Chichicastenango man.*

RIGHT, *Babies go hooded.*

ABOVE, *Sololá market during Holy Week fair. Foreground: Pigs from Quiché region, sold by Chichicastenango merchants. Background: Tents of Argueta (Totonicapán) saddle-makers.*

[PHOTO, WEBSTER MᶜBRYDE, CARNEGIE INSTITUTION – CLARK UNIVERSITY PROJECT, 1932]

RIGHT, *Crossing Lake Atitlán. Chichicastenango traders headed for coast markets. Background: San Pedro volcano.*

BELOW, *Momostenango blankets drying at one side of market (view from church tower).*

[PHOTOS, WEBSTER MᶜBRYDE, FELLOW, SOCIAL SCIENCE RESEARCH COUNCIL, 1935–6]

duplicate every other village's output. Ladinos control much of the craft and they flourish as purveyors of five- and ten-cent-store trinkets to itinerant merchants.

Some pueblos deal more in food than in handiwork. Santa Catarina and San Marcos on Lake Atitlán ship sweet-water crabs and minnows strung on sedge stems. Dried shrimps are very popular, though their shopworn, shriveled aspect is most unappetizing. They come from Tapachula in Mexico. Indians have a way of disregarding political boundaries and import duties; they think of people as belonging to a village, not a nation. Sololá onions are trucked as far as Salvador, and its other vegetables and those of Almalonga near Quetzaltenango supply the whole Republic. They raise all the vegetables familiar in the United States, good sized and finely flavored. Carnations from San Juan Sacatepéquez are wrapped in wet moss, to keep them spicy fresh, and shipped to places too hot to raise them, even to Salvador.

Cooked food is a feature of every market-place. The eating-booths are likely to belong to Ladinas, and there one fares very well. Seated on a wobbly bench under a canvas shade, he who fears no germs may taste real Guatemala cookery. Meat is stewed in red and spicy sauces; tortillas assure that not one drop is lost; corn appears in an infinity of guises, beans are everything from soup to nuts; and coffee, if you like it sweet, is incomparable. That is only a start; there are dozens of dishes. Each region boasts its own; every holiday has its specialty, not to mention such seasons as when the corn is milkiest and sweetest. A sweet tooth can go on a long debauch among the cakes and candies; some very good, some cloyingly sweet. Refreshment-booths offer sirupy ades at a cent apiece. Indian women sell more humbly, with no pretentious table or bench. Their patrons sit on the ground while tortillas brown, and are satisfied with corn gruel, *atole,* white or chocolate-flavored. Many dig their own gourd cups out of their belts; others drink from the vender's cups. They cook over smokeless charcoal, which boils water as quickly as gas. Charcoal is ubiquitous, though a few towns specialize in it, like San Juan Sacatepéquez, near Guatemala, where they have fine oak forests, and Cajolá, near Quetzaltenango. It is carried in nets by the bearers, all dusty black. *Ocote,* pitch-pine, for igniting the charcoal, is offered in tiny bundles or by the stick. In pine woods everywhere fine trees are hacked to death to make them weep and emit resin.

These goods are carried over the roads and trails by a large and active merchant guild. Every village has a few merchants who never stay at home. In some places there are more traders than craftsmen or farmers. One Chichicastenango canton reported twenty-five merchants. Maxeños are called Guatemala's Jews: traders and sharp ones.

I once saw a group of Chichicastenango Indians in the road, men and women heavily loaded, and dogs. " Coming back from a finca," said my driver. " They never take the dogs except when they go to the fincas." " And the women go too? " " Oh, yes. Each man has a wife to go wherever he goes, and one to stay home and keep the ranchito." I have no verification of this. It belongs to my interesting collection of possible misinformation.

On the roads these ambulatory salesmen wear ordinary

dress, but experts claim to distinguish them. Sololatecos nearly always retain their woolen skirt; probably they feel immodest without it. Many are recognizable by a bag, a belt, or the wares. Traders cover a fairly regular circuit. From the highlands to the coast with pottery, textiles, furniture, temperate fruits and grains. From the coast up to Guatemala and Antigua with tropical fruits, coffee, salt, cacao, and balls of raw sugar wrapped in straw. In Mazatenango on the coast, Mr. McBryde counted ten kinds of chile ready to haul in all directions. Salt comes from Tahuexco, where they boil salty sand and filter it so crudely that it reaches the table with a considerable residue of sea sand. From the carrizo palm they make raincoats, firefans, brooms, and roofs, among a host of other things. Cacao is a bean from which women chew the gelatinous pulp before they grind it to make chocolate. They make cocoa by removing the rich oil. Cacao, such an important export in colonial days, finds only a home market now. Coconuts go up from the coast too, and dried iguana for food, parrots and monkeys for fun. In Guatemala or Antigua the merchant reloads with factory stuff for the villages.

One day I watched Sololatecos as they waited for the launches at Tzanjuyú for the first lap of the coastward trip. Each man let his cacaxte down, and freed himself from the cowhide head-piece, worn hairy-side in and molded exactly to the brow. Many men are quite bald from the pressure. The cacaxte is a wooden frame about three feet high, twelve by twenty inches across. The carriers average fifteen to eighteen miles a day with an eighty-pound load, though anyone you ask boasts of carrying a *quintal*, a hundred

pounds, and Paul Bunyan legends abound. When the
launch was ready, each adjusted the tumpline, crouched
against his load, and hoisted himself, slowly, painfully
erect, braced on his iron-pointed stick, the calf muscles
straining round and hard. Even boys, ten and twelve years
old, got up unaided, but some of them needed help for the
trying step down into the launch. Men were considerate,
steadying them, or taking off the bundle with a low laugh.
The little chaps look proud to go with the men, and eager
to carry as heavy a load as possible. One, who had a red
carnation in his hat, insisted upon getting down alone and
paying his own fare.

In the launch I talked with a powerful man who bragged
about his hundred-and-twenty-five-pound load. It may have
been. His cacaxte was packed with onions, garlic, cabbage,
cauliflower, carrots, turnips, and beets, with sacking on the
sides and a straw mat on top. He was bound for Patulul on
the coast. His cargo, bought in Sololá at about one cent a
pound, would bring a hundred per cent profit, less only his
launch fare of thirty cents and a market tax of possibly
fifteen. If he brought back a load of brown sugar, worth
maybe a dollar, he could net a profit of about a dollar and a
half for a three-day journey. An Indian never calculates
his time as worth anything; and my friend carried his commissary with him: beans, coffee, chile, and tortillas or corn
mash. A few sticks of ocote, a lamp, two cups, a coffee-pot,
and a bottle hung on his cacaxte. Upright at one side was
his palm-leaf raincoat, and to protect his back and serve as
bedding he had a blanket.

Going down toward the coast from Lake Atitlán, one

finds them in every hamlet and at all the fincas, where they sell to the workers. Many mules go along those roads too, carrying lime, or grain from Patzúm or other up-country centers. Commonly a man drives his own two or three beasts, though a few capitalists have strings of a dozen or more and hired drivers.

The coast-town markets are notably different from those of Los Altos. Often venders gather under a ceiba tree's dense parasol. Heat shimmers. Children are naked, women bare-bosomed. In Retalhuleu the law requires covering hitherto unashamed breasts, and the women, possibly in subconscious spite, buy the ugliest blouses in the stores. At home they find a gay skirt all the apparel a modest lady really needs. Parrots ride on men's shoulders or perch moodily on baskets, an occasional monkey cavorts under the thatch, and men come riding in strung all over with live iguanas. Here the up-country traders sell out and buy for the return.

I have never heard packing rated as a fine art, but an Indian's packing should be. Indians can pack anything, however knobby, perishable, or weighty. Coffins, ridge-poles, calla lilies, glassware, invalids, an unbutchered beef carcass, bathtubs, and bed-springs are a few of the things they carry with facility. When a man takes his family, the next to the smallest is tied on top of his cacaxte, face up if a girl, face down if a boy. The very youngest, of course, swings from the mother's back. A half-dozen tables or a dozen chairs from Totonicapán are a common load. One pottery load included eighteen huge jars arranged in threes, and twenty-five smaller pitchers. Women use the tumpline in

some places, but as a rule baskets. Men never use baskets.
Every load is balanced to a nicety. Watch a woman move
one mango around until it suits her. Or see a man tie his
load, piece by piece, and then test its equilibrium before he
sets off. They travel at the pace which gives most momen-
tum with least strain, and a carrier returning unloaded fills
his cacaxte with stones in order not to lose the knack.

Sololá is an interesting market because it is near the lake
and midway between coast and highlands, a day's journey
each way. Mr. McBryde studied it in detail for Tulane
University, and I follow his report. Behind the city hall,
people spread their wares on a natural terrace that drops
off sheer to the lake, steely blue at midday, with the volcano of San Pedro a purplish wedge against the sky. The
dominant color is dirt, set off by red splotches of men's
sleeves, kerchiefs on dingy straw hats, babies' caps,
women's wraps, and piles of chile. And the prevailing smell
is onion-garlic, the only combination that can hold its own
against unwashed Cakchiquel-Zutuhil. The exchange is animated. It is big business, and Indian. The few Ladina house-
wives and hotel and chalet people hardly show. At a Friday
market Mr. McBryde counted eleven hundred and thirteen
venders from eighteen towns besides Sololá. Market tax
nets the town about eighteen dollars, and the total business
done might amount to two hundred and fifty dollars.

Even more characteristic is the market at San Francisco
El Alto above Quetzaltenango. Nothing in that region hin-
ders interchange as Lake Atitlán does in the center, so it
draws from a wider radius. The ample plaza displays all

that Sololá can show, with the addition of acres of Momostenango blankets and stacks of pottery from San Miguel
Ixtahuacán, Santa María Chiquimula, and San Cristóbal.
Mr. McBryde uncovered a thriving pottery business among
Olintepeque women. One enterprising dame makes a regular run from market to market through the whole region.
Momostenango weavers come to buy Huehuetenango wool,
and brazil-wood and *palo amarillo* to make their dyes.
Campeche-wood they fetch from distant San Pedro Charcá,
near Cobán. Cobaneros bring it down from the Petén. This
is the most intriguing trade route in Guatemala, for there
are no roads, only trails. Quiché Indians go via Santa Cruz
Quiché, often with their blankets loaded on mules, and
bring back dyewood, hemp, ropes, and petates. The San
Francisco stock market is unique. Hundreds of horses and
mules — somehow the burro does not figure in Guatemala
— sheep and goats, and pigs, and pigs. Fowls too, and more
pigs. Odorous, vociferous, numerous, and unforgettable.
Even more amazing are the men: solemnly unaware of the
weirdness of their clothes, dressed like mountebanks, and
horse-trading as sharply as Yankees or Arabs.

These men of the San Francisco region are even more
inveterate traders than the Maxeños and Sololatecos, and
they make a bigger circuit. San Cristóbal, Momostenango,
and Huehuetenango men are often away from home a
year, and they know most of Central America. But they are
up to date and make their long hauls by truck. On their
return they bring indigo from Salvador; cochineal from
Antigua, where a few bugs are still cultivated; vanilla and

coffee. Coffee is an ever profitable cargo to the uplands from the fincas which sell second-class berries to the Indians.

Everywhere I went I met these burdened drummers on the roads, and always they seemed to be having a good time; they were the best-fixed Indians I saw. I wish somebody would go with them, learn their lingo, get their lore. Doubtless they retail gossip and jokes as our traveling fraternity do, have a girl in every center, and are considered a risky element by more settled citizens.

XII: Totonicapán

TOTONICAPÁN IS A WELL-INTEGRATED LITTLE TOWN, IN-dependent and pleased with itself. It seems to stand firmly on its own feet — one Indian and one Ladino, to be sure; but it does not try to emulate the capital; it is unaware of tourists and makes no concessions to their peculiar require-ments; and no German gargle is heard in its streets. It is Guatemala of today, undefiled. The army officer who dis-patched a telegram for me boasted that Totonicapán has the best climate in the Republic. "A bit icy, to be sure, but very healthy." And indeed it seems to be. Probably all who do not freeze to death come through with the bright red cheeks, apple-firm skin, and vigorous walk so notable there.

When I arrived, the President was expected at any mo-ment. As I had found every town hopefully arrayed to re-ceive His Excellency, only to be disappointed that his visit was unavoidably postponed, I was not much impressed. But the plaza and the open air were more tempting than my hotel room. From the Señora's opulent past it had inherited console tables and a pier glass; a sterner today had finished it off with an iron bedstead, a tin wash-stand, and an electric light bulb on a long string, and it was gelid. The cold of tropical highlands is inexpressible; it is a frigidity that seeps in and is unescapable. The glory of the weather is by day. When the sun goes down, the temperature follows it, and none of the houses are heated. Life in Latin America, gracious as it is, lacks one grace we know: early evening indoors with tea or cocktails and an open fire. It is true that Guatemala's only fuel is charcoal. But Latin Americans are so resigned to discomfort! It is one of their most amiable traits, as they are never fussy. But a Yanqui, irascible and quite unagreeable, would probably have invented synthetic heat long ago and made a whole continent cozy. I noticed that every time I mentioned the cold, which was whenever I put on an additional sweater, the natives referred to the coast. They revel in the crisp freshness of Los Altos in contrast with melting soggily in the stifling lowlands. And in the evening they walk around the plaza.

The streets through which the President would pass were floored with pine, as always, arched with cypress, and many window grilles were hung with cut paper or lace curtains. The national blue and white fluttered from post to post, and across the front of the municipal palace were huge 5's, one elaborately worked in flowers. For Jorge (5) Ubico (5) was completing his fifth year in office. Little brown soldiers were all in the cleanest uniforms: blue dungarees or khaki. They are very military, if they do go in cowhide sandals and carry their duffle neatly rolled in plaid kerchiefs. The Totonicapán home guard won the prize ahead of all the forty-eight troops of the Republic, and it is hard to see how any unit could have been snappier. By half past seven strolling was on in the plaza. Two business men, arm in arm, speeded by in earnest talk. Schoolboys in white trousers and blue blouses walked unconcerned with arms around each other's necks and waists. Señoritas in hard sharp heels clicked stoutly along. I never could see why wearing shoes was considered such a mark of superiority. One need only compare the nerve-shattering pound of the Ladina's heels with the easy glide of the unshod Indian woman. The only Indians in the parade were children's nurses: handsome women in long striped skirts and drooping wraps of blue-greens and beiges. An officer in O.D. with a Sam Browne belt carried a baby girl in a pink ruffled bonnet. His wife in a summery frock disappeared after a few turns and came back in a fur jacket. This is furry tropics, and no mistake.

The plaza has not escaped the kiosk which swept the whole country in the era of scrollwork, and one modern building portends the false progress just ahead. Otherwise the square has true individuality, with arcades all around to shelter the pink and yellow painted walls. It is sad to realize that Totonicapán must run the whole gamut of bad taste before it comes back to its own style again. It still has the virtue of what simple people make because it fits their needs: functional beauty. And then there is no beauty again until a developed taste realizes the truth of usefulness and deliberately returns to simplicity. This cycle is just beginning in Guatemala. Progress is held to consist in imitating foreign ways, far from their own pattern; in using machine-made things, much less suitable and good than what their untaught Indians make.

The President, the word ran, was detained by business in Tecpán. His Excellency would not come tonight.

The band played on. It seemed that they must somehow, some time, just by chance or by the law of averages, strike a harmonious note. But they never did. Blowing and pounding, each man strained his buttons, but he never achieved, or seemed to feel any lack of, connection with his mates. The ambulatory crowd increased. Girls in pairs, going one way; men in pairs the other. Round and round they flowed as Latin American life has gone all through the centuries, centering in the plaza, eddying around the band.

In the morning the boy who served my breakfast announced, surprisingly, that the President had come; was even then in the city hall. I was doubting, but all the other guests ate jumpily. Two clerks, the old druggist; " Licenciado," they called him, because he had a license. And a couple of traveling men. Eggs. And a run to the street. Tortillas and frijoles. Another dash. Coffee and milk getting cold on the table. Sweet bread with the second cup of milky coffee. At last we all abandoned breakfast and stood on the corner.

Indians were there, women with children, everybody waiting. The streets were full of policemen, and then soldiers began to appear. A lad on a motorcycle. Another. A tan car filled with officers in O.D. A dark limousine with the President alone in the back seat: a large dour man also in uniform. He saluted perfunctorily right and left and was gone in a flash. Other cars with officers busy with papers. Trucks. Doubtless repairs are often necessary. The last car was a roadster occupied by one man of that un-

mistakable engineer-stamp. Probably the President elects
at times to go where there is no road at all and the engineer
must make one.

They were gone, but a white-clad orchestra kept right on
playing in the plaza — such a good orchestra that I tried
to ascertain what had so transformed the local musicians
overnight. This, I found, was the President's own orchestra.
His Excellency must have heard a great many local bands.
After the concert the musicians stormed the hotel demand-
ing breakfast for forty men. My Señora was proud of the
fact that she could do it. Beans and eggs, tortillas and
coffee within half an hour and unexpectedly. Meanwhile
two marimbas stationed in the *portal* saw to it that the
air should not be empty of sound. That thin stringy twang-
ing seems to express the whole spirit of Guatemala. It has
character, and it partakes, in an almost lost undertone, of
something savage, be it original Indian or African.

Totonicapán was a prominent Quiché city before the
Conquest, seat of one of the twenty-four noble Quiché families, and a center of culture. Jewelers and potters, painters
and weavers, workers in wood and stone gave it a character
it never lost. After the Conquest Alvarado settled there a
group of Mexicans who named it Totonicapán, " On the
Hot River," after springs still famous. But before this
central highland was open to him, Don Pedro had to deal
finally with the Quichés.

After Tecum-Umán and the quetzal were killed, the
Quiché kings decided on a ruse. They sent sumptuously
arrayed ambassadors to Alvarado and invited him to visit
the royal city, Utatlán. Don Pedro condescended to accept

their visit as apology for their heroic defense of their land;
he was even polite about the presents of low-grade ore they
proffered. He agreed to visit Utatlán with his army.

Utatlán, near the modern town of Quiché, topped a mesa
surrounded by sheer canyons and accessible only over one
narrow causeway. The first sight of that strait path across
the crevasse aroused suspicions which rapidly grew to certainty. The streets were tortuous lanes where horses would
be only an encumbrance. Houses of wood and straw were
highly inflammable. No women and children were in sight.
And the supplies provided for the visitors would not last
out the day. Alvarado hardly needed a spy's report that
the Indians planned to fire the place and flee, leaving the
trapped Spaniards to burn to death. Too wary to risk battle
where the odds were against him, he told his hosts that he
would retire for the night to the plain, where his horses
could graze. He invited the kings to return his visit next
day.

When they came, they were seized, tried by court martial, and burned alive — a not unusual punishment at that
time. But that was not the end. The Quichés were still able
to muster an army. Alvarado called upon the Cakchiqueles
to help. They, who had invited the Spaniards in the first
place, sent four thousand fighting men. With this aid the
Quichés were reduced, their city destroyed, and a new one
founded on the plain, away from all natural moats and
ramparts. Don Pedro then sat down and wrote a letter to
Cortez in Mexico, relating his adventures to that point.
He asked for horseshoes for the coming winter. The conqueror had not yet learned that winter follows spring in

Guatemala. He said that he had named the new town Santa
Cruz Quiché because it was founded on Holy Friday. On
Monday he was going on to Ixmiché Tecpán, the capital of
his allies, the Cakchiqueles.

There the Spaniards were received with every deference:
borne in feather-decked litters, showered with gifts, waited
on by retainers of noble blood, housed in the royal palace.
This palace, like that of Utatlán, was described by the
Spanish chroniclers with a lyricism explicable only on the
assumption that they had been reading the *Arabian Nights:*
with gardens, pools, aviaries, and harems. As the Cakchiquel kings wore crests of eagle plumes, the Tlaxcalans,
never at a loss, called the place Guatemala, Land of the
Captive Eagle. Alvarado, who had not then seen the Elysian
vale of Almalonga, established his capital there with much
pomp, religious mass, and martial music. It was little more
than a military camp, but there was first used the name
Guatemala. Spellings have varied, but the name has belonged to the four capitals, to the Spanish colony, and to the
Republic. Guatemala.

From there, Alvarado advanced upon the Zutuhiles on
Lake Atitlán. Audacious as ever, he forced a drawbridge
single-handed and overthrew a tribe hitherto considered
invincible. With their downfall he had conquered the three
highland nations; and the Quichés, the Cakchiqueles, and
the Zutuhiles were all vassals of Spain.

By this time the prestige of the Spaniards was their greatest asset. Indians who had fought brilliantly at first gradually lost their morale, fought stubbornly always, but without hope of victory. The Spaniards, on the contrary, were

inspired by an irresistible will to win. Put strong men in a
difficult situation and some mystical strength rises. Knowing that the world must be won for God and the King seems
to have been a very sure basis on which to win it. Every
cruelty was then for a greater good, every suffering to
gain some future ease, every disaster only to be turned into
a more spectacular victory.

After each surrender the conquered were forgiven with
embraces and assurances that all was forgiven, baptisms
were scattered broadcast, all were brothers in God. It was
only when these generous conquerors began, later, to check
up their accounts that they concluded the vanquished might
as well express their Christianity in gold. Then imposts
were placed, people enslaved; and revolts ensued. And
the Conquest began to develop a rotary motion. It was not a
triumphant march in a straight line. Every conqueror found
that he had to swing around again over his own track to
punish uprisings.

Alvarado, from his new capital, went on a junket toward
what is now Salvador and demolished the town of Es-
quintla without even the conventional formality of demand-
ing surrender and chastising treachery. On his return he
found the Cakchiquel kings dilatory about producing gold.
He called for more and quicker, emphasizing his remarks
by snatching royal nose-rings out of royal noses. He then
decreed that each ten-year-old child must deliver a finger's
size of gold a day; failure to be punishable by slavery.
It was impossible; there was no gold. Emboldened by a
soothsayer's prophecy of victory, the Cakchiqueles re-

volted, and Don Pedro had to go back to *pacify* them. The
Spanish had a discriminating taste in words!

Gossip persists that Alvarado himself inflamed hatred
against the Spaniards by taking the flower-like Xuchil to
his quarters and keeping her. Many historians deny this.
Don Pedro denied it himself at an investigation in Mexico
of his conduct of the conquest of Guatemala. She was an
old thing, he said, past fifty, and a slave; and anyway the
Indians were always honored to turn over their wives and
daughters to the conquerors. But as José Milla, a historian
who generally discounts all romance, accepts this tale, I
pass it on.

At the beginning of the Conquest it was customary to
appoint the Indian kings and nobles to positions of some
dignity. As pacification went on, a favorite method of punishment was to reduce the whole population to a status close
to slavery. So social distinctions were lost. Romantic people like to cite certain customs as proof that modern Indians
recognize and respect the old patrician families, but no
serious student mentions such things. Most village Indians
are lowly folk who appear — to the superficial observer, at
least — to accept white dominance without question. What
goes on underneath that stolid exterior is probably known
to very few white men.

My hostess, who believes in the Indian's latent power,
told me about Easter Week in Totonicapán. Forty saints
are carried in procession: as devoutly Catholic an observance as one could wish. But at the end walks a man muffled
in a blanket, under which he holds, hidden, an idol and a

machete. Symbols of the day when the machete shall bring the idol back? It is significant that a person who knows Indians thinks so.

Whether or not there is truth in that fantasy, I liked Totonicapán because there, of all the highland villages, I felt the greatest independence of spirit. It has individuality and a desire for expression. It is filled with life, buzzing with workshops. The market extends for blocks around its building. Along the plaza were piles of corn and wheat which they weighed out in old-fashioned balances, loaded on mules or on their own backs, and carried off. Women had vegetables and fruits, and the stalls inside displayed all the variety of dress goods the native weavers make. Every pre-Conquest craft is practiced still. Walking through the streets I got the smell of pine and cedar from open shops where they were making furniture and chests; and the odor of leather from a saddler's, who was finishing off a flat-pommeled saddle with dangling fringes. Jewelers make the silver ear-rings the women like, set with dull or shiny glass beads and sometimes with a bit of real coral. Often I looked through an open door into a patio where a whole family of potters sat on the ground modeling soft clay. And every other building houses a loom or two where nimble-fingered artists make the shuttles fly across big clumsy frames into patterns so intricate it seems impossible they could be followed without guide or chart. But these men make them from memory, easily, deftly, and without paying much attention. At the tinsmith's they were re-fashioning old cans into tubes for valuable documents; an

Indian may be asked at any time for his tax receipt or proof that he has done his stint of road-work. The old costumer was glad to show his workshop where he carves and paints masks and sews dresses for the dances. His profits have educated his sons; both are professional men in the capital now.

At last I strolled up to see the church, which was not particularly interesting, and then sat on the steps to watch boys shooting a ball at a basket on the school grounds below me. Two Indians came out of the padre's house and stopped. The man started toward me, was overcome by shyness, and went back again. She stood waiting. They spoke together. At last he grew bold enough to approach the stranger.

" You are alone? Señora or señorita? I told my wife that you were sad and alone and that we should come to speak to you. Have you no friends? Nobody? You should go to see the padre. He is alone now, and not busy. You could see him."

"Yes," said the woman, " and he is so sympathetic, the padre. Just now we came from there and he was very kind. You see we had candles blessed to put before the holy image in our house, and they stole them, but we don't know who. Only imagine, señora; some thief stole candles already blessed! Well, we waited to think what to do, but at last we came to tell the padre and he was so kind, that one, that he blessed other candles and now I have them here and we are taking them home. . . . Only we saw you here and we came to speak to you because we saw how alone you were and we thought you were sad."

A little girl, passing, put her bundle down and ran to kiss the woman's hand and bow her head for a blessing. " My god-daughter," explained the woman.

My friends went on to tell me their story. Six sons, all weavers. Three married and in houses of their own. Three living at home. They lived, so they told me, in the barrio behind the church, where I could see cobbled streets that ran down between white walls and up again to the hills. Eaves were wide enough to protect walkers in the rainy season. And many houses were painted in the colors that so quickly fade into pastel tones. My friends went at last, having shown me all the courtesy they could. Because I seemed lonely they spoke to me. They extended their friendship, told me frankly about themselves, invited me to their house, and then, offering me the best they knew, advised me to visit the padre. I did, but his cultivated talk about the church situation in Mexico was not so delightful as the pair who came to cure my loneliness on the steps of the church.

In the evening the Señorita from the hotel took me to walk. The Señora was caring for her, the child of a servant; but she was treated like a daughter. Though she ran all day seeing to everything, her heels were inches high, her shining hair was a mass of permanent corkscrews, and her dresses fresh and pretty. Going down the hill the smell of sulphur met us, and people coming from the baths with their faces muffled against dangerous night air. Inside the huge building there was little light to reflect from black water, where dozens of men, women, and children were bathing naked — but not quite unashamed. The women slipped skillfully into the water as they left their skirts; exposed breasts were commonplace. And men turned their backs. But generally the business in hand was all-absorbing. They scrubbed with soap and pumice-stone, with vigor and repetition. They scoured one another's backs and helpless children. They soaked and lolled and then were up and at it again, soaping their hair and some of them their dogs as well.

Then we strolled through the echoing town and down the lanes below the church. The moonlight made all tinted walls like shadowy snow, and the serried roofs were dark steps across brightness. Under the hill was the fountain the Señorita wanted me to see. A wide basin, brimming with water so clear it showed only in starry ripples. She knelt beside it, unaware of me, not touching but almost adoring that living crystal.

"*Clara, clara!*" she exulted. "Clear, clear!"

As we walked back to the hotel she told me about her life. She had visited on a finca near the coast. She had spent two years in the capital, in a convent.

"But to live," she said, "it is preferable Totonicapán. For the climate."

XIII: The Taking of Mixco

DON TONO SUGGESTED AN EXCURSION, "GUATEMALA style." The objective would be to visit the ruins of Mixco, one of the most stubborn citadels Alvarado had to take. Don Tono, whose family used to have fincas near there, said he thought he could get horses and a guide from San Martín. What a relief to settle back and make no plans!

We went out from Chimaltenango. Don Pedro, who in 1525 was not limited to roads passable by motor, went across from Tecpán-Guatemala, where he had been pacifying the Cakchiqueles after the episode of the children and the gold. There could be no enduring peace with the Cakchiqueles as long as their allies, the Pokomanes, held their impregnable Mixco. So Alvarado, who was good at taking impregnable places, marched on Mixco.

From Chimaltenango we followed hairpin curves along bowery canyons and leaf-screened streams to San Martín, higher and cooler and, like all Guatemalan towns, ringed by hills. A Señorita we met there praised its delicious little cold: *friito delicioso!* She was a refugee from what the natives complain of as the terrific summer heat of the capital in April — a heat that seems balmy spring weather compared with July in any city of the United States.

San Martín is a gem of a colonial town, with only one flaw: wires. Its ample square plaza is cobbled and bare, as they were in the old days, with a plain and serviceable fountain. A year ago Don Francisco blocked a move to destroy the fountain, put up a band-stand, and plant trees. May God and all the saints give him strength to cover up that electric wiring and hide the bulbs in colonial lanterns! Every house is a jewel in its own right. Tiled roofs run out into wide eaves, gateways are roofed, and many doors have knockers high up, convenient for a man on horseback. Modern houses are built to conform. San Martín may turn out to be the one town in the world with wit enough to stay as it is.

Don Francisco and Doña Luz took us to see the church. The carved ceiling above the apse is very fine; and there are altars of various periods, even a couple of new ones to indicate that the devotion that makes beauty is not dead. The patio fountain is embellished with stern Maya idols, but the rest of the convent, arches and restrained decoration, has been modeled with good taste. I should have noted more of the church if I had not been so absorbed in Doña Luz as she knelt for a moment, a white wool scarf slipping back on smooth parted hair, her face clear and strong as a fine carving. To see a woman like that does one good. She has ten children, a devoted and energetic husband, servants, and a house to manage. Certainly she has lived and loved and suffered. I shall never forget her face when she spoke of a little daughter who had died. But every experience goes through a nature like that into nobility.

At sunset they rang the bells: four men in the towers

throwing them around with clangs that must have reminded people miles away that tomorrow was fiesta. The first Indians to reach town cooked their supper over a handful of fire in front of the city hall and then went to sleep in the municipal arcade, their gear piled at their heads and calloused feet sticking out of blankets. Only one ragged boy crouched by the coals. Maybe he had no blanket.

Don Tono's modest undertaking to arrange for mounts was lavishly over-fulfilled. Don Francisco offered his own horses, which proved strong and willing. And his seventeen-year-old son as guide. But Guatemala's style goes much further than that. While I sat on the church steps watching the way of the clouds with the new moon, upturned against more rain, the two hidalgos called on the mayor. The white alcalde then spoke to the Indian alcalde, and before dawn four sets of mozos went to work that we might be saved two hours on horseback. There is a good deal to be said for a subject race, if you don't happen to belong to it.

When we drove out of town at six, a red and white flag floated from the white church. On the steps Indians were placing other banners and spreading a carpet of pine needles, and I wanted to stay for the fiesta. In the road we met dozens of people coming to it. San Martineros, men, wear blue coats and white trousers under long woolen aprons. San Martineras, women, wear blue skirts and two huipiles. White and purple, woven in bands of jewel-like figures; or black patterned in magenta and turquoise; or both. We met a man with a marimba on his back, so we knew it would be a gay fiesta; marimbas cost money. Most of the people were taking food to market: vegetables, fruits, and fowls in baskets on their heads, pigs and calves on the hoof.

Our first private road-gang had cut timbers to bridge a gap and were finishing it off with twigs and leaves and dirt. At the next place they had moved a couple of stones and filled up the holes. The third job was a mere matter of leveling down a high center with machetes. I hope they all got back for the fiesta!

Don Roberto, our guide, was what one would expect of his parents' son: well-bred and attentive. He was thoroughly enjoying his vacation and spending as much time as he could on the finca. Next week, he said, the San Martín baseball team was going to play San Juan. From that he moved easily into speculation as to how a fellow might find that underground passage they showed Alvarado at Mixco. Nobody he knew had ever found it, but it must be there.

By that time we had passed the first finca. Nobody lives there now. With motor roads, most finqueros live in the capital, and the provincial social life is gone. Don Tono told tales of his father's youth. How people used to ride from town to town on long visits: ladies in shade hats and veils on side-saddles, and children riding in baskets on mozos' backs. One lady, not so old, remembers how insulted she was when she was considered too young for a horse and had to ride a mozo, kicking at him and scolding all the way.

At the second finca our horses were waiting because the mozo had made a mistake and not gone as far as he might. It was the only contretemps in a perfect trip. And it gave us the fragrant forest uncontaminated by the smell of gas: a forest of long-leaved pine, soft underfoot with fallen needles; and leafless oaks covered, all the branches, with parasitic orchids. It was not the blooming season, so we saw only a few delicate yellow blossoms, almost white; a few white ones, starry in clumps of pale green foliage; and, also in the trees, night-blooming cereus, waxen and profuse of scent. There was an odor of dampness too and of febrile tropical growth and decay. The oaks were hung with curling Spanish moss, pendent in long silver ringlets and stirring not at all. I was reminded of many women in these Catholic countries who go veiled like the oaks and give their strength to other lives. It is a type that probably will never occur in the world again; and to us it is as mysterious and alien as the misty Spanish moss and the fragile orchid plants.

When the descent began we could see how the rivers Piscaya and Motagua converge. Mixco is at their confluence in a warm and productive terrain. We passed patches of jade-colored sugar-cane, rode gratefully into the shade of dark green amate or mango trees and through thickets of spiny mimosa. We startled brilliant yellow and black birds and pure yellow ones, and even emerald parakeets, scolding together in the air. At a stream a butterfly was testing his electric-blue wings in sunshine and shadow. The manager of Don Francisco's finca, Las Pilas, made us comfortable in canvas chairs on a cool porch and gave us orchata to drink while his son saddled up to go with us.

We left our horses at the foot of the eminence where Mixco stands. That rocky trail is too narrow for animals,

even today. By that time there were six of us, the usual rate
of accretion on such a trip. A San Juanero, visiting on the
next finca, had heard about it and come. He was a *chato,*
snub-nose, who sat his horse to perfection, comported himself like a cavalier, and let out syncopated yells of joy when
he felt like it. His mozo was well equipped with puttees,
though no shoes, and a machete to slash the thorny brush
that kept reaching out at us. I had always wanted to see
somebody clear a path with a machete, and here he was,
doing it.

The last to join had been the manager's youngest son,
for whom there was no horse. So he came, as many of the
Conquerors did, on foot and at his own expense, solely for
zest of adventure. Like the Conquerors also he was good at
living on the country. He knew a potable spring. He sepa-
rated some little Indians from wild mangos they were gath-
ering. He found the tart jocotes, which are as refreshing,
when you are hot, as a lemonade. And it was he who spotted
the iguana: the only skin I have ever seen with the iguana
still inside it. It was mottled, an exact match for any dry
stick on the hillside, but that stupid reptile, who must never
have heard of protective coloration, chose to sun himself
against the one red branch which showed him up completely. The boys took after him with a lasso and two
machetes, whooped and jumped their horses, and it was
very exciting. But the iguana got away.

When Don Pedro de Alvarado arrived where we were
going he found himself confronting a natural fortress a
sheer five hundred feet high, and on top man-made walls of
heavy squared stones defended by warriors with no notion

of surrender. No scientific study of Mixco Viejo has been
made. To the untrained eye it looks like a first-rate position.
The town must have made a narrow crescent about three
miles from tip to center, and with only one trail, so narrow
that a single Indian with enough stones could stop an army.
They did, for three months, in a siege that is notable. The
investment was begun by Don Pedro's younger brother,
Gonzalo, with two companies of infantry and one of men
in armor. He was beaten back repeatedly. Instead of starv-
ing out the Mixqueños, he seemed in a fair way to starve
his Spaniards. The defenders were getting supplies through
that secret passage Don Roberto hopes to find.

That was the set-up when Don Pedro arrived with fresh
troops, including thirty mounted men, a company of crossbowmen, and many Indians. His captains, in conference,
agreed that the project was impossible and advised living
to fight another day. Alvarado knew the secret of the Spanish conquest of the Americas. They had to win, every time.
Defeat was unthinkable. Fail here, and every Indian nation
in Guatemala would take to an impregnable rock. He found,
as we did, that he had to leave his horses. Mixco is no
cavalry job in any age. First he tried to weaken the defense
of the passageway by a feint on the other side. But the
Indians, who recognized that Spanish custom, met him
with such a deluge of stones and poisoned arrows that even
Don Pedro hesitated.

At that desperate moment Indians from Chinautla appeared in numbers to aid the Pokomanes. Enemies behind
as well as in front. But it was their chance to demonstrate
that invincibility which was the white man's greatest asset

in fighting Indians. The most spectacular performance was that of a youngster named García de Aguilar and his horse, who kicked to such good effect that he killed several and wounded many. Aguilar is said to have held off four hundred Indians until six comrades came to his rescue. Whether or not these numbers, given by the Spaniards, are precisely correct, they give the idea; six Spaniards naturally outnumbered four hundred Indians.

Alvarado hoped the Pokomanes would come down to help their allies, but those canny savages stayed where they were and watched. The Chinautlans, weary of doing all the fighting and convinced of the Castilians' superhuman powers, capitulated. They revealed the secret entrance, and Don Pedro was able to cut off supplies from the town. His real problem was still the disputed trail, and he ordered a daring attack. A string of men, one with a shield and the next with crossbow, should advance and never rest until they made it. An intrepid soldier, Bernardino de Artiaga, volunteered to lead. A heavy stone crushed both his legs. Another took his place, and another. Like a file of indomitable ants they kept coming and falling back, man after man, crushed and broken, until one miraculously reached the top. That meant the end. According to the ratio established by Aguilar, that one Spaniard could stand off hundreds of Indians until his mates reached him. So Mixco fell. Some people, many women and children, tried to escape through the subterranean way and were slaughtered there. Some jumped. Many surrendered. The Spaniards, as was inevitable, had won. Alvarado ordered the city burned.

The Pokomanes' treason — that masterful Spanish command of words again — was punished by removal to a place they could never hope to defend. Many of the Mexican Indians settled there among them, so modern Mixco is more Mexican than Pokomán, and the women wear a belt that comes from Mexico, probably with no idea why they follow that custom. Only one soul would not go, so the Indians of San Martín say, and at night she may be heard wailing, the pitiful sobbing plaint of a tortured child.

I doubt if the Spanish army was any more exhausted by their three months at Mixco than was one modern gringa by an hour's climb at midday in a climate that knows no delicious little cold. And I am sure they found no relief equal to our rest at Las Pilas, where the Señorita met us with cool orchata. We lunched on rice and black bean soup, eggs in spicy chile sauce, hot and tender tortillas. After that I had a nap in a room that the light entered only through bamboo slats and the net that screened my slumbers. Gautemala style is never better than when they advise a siesta.

XIV: Costumes and Textiles

To ACQUIRE KNOWLEDGE OF GUATEMALA TEXTILES, ONE first assists at a session of mourning over how alarmingly the art has declined. Costumes are contaminated with factory stuffs, mixed as to style, or not worn at all. And weaving, " since this horde of tourists, my dear, paying high prices for atrocious work, is slovenly, careless, and coarse beyond words." I venture that when Doña Beatriz came out as Alvarado's bride, she heard the same plaint from ladies who had been before her.

Guatemala, in spite of all, is most remarkable for its weaving. Experts from other lands are incredulous that such intricate patterns, like tapestry, cross-stitch, or tufting, such varied textures as shadow designs, crepes, nets, and effects like Mexican drawnwork, can be done on the simple looms the Indians use. Once convinced by seeing, they proclaim Guatemala's weaving one of the world's outstanding folk-arts. Krishnamurti, Hindu mystic, is quoted as saying that his country produces nothing better of its class. The Carnegie Institution created quite a flurry in New York with costumes assembled by Mrs. Oliver G. Ricketson, Jr., and textiles designed by Miss Ruth Reeves from Guatemala mo-

151

tifs. Mrs. Matilda Geddings Gray has presented Tulane University with a collection of sixty-one complete costumes, including the various types used in many villages. This is the most scientific exhibition so far, but Mrs. Gray claims to have made only a beginning. There are about two hundred and seventy-five distinct costumes in Guatemala. In some cases the differences are slight: the tying of a kerchief, the arrangement of stripes; but in many they are striking enough to be distinguishable at sight. And so extraordinary that a leading Paris designer is reported to have a scout out among the villages, whose observations may some day eventuate in a Guatemala season.

In Guatemala alone this opulence is still unappreciated. Exhibitions of these costumes must be sought in other countries; Guatemala has none. At state fairs the proudest showings are of handiwork copied from women's magazines. Often no native weaving is shown, and if it is, it is poorly chosen and without appreciation of what is good. Above all, no effort is made to hold the Indians to their own highest standard. Guatemalans in general cannot grasp what foreigners make such a fuss about. Ladino dealers in the capital complained because North Americans prefer old to new goods, and newspapers played it up as subtle proof of Yankee snootiness. Some editor missed an enviable opportunity to point out that if modern loomcraft were equal to the old, as well done and the product as fadeless, it could command a world market. Some reporter should compare, for instance, a modern kerchief from Palín, loose enough to stick a finger through, with an old one, even of mesh, dainty in design, edged with tiny dots like enamel, and bright with softly unfading vegetable dyes. The middleman naturally spurs his weavers on to fast work for a quick turnover. To him the maintenance of a unique village craft is less than nothing. If he can make an issue of a discerning buyer's refusal of second-rate work, he, of course, will. The Indian in Guatemala, as everywhere, prefers to do his best, for he is essentially an artist who values good work for its own sake.

The government might do much to maintain the craft, to give the Indian a sense of his own value, and to educate its people in general by making a complete collection of native costumes before it is too late. Any village would be honored to send its best to the capital, and sedulous collectors would be sure to find priceless old examples of dress and design. And what a gorgeous show for the national museums! It offers, also, another route into that unknown Maya world, for a people as tenacious of the old as these Indians in-dubitably weave much lore and legend into their clothes.

So far, nothing on Guatemala dress and weaving has been published except a brochure by Mrs. Lily de Jongh Osborne for Tulane University, and an even slighter leaflet by the Carnegie Institution.

Mrs. Osborne was born in Central America, has lived most of her life in Guatemala, and has one of the best of many private collections of costumes. Loving fine weaving and knowing the workers as friends and intimates, Mrs. Osborne not only elucidates the technique, but gives many hints of tribal custom and class symbols.

In Guatemala clothes not only make the man; they reveal him. I am told that only pure-bred Indians wear the native

dress in complete correctness. Any tyro can learn to identify the people of a dozen villages driving from the capital
to Chichicastenango. A knowing person often can tell from
what tribe the man descended, his official position, on what
business he is bent, and to what social level he belongs.
What an Indian wears is never a matter of personal taste;
it is custom, that ubiquitous god of the primitive.

Unluckily none of Alvarado's host liked to draw, so we
have no pictures of sixteenth-century Guatemalans at work
and worship and play like the delightful sketches Padre
Sahagún made of the Mexicans. But from written accounts
certain raiment can be definitely put down as pre-Conquest
in Guatemala. The woman's upper garment persists unchanged. A square of cloth with a hole for the head, joined
under the arms — and that is the huipil. The skirt in its
earliest form is only a rectangular piece wrapped around
the hips and held by a twist or a sash. This mode has endless variations. The huipil may be in two pieces as at San
Antonio Aguas Calientes, or three as in Cobán. It may be
too short to connect with the skirt as at Palín, or long enough
to serve as a petticoat as at Quetzaltenango. It is usually
worn inside the skirt, but women in the mountains above
Huehuetenango let theirs hang loose below the knee. Sometimes it fits the arm closely; sometimes it hangs free. As a
rule it is a heavy and modest covering. Only in Cobán does
the netted huipil show the brown skin through the mesh. In
cold places, like San Martín Jilotepeque and Patsicía, an
extra huipil is worn for warmth, and in many villages a new
one serves as a wrap until the old one falls apart or a newer
one is finished. The prevailing wrap is a rectangular cloth

which also serves as carrying cloth or is folded on the head
for protection. A few villages have characteristic coiffure,
like Santiago Atitlán, where the head is encircled by a
long narrow belt wrapped like a halo. At Senahú a rope of
orange wool makes a massive, clumsy queue. This is the pre-
Spanish woman's wardrobe. Sandals belong to men, as do
hats. Traditionally each woman makes her own huipil, weaving in tribal symbols familiar to her from infancy, making
it as true and as fine as her skill allows. Buying clothes is
a recent innovation. And making things to sell is still futur-
istic. That is why it is hard to buy good pieces and why tourists so surely corrupt the craft. Anything will do to sell;
good work is for one's own use.

The ancient Maya was probably much less clothed than
his modern descendant, though the upper classes may have
been smothered in feathers and skins like the figures on the
stelæ. One might deduce from the way certain villages tuck
in the tops of their trousers that they knew the gee-string
before the Spaniards got them breeched. In Tecpán they
produce a folded effect for which English certainly has a
word. But most modern dress indicates that monastic modesty was bound to clothe the aboriginal nether man as soon
as he was baptized. Santiago Atitlán and San Pedro de la
Laguna wear what can only be described as panties, loose
and at the most awkward length, and adorned with amusing
figures of men and beasts. The monks' own habits and sundry Spanish suits survive in grotesque parody. But before
he was converted the Indian probably wore something not
too far from the gee-string, the Sololá skirt, or the dark
blue jerkin of San Antonio Aguas Calientes. He had no

shirt, but he used a mantle, which served like today's blanket. He wears a sash, elaborate as in Chichicastenango or plain and coarse, but always red and magenta or noticeably striped, and brightening to the drabbest modern garb.

The hat, as the Guatemalan Indian uses it, can only be described as a sartorial error. He is much handsomer, if he only knew it, with his turbaned kerchief, the *sute*. The Sololá man in his checked skirt over dirty white drawers and his Gibson sailor hat suggests nothing so much as a sadly dissolute Camp Fire Girl — an effect enhanced to the point of burlesque by his complacent solemnity. The prevailing ugliness of the Indian's hat is probably due to the fact that he follows European models; but from twenty to fifty years late. Just now cork helmets threaten to supersede Fedoras and boaters, which are especially chic on men from San Martín Chile Verde. In their long red-striped white gowns, with pantalets peeping coyly out below and flapping unsewed robes on top, they are like bedraggled long-tailed birds. And when they tuck the monk's gown up over brawny legs to wield a machete or a shovel on the roads, the effect is too ludicrous even for laughter. But I prophesy that this very ensemble will emanate from Paris some day as a redingote with white underdress and sleeves dashingly embroidered in red and purple. His " jeweled sleeves " are the Chile Verde beau's great pride. This apparel is outdone only by the striped trousers of Todos Santos; or the long-tailed coat of Aguacatán. Unmistakably Spanish are the jackets, embroidered or frogged and embellished with a plethora of useless buttons. San Pedro Sacatepéquez is distinguished by a red one, gay enough for

ABOVE, *Woman of San Sebastián Retalhuleu, sewing up "suyucal" (rain-cape) of corozo palm leaflets.*

[PHOTO, WEBSTER McBRYDE, FELLOW, SOCIAL SCIENCE RESEARCH COUNCIL, 1935–6]

RIGHT, *The sun symbol is said to belong to the nobility.*

[PHOTO, EICHENBERGER]

BELOW, *Men (father and son) of Todos Santos, headed for Mazatenango to buy cotton (photo at Pueblo Nuevo).*

[PHOTO, WEBSTER McBRYDE, FELLOW, SOCIAL SCIENCE RESEARCH COUNCIL, 1935–6]

BELOW, *Chile Verde men.*

[PHOTO, SERRA]

LEFT, *The ruined monastery of La Merced, Antigua.*

BELOW, *Palace of the Captains General.*

[PHOTOS, EICHENBERGER]

a bell-hop in a tourist hotel. Many men carry bags which they knit on steel needles as they go about their business. Henequen and jute are used for bags as well as nets and ropes, all of which men make. They do their own embroidery too, working in caste or tribal symbols.

Indian women, whom we left in their primitive skirts and huipiles, keep up with the times also. They say the Cobán blouses, peek-a-boo as they are, represent a Christian step ahead. For the Dominican missionaries who carried the gospel there were so embarrassed by the widespread lack of coverage that they offered up their mosquito bars. In a malarial land that was a Christian sacrifice worthy of suitable celebration. Round-cut necks connote the white woman's influence, as do all ruffles and embroidery. San Cristóbal women embroider a bertha with gaudy flowers, and Cobán features embroidery for dress-up. Santa Magdalena embroiders a mass veil, and the fiesta huipil of Totonicapán is dark blue patterned in loosely twisted silk; not nearly as effective as the work blouse. Parts are joined by the *randa* — a satin stitch of silk or cotton which varies from a thread to a two-inch band. The wider the randa, the more wealth it denotes. Another sure trace of the white woman is full skirts, most notable at Quetzaltenango.

All these costumes, of both men and women, seem to be a melange of Christian morality, European wool, and Chinese silk superimposed on the indigenous taste for scant covering and native cotton. According to the legend, it was Hunahpú, the Cakchiquel culture hero, who gave cotton to the people. Certainly the Mayas maintained colonies on the coast for its cultivation. Wool, which the Spaniards intro-

duced, must have offered enough comfort in the frigid highlands to compensate, or almost, for the horrors of the Conquest. The Indians made it their own at once; their blankets
are strong in design, waterproof, and everlasting in color.
At Momostenango they use some vegetable dyes and set
the color by soaking the blankets in hot sulphur springs.
But the preferred black is natural, which accounts for the
sinful aspect of Guatemala's sheep. Silk, the other imported
fiber, is bought ready dyed. When its use began I was unable to learn, but old ladies recall that when they were
children the nurse had a silk skirt for Sundays. And a storekeeper in Antigua averred that she had sold Chinese silk
over that very counter for fifty years. She showed me how
it has always come, in paper packages covered with Chinese symbols. It seems likely that silk for weaving was imported in colonial days when so many luxuries came from
the Orient. Silk appears more in ornament than in fabric,
though the Indians of San Marcos and San Pedro are as
gay as sunshine in their orange and yellow skirts, partly if
not wholly silk. All these materials are used in combination.
Wool is woven with cotton, as in the shawls, and with silk in
skirt lengths. Most head-bands carry the design in wool or
silk on a cotton warp. Even rayon has reached Guatemala
to replace silk, especially in patterned belts.

Dyeing has always been an important art. The Mayas,
like the Tyrians, had their sacred purple. In season men
waded out into the sea to scrape the mollusk off the stones
and stain the thread right there. That brilliant and enduring
hue has almost given up to commercial dyes now, as have
cochineal red and indigo blue, also native to Guatemala.

Some day that country will be advertising for an old Indian who can make and use the vegetable dyes which may soften and grow more vibrant as the cloth wears thin but which never fade in sun or water.

The details of dyeing, spinning, and weaving are for the technician to expound. Each region has its special methods, though all are primitive. A spindle dancing in a bowl may be seen anywhere. Women use the simplest loom, hung from a rafter or a pole and held by a belt as they squat on their heels. With that, a couple of smooth sticks, and a pile of colored cottons, they evolve the most difficult designs with no guide, from memory entirely. The pattern is made by slipping the colored cotton, silk, or wool into the white or black cotton warp. This is the finger weaving which makes Guatemalan textiles look like embroidery. Each woman works her own mark into every piece; no two are alike. She may use a symbol of her tribe, her family, or her caste; or a personal motif. But the patterns as a whole are prescribed by ancient and inviolable custom. Easy to identify are the sun, moon, and lightning; corn, cactus, and other plants. The Cobán shadow work often shows deer, rabbits, or birds in heavy work on the open mesh of the monks' mosquito netting. The plumed serpent, which goes back to Kulkulcan, is used in many places, but the turkey seems to belong to Quetzaltenango. The double-headed eagle, wherever it appears in the Americas, is assumed to be the Austrian bird introduced by the Spaniards when Charles V was Emperor. But a San Juan weaver explained that their eagle represents the two-faced god, though he recognized the Austrian emblem as a bird from across the sea.

In Mixco, founded by Alvarado when Mixco Viejo fell, the women's belts show designs of human figures holding bunches of feathers and double-headed doves. Those belts are brought in by traders from Oaxaca and the Mixceña will have no other, though nobody knows why. Her huipil comes from San Pedro Sacatepéquez, her skirt from Los Altos, and the red or blue striped and fringed napkin on her head from San Raimundo. Obviously a light-headed woman with no stability in dress!

Men weave on clumsy foot-looms and are much more exploited than women. Often a boss has six or eight men working for him in big dark rooms, with small boys bobbing up and down like gnomes to shift the heddle frames. They make the skirts, wraps, some huipiles, and many adaptations for the tourist trade. Table-cloths and napkins, even cocktail napkins — surely the farthest cry from ancient Maya. The skirts are patterned in the dyeing of the thread. Yards and yards of cotton are wrapped so tightly that regular sections stay white when the thread is dipped. And it is so cunningly done that in the weaving those white spots work out into regular designs: the tied and dyed technique.

Though custom prescribes what shall be worn, custom recognizes feast days and the world-wide need for dressing up. It is a very poor Indian who does not have something new for Easter and a veil, a hat, or jewelry for church or cofradía. The church outfit may be only a white veil over the ordinary dress. A bride generally has a special headdress as well and often the necklace which her grandmothers have been assembling for generations. Old sea coral is strung with coins of many ages and anything else to catch the eye. The heavier, of course, the better. None of the weight and distinction, but only the shine carries over into the modern displays of cheap beads: another count against the German importer. The man, so stunning in his sute, is prone to dress up in one of those deplorable hats. Add to this the official cane and the pompous walk of a lodge member on parade.

The grander the occasion, the more apparent the white man's influence. In Guatemala as everywhere the Indian seems more admirable in what he is and what he does the more he is let alone. Guatemala weaving at its best is unexcelled. Guatemala weaving exploited for tourist trade is in danger of ultimate loss unless the white man will set the stamp of his approval on the good rather than the false.

But it is not too late. Guatemala dress and how it is made have begun to attract serious students. Ethnologist, archæologist, and historian may establish a pet theory there, or see it disproved. The interior decorator, the modiste, and the costumer might build a reputation for great originality on these Indian modes. Only the milliner would have to walk warily. But by eschewing any hint of the erstwhile London cabby's hat and holding tenaciously to toques and turbans, even he might profit much.

XV: Antigua, the Capital

ANTIGUA IS A PLACE TO GROW LYRICAL ABOUT. NEITHER city nor village, neither highlands nor tropics, it offers all the blessings of the perfect mean. A lady of rather crude perceptions complained of it: " In the heights I feel cold. On the coast I feel hot. In Antigua I don't feel." Here is nothing so sharp as sensation; a pensive musing, rather. Magnificent buildings are telling evidence of centuries of destruction, but in today's sunny calm it appears unlikely that anything will ever happen in Antigua again. Even the volcanoes that dominate every vista, majestic and blue, are tamed to the gentle ways of a town of aristocrats. But it is not altogether the equable climate nor the repose. The place has character too. Its broken palaces and convents are like the poverty of one too great for pretense; an old noblewoman too wise to blur the glamour of her age with tawdry imitations of youth.

That this continues true of Antigua is due to the good taste of the Governor, Coronel Carlos Cipriani, who proposes to see that real distinction is not lost in modernness and mediocrity. When he took office, progress had already cast its shadow from the electric building leering corner-

wise between low tiled roofs. Nothing can now restore the
old colonial house that was sacrificed there, but maybe the
Colonel will think of a way to suppress the crass imperti-
nence of the theater. Otherwise the plaza is in harmony with
its past. The squat sixteenth-century arches of the palace
and the equally solid city hall are still sturdy after four
hundred years of service. Pepper and mimosa trees shade
the grassy park, and around the promenade are clipped
yews and four statues in the Rogers-group tradition. Judging by their war feathers, helmets, and shields, these sim-
pering females must have meant the races of mankind or
the continents in the nineties. They should never be removed, but it will be an improvement to have the old fountain back. A tale is whispered of a statue which once
adorned that fountain: something so scandalous that gentlemen forbade their womenfolk to walk out while it stood
there. Doubtless a nude. One wonders if some far-sighted
citizen preserved that work of art for a more tolerant age.
All over town, citizens, whether they like it or not, are chip-
ping decades of paint off natural stone door- and window-
frames, often to reveal the family crest. Thanks to Coronel
Cipriani, Antigua will remain the one unspoiled colonial
capital in Spanish America.

The history of La Capital Antigua is framed between two
epochal catastrophes: the flood that inundated La Ciudad
Vieja at Almalonga in 1541, and the shattering series of
earthquakes that caused the government to leave it in 1776
and found the modern Guatemala. Within that frame Guatemala, the Ancient, was the proudest city between Mexico
and Lima. The Spanish built cities, not crude frontier towns.

Wherever Spaniards went they took their civilization: finished, orderly, comparable in its hieratical completeness
with the Catholic Church which advanced beside it. The
Conquerors were no rough pioneers with gun and ax. They
were noblemen and knights. They brought priests and law-
yers, doctors and teachers, and I don't doubt a full quota of
rogues. But they knew how to deal with them. Everything
was done correctly and with form. From the Conqueror's
first declaration, as he stamped on a new shore, that it and
all its inhabitants and all its hinterland even unto the South
Seas belong then and forever to Their Most Catholic Majes-
ties of Spain — from then on, every act was recorded by a
notary, attested by witnesses, blessed by the Church. Much
as civil and clerical authority might be at loggerheads —
and they were, especially about dealing with Indians —
they stood staunchly together for discipline and order.

Every town was laid out according to plan. Church; government buildings; plaza with market; fountain; hospitals;
prison with scaffold; quarter for Indians. Life followed
lines as rigid. Everyone knew his place and had to stay in
it or answer for his temerity. Everyone was responsible to
somebody. Every ship from Spain brought a royal snooper,
Visitador, to audit the books, hear the gossip, put everyone
on tenterhooks. No man so powerful or so secure that he
was not in danger from enemies who could get the ear of
the Visitador. Twice Alvarado had to go to Spain to answer
charges.

During his first absence his brother, Jorge, left in charge,
moved the capital from Tecpán-Guatemala to idyllic Alma-

longa on the slope of the volcano of Hunahpú. Charles V,
then Emperor of most of Europe, all the islands of the At-
lantic, and all the Americas, granted that city the title of
Most Noble and Loyal City of Saint James of the Gentlemen of Guatemala. He also endowed it with the coat-of-arms
which endured as long as Guatemala was a colony of Spain.
A spirited Santiago on a white horse leaps agilely across
three volcanoes, two crowned with crosses, the other, un-
regenerate, with smoke and flames.

Alvarado, on one of his trips to Spain to answer charges
against his administration, proved that he could play the
courtier and politician as well as the soldier. The nobleman
then most influential at court was the Duke of Alburquerque
who chanced to have a charming young niece named Francisca de la Cueva. When Don Pedro started home again, he
went as Captain General and Governor of Guatemala, no
longer a dependency of Mexico, and with the additional title
of *Adelantado*, which might be translated He Who Has Gone
Ahead. He took with him his bride, Francisca de la Cueva,
and a priest named Francisco de Marroquín, who was to
prove his most sagacious adviser. Doña Francisca, not des-
tined to be the heroine, died of a fever in Veracruz. Two
years later Alvarado, in Spain again, married her sister
Beatriz. Doña Beatriz was said to be beautiful, and the marriage had the added advantage that the Duke of Alburquerque was still uncle. The Adelantado, cleared again and
confirmed in all his honors, rights, and titles, wrote gayly
to the young knights in Guatemala that his bride was attended by twenty maids of honor, all of good family, hand-

some, and well dowered. Carried into the Most Noble City
on the backs of Indians, the girls from Spain were amazed
at the elegant city they found.

The life of that decade is delightfully described by José
Milla in *La Hija del Adelantado: The Daughter of the Adelantado*. By this time, that Doña Leonor who was born while
her father was conquering the Quichés was a young lady
with two suitors. Don Pedro, believer in marriages that
counted for something, favored his wife's brother, Francisco de la Cueva. Leonor loved Pedro de Portocarrero, her
father's close friend, a most honorable knight. The novel,
enthralling as one of Scott's, deals with intrigues, infidelity
in high places, poisonous herbs and wicked herbalists, with
tournaments, and dark plots circumvented at the last moment; with Portocarrero's surrender of his lady love and
all his hopes, and with his daring rescue of her at the end.
As a matter of fact, Doña Leonor married both the gentlemen. After Portocarrero's death she lived a long life as Don
Francisco's lady, and her son was considered Alvarado's
only legitimate heir.

Alvarado, better suited to action and conquest than to
sedentary administration, set out in 1541 for Mexico. He
had previously failed in an attempt to force Pizarro to
share the wealth of Peru. This time he was bound for the
Isles of Spice, outfitting in Mexico. In Jalisco he had, as
so often happened, to pacify revolting Indians. In a place
of no note, a clerk of no importance, riding a horse he could
not manage, let the beast stumble, fall, and roll down a
hill onto the Adelantado. Alvarado tried to free himself,
but he was caught, crushed, mortally hurt. As he lay dying,

the Conqueror made a remark which must rank as one of the most characteristic last words of great men.

" Serves me right," he groaned, " for bringing a damned fool who couldn't handle his horse! "

When the sad news reached Guatemala, Doña Beatriz was stricken with grief, but equal to the occasion. She robed herself and her dames of honor in trailing black velvet and had her rooms painted and hung with black. Even the candles in their silver sconces were of black wax, and the stones of the court were polished with black oil. In that lugubrious setting, the widow had herself appointed Governor and she signed all papers *La Sin Ventura*, the Hapless One. She cursed the Blessed Trinity, the Virgin, and all the saints.

The people knew that evil must come of that, and it did. In September 1540, month of the heaviest rains, there fell such sheets of water as had never been seen before. For days it poured in cloud-bursts, deluges, until the streets ran sluices of water, the houses sank under the onslaught, and people struggled out only to go to church and pray. On the night of the 10th the volcano burst open, loosing the flood that roared like a tidal wave down the canyon. People thought that Hunahpú was erupting water instead of fire. As the lower floors of the palace were inundated, Doña Beatriz, with an illegitimate child of Alvarado's in her arms, fled to her chapel on the roof. But her prayers were too late. Her brother, Francisco de la Cueva, battled fiercely to reach her, but Doña Beatriz and her funereal ladies were submerged with the palace, and Don Francisco could only cling to a tree and see her refuge washed away. Nothing is left of her palace now but part of the chapel, and the old city has no other name but that: La Ciudad Vieja.

The people wished to deny Doña Beatriz Christian burial because her cursing had brought its just punishment, but Bishop Marroquín had her fittingly interred in what was left of the church. Later her remains were buried with her husband's under the high altar of the Cathedral in the new city. That time they built in the valley of Panchoy, Dry Lake, at a safe distance from the volcano. Only in occasional heavy rains does the trickling Rio Pensativo rise and threaten to overfill the lake again.

The Bishop and Don Francisco steadied the people through the interregnum, but when the new Governor arrived, the Bishop was free to settle Alvarado's estate as executor. The Conqueror, like so many men of action, was always able to finance an expedition to Peru or the Orient; but he had great difficulty in paying the cook. His fortune was not considerable, and the Bishop caused much grumbling by his disposal of it. He paid all servants, all small claims; freed Indian slaves, but not Negroes; put mineworkers on the basis of free labor; and allotted what was left to the maintenance of Alvarado's illegitimate children. Don Pedro had also left money for charity to ease his conscience.

The new administration was much pestered by the zealot Bartolomé de las Casas, who preached a ceaseless, fervid campaign against maltreatment of Indians. Guatemala had followed the custom of granting groups of Indians to white men, known as *encomenderos*. In theory, the natives were apportioned among Christians for religious instruction. In fact, it meant a good deal of practical experience in agriculture, animal husbandry, and the panning of streams for gold. The Indian was a slave even if he was not so branded and designated. Las Casas had seen this practice in the West Indies, where its horrors were extreme. He had even been an encomendero, a fact which caused him bitter regret all his life. In atonement, he suggested the introduction of Negro slaves. Negroes, unfortunately for them, were so hardy that they survived and multiplied under treatment that exterminated the Indian race.

Las Casas went repeatedly to Spain. Remarkable that in an age considered so narrow this monk could always get a hearing before the King, where he minced no words in accusing the encomenderos — and among them were the most powerful men in Spain — of heinous crimes against their dependents. He was actually given the title " Protector of the Indians," and a roving commission to go where he liked, see what went on, and report. He was a Father Coughlin, a Billy Sunday, vociferous and truculent, with the lack of balance of such men; but he got things done. The Laws of the Indies were largely the result of his agitation, and more humane laws for the protection of a subject people have never been known. Las Casas's story offers strong proof that Spain was honest in her desire to convert and civilize the Indian; that the entire Conquest, with all its cruelties, was justifiable to her on that basis. Every ship from Spain brought orders that slavery must be abolished, that natives must be kindly treated. But nothing was ever said of lighter tribute. Endless wealth was expected to roll in as free and open-handed gifts. Las Casas was so radical as to say that Indians could be converted and even mulcted of a good deal by peaceful means. He was later given a chance to prove how right he was. But he could not change human nature so quickly. He could only set up a standard still far ahead of our own civilization.

Las Casas achieved greatly, but Bishop Marroquín, as a scholar and a diplomat, accomplished much too. It was he who got lands allotted to Indians. It is due to their first Bishop that so many Guatemalan Indians own the lands they work. He was influential in founding schools for Indians as well as whites and in bringing orders of monks and nuns to staff schools, hospitals, orphanages, homes for the old and destitute. With his own funds the Bishop built a home for orphaned girls and in his will he left twenty thousand pesos and a large estate for the founding of a university, a project he had been unable to realize.

The Bishop's palace was in the village now called San Juan del Obispo. In the city lived Doña Leonor, lady of Don Francisco de la Cueva. Her house still stands, plain and substantial, at the corner of the street named for her La Calle de la Princesa Xicotencatl and La Calle de la Concepción. In Calle de la Universidad, Bernal Díaz del Castillo, aging but very clear of memory, was writing his *True History of the Conquest of Mexico*. If he talked as he wrote, he must have been a stimulating guest. I like to think that Doña Leonor invited him often. What tales he could tell of her grandfather, the Tlaxcalan chief, of her father's impetuous youth, of how her mother escaped with Malinche from the collapsing capital of the Aztec kings! And if the Bishop took chocolate as well, suave in his rustling magenta,

what a company that would be! Hardy conqueror, cultivated priest, and daughter of an Indian and a Spaniard.
Such is the proud heritage of Spanish America!

Another type who figures in Antigua's history was
Brother Peter de Betancourt, called the Saint Francis of
Guatemala. While Las Casas raged and the Bishop pursued
his softly wise and diplomatic way, Hermano Pedro, poor,
simple, and unlettered, passed through the streets at night
with his bell and his lantern, seeking the sick and distressed
to aid them. At last his humble house could not hold all the
needy, people helped him, and they established a hospital
which still carries on his work: the Hospital of Hermano
Pedro de Betancourt. Naturally miracles are told of him.
Once, they say, a poor man came asking for food. Hermano
Pedro, having nothing to give him, picked up a lizard. " Put
this in your sack," he said, " and see what you find when
you get home." The lizard's skin, it is related, was filled
with precious jewels which the man sold and relieved his
distress. Even today simple people go to Hermano Pedro's
tomb in the Church of San Francisco, tell their troubles
to him, and put their ears close to hear his reply. To them
he is a saint, though the Church has not canonized him.

All Hermano Pedro's work was not with the poor. This
is a story of a different kind:

The Royal Councilor Alvaruenga lived in Calle de la
Nobleza in the house known now as Dorothy Popenoe's.
Every night, to the Councilor's disgust, Don Alvaro de
Asturias came to court his daughter, María. Don Alvaro
was of noble birth and lived in the Casa de los Leones, but
there was enmity between the families. The Oidor, over-

borne by hate and pride, decided to put an end to it. One night the young lover left María's iron-barred window as usual and started home. He met the sereno, making his rounds with staff and lantern, chanting the hour, the temperature, and " All serene! " Then Don Alvaro turned the corner near San Francisco where the Virgen de la Luz glowed in her candle-lit niche. An Indian, muffled in a dark blanket, waited there. When the sereno passed again, near dawn, he found the body of young Alvaro, stabbed, just under Our Lady of the Light. The murderer was not found. María, desolate, entered the convent of La Purísima Concepción, the wealthiest in Guatemala and the one about which the apostate monk Thomas Gage recites such scandals.

Months passed, bitter, agonizing months for a Royal Oidor, aware, as his age was, of the yawning pit of hell just before him, of devils looking over his shoulder, of the dangers of either seeking or avoiding confession. At last, fear-driven, he went to consult the humble Brother Peter. That one exhibited no surprise. The Indian had told him all about it. He was not considered guilty; a slave, of course, must obey. Alvaruenga begged for help. Brother Pedro could offer none, but like a good psychologist he told his penitent that he himself would know what to do. " Follow the guidance that comes to you," he said.

The Oidor returned to his home where a barefooted bowing menial opened the door. Beyond the entrance was the patio, aglow with sunset at that hour and aflutter with birds nesting in the great cedar tree. Against that peaceful light he saw not the flowers and the fountains that were really there, but a gallows — black and awful, and final.

Then he knew. The next day he used his privilege of calling the council together and confessed. He was hanged from such a gallows as he had seen in the patio. Pedro de Betancourt stayed by him until he mounted the steps, sent him off, perhaps, at ease.

The council had plenty of worries. If pirates were not threatening the coasts, malcontents were complaining to Spain. Ships from home brought new exactions or failed to arrive. As the colonies were forbidden any industry that might compete with Spain, they were often short of wines or olives or other essentials. Always there were Indian troubles. Pressed too far, those thankless savages had a way of taking to the bush and having to be reconquered and reconverted. Negro slaves were brought in because the natives did not breed fast enough, even when marriages were forced at the earliest possible age. Or they just supinely died. A most ungrateful lot, whose laziness, then as now, was an unfailing topic of conversation.

But on that underpinning, wobbly as it sometimes seemed, the Spaniards erected a life that must have compared favorably with that in European cities. At its apogee, in the eighteenth century, the Most Noble and Loyal City had a population of thirty thousand. The upper class lived in stone mansions, some with balconies, all with ponderous carved doors and glazed windows. The rooms were furnished with brocades and tapestries, paintings and statues, crystal, porcelain, and silver, and fine furniture. Ships from China and from Spain brought luxuries of two worlds, and nothing was too cumbersome or too heavy to load on an Indian, or a team of Indians, and fetch in from the coast.

These aristocrats went forth on blooded horses or in carriages. If there were not many titled folk, there were more than a hundred families who had carriages — the mark of superiority.

For mental and spiritual sustenance there were twenty-six churches, each one a treasure-house of art. The Cathedral, with its three naves and sixteen chapels, was adorned with much gold leaf on carved wood and with statues of the Virgin and the Apostles in marble and bronze, inlaid with mother-of-pearl. The University, founded in 1676, ranked as sixth in the New World. There was a printing press. There were two schools for boys, one for girls, eight monasteries, five nunneries, three beaterios, two hospitals, two prisons for men and one for women. Guatemala then must have presented such a picture as we associate with our North American colonial days. Powdered wigs and colored smallclothes, lace ruffles and snuff, curtsying ladies, and talk — under the breath certainly in Catholic Guatemala — of the wild new ideas in France. They probably felt very secure from anything so upsetting.

In 1771 the Governor died of a fever contracted on the coast. In '72 the King appointed his successor, Don Martín de Mayorga, who proved much more destructive to the lovely capital than many earthquakes. On May 11, 1773 he landed after sixty-one days at sea. By June 11 he was within a day's journey of the capital, where an elaborate reception awaited him. As he rested at the Finca Cabrejo, the earth began to tremble. It made the new Governor nervous. He lacked training in the earthquakes which had been intermittently shaking Guatemala for the last thirty years.

When he reached the capital, the city officials stood up as well as they could through the speeches and fireworks, and tried to settle down to work. But the earth was never still. Tremblings became shakes, shakes became quakes.

By Saint Martha's Day, July 29, even the strongest buildings rocked. Men had to crawl through the streets. The four legs of beasts did not suffice to steady them. Trees lay with their branches on the ground. Tiles and stones leapt in the air. Nuns fled to the country, for wattled huts were safer than stone temples. Prisoners were released. A monk saw the Virgen de la Luz dance in her niche and ran, crazed, until he fell dead. Processions of penitents whipped themselves through the streets. Priests prayed without ceasing. Day was dusk with dust; night a black horror lit by rivers of flame flowing down the volcano. Those who could not find priests to confess them ran through the town crying their sins aloud. The Cathedral priests took out the famous Jesús del Perdón and set it up in a hut, where people knelt by hundreds, burning their candles. Indians fled to the mountains and had to be lured back with threats and promises. Priests never rested. They gathered what bodies they could for Christian burial. Robbery became so common that the death penalty was decreed for almost everything, and a gallows set up in the plaza. Rains brought the Rio Pensativo up to the danger point. Everyone who could fled, including the Governor, who was not used to such an unfirm terra. Then the quakes ceased, and people came back to try to restore their homes. But in December quakes began again, and Governor Mayorga was through.

He decided to establish his capital at *La Ermita,* the

Hermitage, in the valley of the Virgin. Mayorga interpreted as a command the King's permission to move and
used it to force unwilling citizens to desert their homes,
lose their investments. It was a long battle, but the Governor
was a strong man, thoroughly frightened, and he overlooked
nothing to make life intolerable in the old city. Repairs
were prohibited, even to roofs or gates or water-pipes. The
University faculty, whose fine buildings were newly finished, held out against the move, but at last they capitulated.
Indians were beaten into baggage trains that moved day
and night across the mountains carrying wheat and corn
from Quetzaltenango and Sololá and from Antigua everything portable. Not only furniture, but altars and screens,
portals and statues, iron grilles and fountains. Palaces,
convents, and churches were left stripped and unprotected
in La Antigua Capital, the Ancient Capital, while their
owners lived in grass huts during the building of the new.

Guatemala, going along with history, achieved character-
lessness. Antigua, deserted, mellowed into tranquillity: the
unique example of a Spanish colonial city, untouched by
modernity. Happily the people who gradually drifted back
there to live have done nothing to mar its calm, deep as the
peace of one who has known suffering and come to evalu-
ate it correctly. Perhaps the magnitude of Antigua's tragedy
dwarfs all others into true perspective. More likely it is just
that the cobbled streets are unchanged and that grass grows
between the stones. Many of the houses are the original low
structures, built with thick walls and buttressed to withstand
earthquakes. Every street soon meanders off into a leafy
lane between moss-covered walls. Behind them are traces

of old convent gardens where heliotrope and roses border the damp paths, and crumbling fountains still play. Children and birds chirp wherever there are trees and water. Sunny days are never hot, nor winds biting. All day it is quiet, and at evening night-blooming flowers scent the air and only fireflies illumine the empty alamedas.

XVI: Hot Tropics and Bananas

THE RAILROAD FROM GUATEMALA TO PUERTO BARRIOS crosses deep canyons on dizzy trestles and drops in a few miles from an altitude of five thousand feet to sea level. Like an educational film, it unrolls a complete geography lesson from mountain top to seashore. But the railroad itself and the story of its building are more interesting than the country it crosses. For this is one of those triumphs of Yankee enterprise and engineering which made North American capital so dear to ambitious dictators half a century ago and so dangerously imperialistic to some Central Americans of today.

Back in the eighties President Barrios was stung by the prevailing bee for expansion and development by means of railroads. By dint of much effort he got a few miles of track laid. After his death his successor carried on, but the road was not finished to Puerto Barrios until a Yankee appeared. Myron Cooper Keith had already won fame by building a railroad in Costa Rica, where they said, in proof of Mr. Keith's greatness, that a dead man lay under every tie for twenty-five miles. Sanitation and care for human life did not much concern a promoter in those days. That

178

three of the dead men were Mr. Keith's brothers only adds pathos to the tale. Mr. Keith's history is a Richard Harding Davis tale of strong men hacking a way through jungles to lay steel rails, bridging torrents, dying of tropical diseases or surviving as tropical tramps, subsisting on liquor, and figuring as Mr. Davis's raconteurs. Indians and Negroes from the West Indies were the wielders of machetes, the sweating crews that laid the tracks and provided the stuff of revolution when the course of business called for revolution.

Mr. Keith was not only a construction engineer; he was one of those daring financiers whose business acumen, political skill, and boundless acquisitiveness made their buccaneering so picturesque. Encouraged by President Barrios, he procured staggering loans in London banks, risked all he had many times, and won fabulous rewards. The International Railways of Central America were designed to connect all the Central American countries. Many politicians have tried to unite them all into one republic. Both those dreams are still unrealized, and the road's principal importance to Guatemala is that it links the capital with the two ports: San José on the Pacific and Puerto Barrios on the Caribbean. And that it hauls bananas. But that comes later.

As the terrain shelves off from the central highland, the train runs for hours through scorched desert, the only arid stretch in Guatemala's miscellany of climates. The villages are stupid railroad towns, and the people that mongrel type of Indian going Ladino which combines the worst features of both. These are the folk who make sentimentalists yearn for the uncontaminated primitive who is dignified by a steady adherence to his own mores. Below El Rancho, where the bus takes off for Cobán, heat settled moistly upon me, and I knew that my search for hot tropics was rewarded at last. We followed the Rio Motagua, whose recurrent overflow fertilizes fecund growth. No hut is too poor to have a thickly branching date palm, a coconut or two on slim gray stems, and a breadfruit tree, standing apart, shapely and of a rich green. Bananas edged the fields of corn and garden truck. A people whose back yard yields so much can be exploited, but never to the point, surely, of starvation.

Below Zacapa begins the domain of the United Fruit Company, which the natives dub La Frutera. Charles David Kepner and Jay Henry Soothill have called their study of its activities *The Banana Empire,* on the ground that it extends over more than one nation and that its might is felt in international relations as well as in finance. Bananera, between Zacapa and Puerto Barrios, is its capital. Seven thousand employees, foreigners in positions of responsibility over native foremen and laborers, inhabit a swampy region many miles in extent. On the Indian-Spanish blood base, these people seem to be evolving a new race. Nordic strains are discernible in pale eyes or streaky hair, and Negro blood has tarred the entire population. Chinese merchants stand coatless in front of almost every store. Near one of them I saw a moon-faced yellow child with frizzly African wool. And a cinnamon-colored baby in the arms of a Spanish-looking mother was fondled by a monkey dangling from a tree. By that time I was ready to believe anything, and the Carib youngsters in Puerto Barrios make a touch of monkey blood seem only reasonable.

These people of blended races and color live in company houses set on stilts, and pass their off hours swinging in hammocks under them. Their houses are not screened, as the higher employees' are, though the country is dangerously malarial and the company makes great talk of its fight against malaria. The roofs are corrugated iron. I asked why they did not use tile or thatch as both cooler and prettier, and was told that sheets of iron flying through the air on stormy days are easier to dodge than tiles, and that cisterns fill most readily from iron roofs. The workers deal in company stores, and though they are citizens of Guatemala, with the right to vote, they can almost never be bothered to go to town to do so. They are subjects of La Frutera. If they ever think of any other possible condition, no casual passer-by would suspect it. Leisurely women with baby on hip in rooms open all around, slack men swaying in hammocks, a few animals, bare ground clean of debris, and bananas shutting in every outlook. The foreign upper crust seem just as restricted, in spite of their screened club houses, tennis courts, and golf links. They might as well be living on an island. It is not only because swampy country with fantastic plant forms looks like a sea, but that white men repulse the human life around them. They never see the Indian-Negro-mestizo as an individual or a race with creeds and customs and a psychology that are human and worthy of understanding. And a conception of him as a man with rights, and all that, is so remote as to seem ludicrous in connection with a company man's mind. The banana-worker is a hand, good or bad, worth enough care to get his maximum of work, but impersonal, distant, uninteresting. Even Guatemala is less than nothing to these isolated Nordics. They inhabit company compounds, fill days with bananas and company gossip, and go home to England or the United States without having touched a foreign country at all.

At Quiriguá I met the exception. As I stepped off the train a tall Scot introduced himself as Clark, manager of the company hotel. He and Mrs. Clark made me at home in a cool house with more screens than walls, set above lawns to catch the breeze, and commanding that waving immensity of bananas as a ship the ocean. The Clarks recommended good Scotch as the best protection against the malarial mosquito, and the morning light for the ruins. Fortified as advised, I chose to visit the monuments that evening instead of in the glare and heat of day. A hand-car ran us out and a few steps through jungle brought us to the stelæ. When La Frutera cleared the forest to plant bananas, this patch was left as a setting for the last Old Empire city. In pale twilight we wandered through the ruins and I heard what all comers hear and was hypnotized as at Copán by the mystery of the persistence of things after the beliefs that vitalized them are lost.

This site has been known a hundred years; a whole procession of archæologists has dug and pondered here. The seventy-five-acre archæological reservation was set aside and is maintained by the United Fruit Company. Here in recent years the Carnegie Institution has cleared the carv-

ings of moss and set the stelæ in cement bases and surrounded each one with a heavy wire fence. For this is the
Maya ruin most accessible to the casual traveler, who is not
above leaving his name or collecting a souvenir. The stelæ
show some of the finest carving in the entire Maya area. I
was arrested by face after face, highly personal portraits,
beautiful and serene, strong and noble. It is impossible to
describe these things, silly to try. Enough information to
satisfy the unscientific visitor has fortunately been assembled by Sylvanus G. Morley. With his *Guide to the Ruins of
Quiriguá,* one may spend hours looking at the monuments,
learning the story of their discovery, their place in the
scattered records of Maya history, getting some feeling of
their significance to the student.

As Quiriguá was colonized from Copán, it carries on as
one would expect. Carvings are deeper, more rounded,
more realized, sometimes even to the point of over-elabora-
tion. Quiriguá is notable also for its zoomorphs, animal-
shaped altars, which, like the stelæ, were set up as time-
markers. Just what animals are represented it is hard to
say. Some might be toads, if they did not have horns and
tails; some might be crouching beasts if they did not show
feathers or fins. Only one, Zoomorph G, is identifiable beyond all doubt as a jaguar.

Near each zoomorph stands its altar. As I stood beside
the one marked O, better described as that of the Masked
Dancer, looking at that vital figure in movement I wondered
what it might mean to a descendant of those people. One
Indian said: " I like these things because Indians made
them." As we watched the dimming of the late light, a

group of Indians came single file out of the bush and disappeared noiseless as specters into it again. The ceiba and mahogany trees were very still, and only a shy breeze rustled the fan-topped palms. Mr. Clark told me of an archæologist, younger then than now, who once laid an Indian guide out on that stone and intoned a Maya prayer over him, to get the atmosphere. The Indian, understanding perfectly that the wild white man was offering his living heart to the gods, leapt up and ran. I laughed. The spell was broken, but at twilight, in a place like that, anything could be.

By the time I was ready to consider bananas in the morning, Mr. Clark had done a half-day's work; a banana man's day begins at dawn.

We started with a sketch to show how the herb — the banana is the largest of all herbs — develops from a corm. It is a virgin, and the whole plant is held ready-formed in a triangular particle like a corn in the foot — miniature, but complete, to the fingers of the fruit. As it grows, the foliage pushes up inside, unfurling leaf after leaf; the leaves rise and unfold until of their own weight they fall out into the familiar drooping form of the plant. Last comes the blossom, heavy, purple, phallic-looking, and above that show the fingers which will develop into bananas. At first they turn upward in delicate yellow whorls. Later their weight bears them down and they turn leaf green. One bearing ends the plant, and then it requires skill to decide when to cut it down, which of its many shoots to save, and how to space them. Five hundred plants to an acre are the average, but that varies according to soil and weather conditions. Aside from pruning, the plantations must be kept cleared of underbrush as fire protection and vigilantly watched for blights.

Bananas, like so much good food, were brought to the Western Hemisphere by a monk: Fray Tomás de Berlanga, who was later Bishop of Panama. He is said to have imported some plants, in 1516, from the Canary Islands to Santo Domingo, where they throve. In the eighteen hundreds several ship-loads went to the United States, but sailing ships were too slow and nothing came of it until Captain Baker of Boston began shipping bananas in steamships in 1880. Out of that grew the Boston Fruit Company, incorporated in 1890. They tried to develop bananas in Cuba and Santo Domingo, but sugar-cane won in those islands, and it was not until the Boston Fruit Company discovered the mainland that big things began to happen.

As far back as the seventies, Mr. Keith, seeking cargo for his railroad in Costa Rica, had hit upon bananas. By the beginning of this century, many banana farmers were shipping fruit to New Orleans. Prices were fixed by keen competition, both in Central America and in the markets of the United States. It was the heyday of rugged individualism. Then, just when the Boston Fruit Company was on the lookout for new lands, Mr. Keith's New Orleans associates went into bankruptcy and two strong men met. Mr. Andrew W. Preston, president of the Boston Fruit Company, and Mr. Myron C. Keith, president of the International Railways of Central America, agreed that one rugged individual in the banana business would be sufficient. So they combined to form the United Fruit Company, which bought out the seven subsidiary companies of the old Boston Fruit and acquired, in one way and another, the control of most competitors in both hemispheres. The neat result was that the new company had the bananas, the railroad and steamship lines for shipping, and the market for selling them. Gentlemen prominent on La Frutera and the I.R.C.A. maintain that there is no connection between the two corporations. But they are undeniably on speaking terms. Mr. Keith was first vice-president of the Fruit Company from 1899 to 1921; Mr. Preston and other officers of United Fruit have been on the board of directors of the railroad.

The advantages of the union were great. Raising and shipping bananas is a risky business. Whole regions may be razed by storm, devastated by disease. In such cases a company of imperial extent and mastery can make its market, and its profits, from another country. Its wealth enables it to command the best technical equipment and scientific knowledge. The United Fruit, for instance, owns and operates the Great White Fleet of ships, especially constructed to keep bananas at exactly the right temperature. All these advantages and others are set forth most eulogistically in Samuel Crowther's *The Rise and Romance of the American Tropics*. Mr. Crowther skips lightly past the facts, which Mr. Kepner and Mr. Soothill dwell upon, that all independent banana-raisers must sell to the United Fruit and ship over the International Railways. The combination, according to the last two authors, is the most powerful influence in Central America: economic imperialism *par excellence*. These books offer convincing confirmation of one's prejudices, whatever they may be. Those who think the little brown brothers have a right to their own will like Mr. Kepner and Mr. Soothill better.

Modern commercial methods have not put an end to the romance of strong men in bitter strife. The last exciting tale is that of the rise of Samuel Zemurry, now president of United Fruit. A Bessarabian immigrant, he drifted south to New Orleans, where he made a contract for all the United Fruit Company's *rejects* — bananas too ripe to ship inland. By underselling the big company, he brought them to see the advisability of assisting him to go into the banana business in Honduras. In time he incorporated the Cuyamel Fruit Company, which became the United's most annoying competitor. The United Fruit makes a policy of encouraging independent growers, but companies it sets its foot on firmly. This policy was not a success with Mr. Zemurry. There are exciting tales, also in the style of Richard Harding Davis, of Mr. Zemurry and the " Incredible Yanqui," Lee Christmas, and how they sailed from New Orleans under the noses of the United States Secret Service with arms for a revolution in Honduras. There is the story of how Mr. Zemurry, in Boston in 1932, held up the board of directors of the aristocratic United Fruit at the point of twelve million dollars' worth of stock and lifted the company right out of their hands. Mr. Zemurry is now managing director in charge of operations and he has replaced many young Harvard graduates, sons of sons, by gentlemen of a type Mr. Zemurry likes better.

The company, they say, is making even more money than before. It owns approximately fifty thousand acres of banana land on the north coast of Guatemala and it handles all the bananas that anybody raises. It pays the government fourteen thousand dollars a year for the right to operate, as well as an export tax of one cent per stem. In return the government allows construction material to enter with little or no duty. The company has had its ups and downs, but as long as Central American presidents continue friendly toward foreign capital, bananas are indeed gold to Boston and New Orleans. After the merger with the Cuyamel Fruit Company and Mr. Zemurry, the capital stock and surplus of United Fruit, all earnings of the business, amounted to about $206,-000,000. In the worst years it has never passed a dividend, and its early investors have, according to Mr. Kepner and Mr. Soothill, averaged no less than seventeen per cent a year on their money. Mr. Crowther's thesis is that all this has been of immense value to the Central American republics. If so, it should inspire us all to altruistic endeavor in foreign lands.

I gleaned this information later. That morning Mr. Clark of La Frutera stuck to banana culture, the troubles that beset the company, and what it does for its employees. Its troubles include flood and storm, plant disease, and loss in shipping. But the greatest of all dangers is that banana lands wear out. Mr. Keith's concessions from the government were for ninety-nine years. There are fifty years still to go, but the lands are weakening fast. The company maintains a botanical department under Dr. Wilson Popenoe, which constantly studies improved methods of agriculture, of fertilization, of everything to increase production. It is even reaching out to acquire lands on the Pacific coast. And it is experimenting with cacao, that ancient source of wealth for Guatemala. It may be only a matter of time until flamboyant advertisements are assuring us that only by drinking cocoa can we remain slim, fragrant, and alluring.

The company boasts that it pays five million dollars a year in wages and salaries in Guatemala; and that its lands, productive and habitable now, were a worthless and dangerous swamp when they were taken over, forty years ago. It encourages the natives to use mosquito nets, to sleep off the ground, and to wash their feet. That has to do with hookworm, though; not with malaria. Jamaica niggers are smarter about taking care of themselves, and better banana-workers generally, than Indians. The most hopeless human proposition, Mr. Clark said, is an Indian just down from the hills. He is puny, lacking the arm and back muscles necessary to swing a heavy stem, and he has no feeling for a banana plant. The second generation is pretty good. At that point a twelve-year-old boy passed us, and Mr. Clark caught his arm to show me the heavy muscle, had the lad lift a stem to demonstrate his skill, and let him go, grinning with pride as a real banana fellow. These youngsters are even developing judgment about pruning, the most technical part of banana culture.

It takes experts to treat bananas right and to get them finally to our tables, evenly formed, golden yellow, and unscarred. To know when to cut is an art in itself; to catch the stem when it is fully matured but still green, with as much weight in fruit and as little in stem as possible. A good average bunch has about a hundred and seventy bananas or fingers and weighs around seventy pounds. One man cuts, another catches, a third hoists onto a cart driven by a fourth

who hauls the load to the train. Both cart and railroad car
are heavily padded with banana leaves, a pampering that
aroused the indignation of Carleton Beals, writing in *Banana Gold*. Mattresses for bananas, and people packed in
on hard seats! But these bananas must meet the exactions of
the market in the States, and so far there is no demand for
the particular human blend the United Fruit Company produces. Or maybe for any human blend.

The preferred banana is the Gros Michel, so familiar at
the grocery-store. From its padded railroad car it is lifted
tenderly onto the United Fruit Company's ships, built to give
it the best conditions. Refrigeration, ventilation, even heat-
ing are provided to deliver the fruit to the jobber still green.
It must by no means ripen until it hangs in the middleman's
storeroom in the States. The company would like to develop
our taste for a larger variety, but so far only a few luxury
shops will handle anything new. There is a great and de-
lectable variety, from a tiny sweet mouthful to a husky
plantain too crude to eat raw, but rich and palatable when
cooked; and we may learn to like them all.

Mr. Clark said that all Pacific-coast bananas are hauled
across and shipped from Puerto Barrios. " The Grace Line
lands its passengers at San José," he chuckled, " but bananas are more fragile than tourists and can't stand that handling through the surf." So there is something more fragile
than a Grace Line tourist!

In this connection, illuminating figures are cited in *The
Banana Empire* to prove how much cheaper it is for a
Pacific-coast finquero to ship his produce across the conti-
nent to Puerto Barrios and out on United Fruit Company

steamers than to a much nearer port on the Pacific. Rates for shippers close to Puerto Barrios are often quite high. This works a hardship on shippers of coffee, many of whom are native Guatemalans living on the Pacific coast. The government has not been able to cope with the situation.

Mr. Clark did not go into this. Banana-workers, he told me, are paid by piece-work. A superior cutter can earn six or seven dollars a day three or four days a week during the three months' cutting season, though nobody does. Some cutting goes on all the time, but most men face months of idleness. When they work, seventy-five cents a day is an average earning. I was interested to note that Mr. Kepner, taking all the facts into consideration and writing from a critical point of view, bears out this conclusion. He puts it at less than $1.25 a day. Compared with the pay of other Guatemalans, it is a good wage, though the banana-worker has poor or no land to till and has to feed himself, while the Indian on a coffee finca is given land and some food. Mr. Clark said that most laborers put in about four hours before retiring to the hammock under the house. Mr. Kepner puts the day's work at from six in the morning to two in the afternoon, though he states that the task system and the Indians' lack of time sense make it difficult to estimate how much time they work.

Aside from pot-bellies indicative of hookworm and the lean malarial victims, the people I saw looked well fed. Dr. McPhail in the company's hospital said they get a fairly well-balanced diet of vegetables, meat, and fruit. He confirmed the Public Health Department's findings about high infant mortality and the prevalence of parasitic diseases.

The company fights all that by inspection, bi-monthly blood tests, and treatment when needed. Every wage is docked two per cent to cover that work and all hospital care. The hospital at Quiriguá is one of Guatemala's institutions. Many Guatemalans get no pleasure out of an illness unless they can go down to Quiriguá and Dr. McPhail. Dr. Mc-Phail is an old Scotch bachelor and everybody's best friend. When he started with the company in 1907, his hospital consisted of a bicycle on which he pedaled up and down the track with plenty of quinine. The natives had very little use for quinine in those days, but the doctor did a thriving business in pay-night carvings. Now there are fewer drunks, fewer fights; and the natives love to get into the hospital. Dr. McPhail's only rivals are the witch doctors. The day I was there the police gazette carried an item about one who had charged eighteen dollars for his ministrations.

The hospital is well equipped. The doctor says the company has never refused him any apparatus he asked for, so he has excellent operating-rooms, with X-ray and all the gadgets, and space for two hundred beds. The worker's two per cent covers whatever he may need. He pays for his family if he can, but few can and Dr. McPhail, gruff and humorous, is said to turn nobody away. He took me about. We looked in on a woman whose appendix had been taken out that morning. Another woman sat beside her baby, whom she brought in every week for a few days of correct feeding at hospital expense. Cancer had taken both her breasts. A plump baby was sleeping quietly with bandaged neck. A big tumor had just been removed. Another child, an appendectomy case too, stopped fretting when the doctor spoke to him.

I rode on to Puerto Barrios through banana groves, along lines of cars bulging with green bananas and graying leaf mattresses. I passed company towns, company stores, company telegraph and radio stations, company employees of every caste and race, of almost every degree of human culture. On the dock at Puerto Barrios I watched huge black men load tons of green bananas. Men of muscle, slipping strongly under wet slick skin, men with empty, dull, or smiling faces, chanting to help the rhythmic heave, or jabbering that almost inhuman singsong of the Carib speech. Democracy must come, I thought, but it will take those men a long time to know it.

XVII: Hospitality and Pirates
on the Rio Dulce

PUERTO BARRIOS, REPUTEDLY THE FORLORNEST OF ALL
tropical ports, flaunts enough South Sea flora and fauna to
conjure up numberless romantic ragtags of history and fic-
tion. Ships in the sluggish ultramarine harbor fly flags
from everywhere. The shoreline is rendered outlandish by
crooked palm stems and tattered bananas forever soughing
in the wind. And the natives, shuffling along to their strange
talk, both harsh and musical, are as ludicrous as comedy
niggers — long shambling niggers with big flat feet and for-
ward-thrust heads. Negroid as they look, they are Indians
with only a touch of African blood: the Caribs whom
Columbus saw and miscalled cannibals.

The town is of La Frutera, and nearly all its buildings
are those yellow company houses. Tourists from the Great
White Fleet are shunted directly aboard the train for the
capital, but for the eccentric traveler who goes unescorted
there is a hotel, well screened. Double screens at the doors,
screened porches all around, and double doors at every
room make it seem impossible that a mosquito could ever
get in. Puerto Barrios is really malaria-infested, and the
safe thing is to stay indoors after dark. The maleficent

anopheles is the buzzless night-flyer; the mosquito who
warns before he bites never carries the disease.

The hotel is operated by Germans with lamentable in-
ability to sense what would appeal. The diet would be suitable, I should think, in Hamburg. Meat and potatoes,
pickled beets, hot puddings and sauces. With a market piled
with tropical fruits, you may get stewed prunes. I left it
finally in a pet because the manager, having interrupted
my breakfast to complain of the inferior and unreliable
natives, neglected to provide the promised porter to get me
to the wharf. When I realized that he had done nothing, it
was five minutes to eleven and the launch left on the hour.
And if I missed that boat there was not another for a week.
Well, I didn't. The barmen called a houseboy who got the
bags as far as the porch. Farther he could not go without
encroaching on the rights of outside porters. But he summoned another who set off to find a licensed cargador. The
manager was nowhere to be seen. But that harried person,
found in every organization, who does all the work, gets no
credit, and always shows up when annoyed customers boil
over, bustled in just then right in the track of my wrath.
Wearily resigned to a scolding public, he took charge and
got me off, vowing again that if there must be inefficiency,
as apparently there must, I prefer it embodied in a brown
and pleasant person and expressed in mellifluous Spanish.
I am entirely opposed to ineffectual Aryans.

The launch was as scrubbed as your kitchen table. The
boy who took down my name, age, place of departure, destination, and why, was one of those Livingston niggers, surely
the funniest people in the world. His trousers were hitched

up to his armpits by one string, his shirt was about half a shirt, and his sugarloaf hat spired high. He spoke Spanish with the oddest accent: Carib. Women of his race, in clean dresses and pink ribbons, lay on the deck making the most of a quiet hour for a snooze. One or another poked her head into the cabin, grinned at me, and touched my things. Inquisitive and forthright as children, they were as inoffensive.

I had heard of the Carib's strong tribal solidarity, with their own voodoo; their cabalistic rites with who knows what sacrifices of children; and their own king. One man told me how he got no service until someone introduced the king, and at that wizened little Negro's word porters appeared like magic. I hoped to see the Carib king. Another related that a young lady visiting in Livingston less than thirty years ago found a baby's hand on her pillow; an amputated, desiccated, black infant's hand! What with her faint and restoration, she never learned what it portended. I longed to be one of those travelers who stumble on all sorts of mystery and magic. But my first concern in Livingston was to find a room for the night.

The town straggles over a hill with yellow frame houses and a pure black personnel. The boy who lifted my bag found it pretty heavy, so he hoisted it onto his woolly head and trotted along as easily as though it had no weight at all. The hotel, a huge building, had no rooms. The heat was vibrating, alive. My boy, undiscouraged, ducked round a corner and brought up before an even dirtier house with screen doors sagging open, rags and bones on the ground among the dogs, and a broom that someone had dropped without sweeping. A woman who rushed out to pick it up said she had a room, and jerked open a sticking door. It was a dark hole, furnished with a camp cot and a chair, and hotly fetid. I asked my guide to lead me to Mr. Parrish, the United Fruit man. Even as an intrepid traveler I felt that more comfort and less atmosphere was highly desirable. Two wenches leaning over the fence said Mr. Parrish had gone to Barrios, and said it in excellent English. All Caribs, I learned, are linguists. Besides their own tongue, they have Spanish and English at least. Many know German too. We walked back to the main street, where the heat was violent, surging back and forth between bare boards and bare baked sand.

Someone in the capital had said: " If you are in trouble, get in touch with Don Pablo Doescher." I thought of the typical small-Guatemalan-town German with maybe a native wife. The boy said: " Yassum," and we set off.

We approached a spacious bungalow with screened porches, a row of coco palms in front, a bougainvillæa over the gate. From the front door I looked through the house to another porch and flowered hills along the Rio Dulce. In the shadowy hallway two white-clad people were taking coffee. Frau Doescher met me at the door, and the minute her kind hazel eyes smiled at my red-faced hotness, I knew I had found a refuge in a weary land. In a minute I was sitting in that breezy lounge among polished mahogany and gleaming silver and asking where they thought I might stay for the night.

Frau Doescher said, as though it were nothing at all: " I think I'll tell them to put up a bed for you here."

A late lunch was served me by an ebony Willie in starched white. I made the mistake of asking if he were Carib, no less than an insult to a citizen of Belize, where they refer to themselves as British " objects." Willie's grandfather was German, but his grandmother, Frau Doescher's cook, was black Belize and very British. She had been reading, she said, that her countryman Bernard Shaw was coming to Guatemala. A lady who kept up with the home news.

My host, when we got around to facts, pooh-poohed most of the lurid tales I had heard. In his thirty years in Livingston he had never heard of a Carib king. But he agreed that the Caribs do have strong tribal solidarity, many customs unknown to whites, and the only Indian language white men do not readily learn. If they continue to practice ancient rites, it is very secretly. Don Pablo doubted cannibalism and the withered baby's hand. The only dance white men see is a Christmas celebration in which all the actors are men, though some are dressed as women. In general they are good Catholics and very moral, both sexually and as to thieving.

" I don't say," said Mr. Doescher, " that if a case of whisky broke, they wouldn't take a bottle, but stealing as we know it in civilized countries, they know nothing about. We never lock up anything, our houses, even our valuables. Of course, all that will change with civilization. . . ."

In the evening a couple of young Germans came in. Over the radio we heard British, French, and German statesmen discussing the Locarno pact. I was interested to watch those Germans, to see how disturbed they were by rumors of war.

Herr Doescher especially is of those kindly, humane cosmopolites who must finally end a civilization founded on war, a civilization that takes stealing for granted as the Caribs never could. When Big Ben struck four o'clock, ten in Livingston, I decided to go to bed, weary with the annihilation of time and space. My room looked out across the wide lawn and the Rio Dulce. As the early light came I could see the golden splashes of the flowering trees of San Juan. The morning was very fragrant, and Willie, at breakfast, as crisp and multilingual as ever.

As Don Pablo walked with me to the launch, a man handed me a ticket. They are apt to ask money for a ticket at any time, so I stuck it into my purse without looking at it. Hours later I discovered that I held a pass the length of the Ferrocarril Vera Paz, " *incluyendo hospedaje* "; a day by launch, five hours by train, and hospitality for the night in the company's rest-house at Panzós. And all as quietly as though it were nothing at all! To people as kind as the Doeschers it may have seemed nothing at all. To a stranger in a strange land it was one of those cockle-warming experiences that will be remembered, I know, when I am old and tired and the world may seem dull or unkind.

I was the only passenger, and I sat aloft in one of the Doeschers' porch chairs. I could make out the shapes of men in boats, very black in the pearly dawn. Victor, the launchman, said they were fishermen. They ship fish to the capital all the year, but especially during Lent. The river tunnels directly into mountains, between steep cliffs covered to the top with heavy growth. It was solid green, varied only by the flowers of San Juan and the white fluff on the bare lanilla trees. The river was oily, deep blue, and the dawning slow. At first there was only the silky run of the water under the prow. Then birds stirred and finally began to sing in high clear notes. The whole trip was soft and smooth and clear. No effort, no confusion, and natural loveliness the entire length of the river, for man has touched it scarcely at all. We saw a few Indians paddling canoes under the bank, the whole picture sharply reflected. A couple of thatched villages showed among banana groves, but the government has forbidden any more clearing for farms. The Rio Dulce is to be preserved as virgin wilderness. We saw few flowers, but the air was fragrant with hidden orchids. Victor proudly pointed out the Piedra Pintada on which travelers carved their names about 1900. It will be a couple of centuries before those names seem anything but a blot on the landscape.

When day was full, there were birds to watch all the time; more herons than anything else. Big blue ones, smaller gray, one almost black, and the snowy great herons that stand like white flowers on long stems and fly tiltwise with slow curvettings against the green as though conscious of their astounding pulchritude. Pelicans, mostly beak. The kingfisher showed his skill by dropping, a black plummet, on a fish from above. Orioles flashed by, and a few parrots rose clamoring from the mangroves. The water gave off a light mist and for hours there was chill in the air.

People were more scarce than birds, but we passed a hamlet now and then, with little patches of corn and sweet potatoes. Corn-tassels looked very incongruous in that jungle, but I reflected that wherever the Indian has trod, there springs maize. As the stream narrowed, we ran close to its verdant banks and saw occasional orchids, pale lavender, and wild sweet-potato blossoms, just as exquisite really, if only they had a more seductive name. When the sun got hot and high, I had my chair moved below, and gave up completely to the languorous heat, which made all living things still and slothful. We passed landing stages and now and then we met a clumsy scow loaded with coffee or bananas. At the Fort of San Felipe we stopped to deliver mail to two Germans in a boat. Only a vine-draped shell of the fort stands now, and there is not even a memory thereabouts of the heavy chain strung across the river to keep pirates out of the lake. But in its day this fort was Guatemala's last hope of safety.

From the time of Elizabeth of England for a hundred years corsairs sailed the Caribbean trying to get a share of the wealth of the Indies for England, France, and Holland, whose colonies did not yield such loot. Guatemala exported indigo, cochineal and liquidambar, hides and cocoa, balsam, vanilla, and gold. And the galleons returning from Spain carried wines, which the colonies were not allowed to grow; manufactured goods they might not make, new colonists, orders from King and Pope and officers of both. Spain took to sending ships in fleets, but the pirates grew bolder until they actually sailed up the Rio Dulce and into the sweet waters of Lake Izabal to scrape the barnacles off their hulls, restore their health on fruits and fresh meat, and pick up what they could from the overland trade. The regular route from the capital was across the mountains by muleback and manback, down the river, and so to the sea. Hence the well-manned fort and heavy chain.

Of pirate tales there is no end, but the favorite buccaneer was Sir Francis Drake, authorized by Queen Elizabeth to harry Spanish shipping all he could — a charge he fulfilled to admiration. He began at Nombre de Dios on the Caribbean, but gradually he worked inland. On one raid he violated a high-born widow on her own estate, and had a son by her who figures in José Milla's novel *El Visitador* as Francisco Molinas. His family is said to be important still in Guatemala. Drake was a foppish pirate, who always dressed richly and had his red hair curled and pomaded. On his ship, the *Golden Hind*, meals were announced by an orchestra of violins and served from crested silver plate. His cabin was hung with pictures and tapestries of great value, many of them gifts of Her Majesty. A personage sure to be admired by the splendor-loving Spaniards!

During that century of license on the high seas, no colonial governor had a night's peaceful sleep. Any day word might come of the loss of an invaluable cargo or of a coastal town laid waste. Every governor had his way of trying to meet the menace. One sent out an expedition of youths of the very best families, blessed by the Church and supported by crossbowmen from the Alta Vera Paz. But after months of futile campaigning against an enemy who could so readily go down to the sea in ships, the young gallants returned bedraggled and unsuccessful. Another Governor, more practical, proposed the purchase of fifteen or twenty Negro slaves to be planted in the swamps along the Rio

Dulce. He was sure that what with neighboring Indians and procreation, they would soon build up a population large enough to keep the road clear and safe. The weakness of this program was that runaway slaves were apt to make friends with pirates and keep them supplied with corn and meat. Actually nothing worked until political changes in Europe put an end to piracy, or at least piracy of that kind.

Beyond Fort San Felipe's ferny shell we rounded the curve and rode out upon Lake Izabal, twelve leagues long and six wide, with fine fishing — everything from perch to tarpon. The lake was gray under an overcast sky, and the hills around a quiet shadowed blue. Time no longer existed, only the gentle sighing motion of the launch, hung in silent space, now that no river banks hemmed us in. So it was with a distinct shock that I saw we were approaching a settlement. It was Estor, Victor said.

" The company used to have a commissary there," he explained, " and the English word for that is *estore*, so they call it that."

At Estor we picked up a passenger, whom Victor introduced with pleased pride. " Now you have a very good traveling companion, Dr. Fulano de Tal, who visits all the fincas along here."

The doctor rattled off all the customary greetings and proceeded to entertain me with such praises of the places I could never hope to see that I could hardly look upon the wonders at hand. His arduous duties had left him no time either to bathe or to shave for, I should say, quite a few days. His equipment, however, was most up to date: Leica camera, field glasses, and in his pocket, besides his comb, pen, and pencil, a clinical thermometer. Needless to say, I greatly preferred the company of the modest Victor, who, now that I was so well attended, had retired above.

We soon left the lake for the Rio Polichic, narrower than the Rio Dulce, more winding and sluggish. Matted lianas draped the trees, which crowded closer, almost menacing. Mammoth ceibas and sky-scraping palms reached above clumps of bamboo, waving puffs of Bermuda grass, coarse-leaved plantain, and a slender reed almost as delicate a green as sugar-cane. The midday heat brought out swarms of yellow butterflies. The only other color variants were orchid lavender and the occasional flash of a bird. Herons were always with us, sleeping now. An iridescent kingfisher slipped out of a thicket and in again.

The doctor went above to eat his lunch, leaving me not too lonely to solace myself on sandwiches, iced beer, and fruit. That led to a nap, which was just reaching a peaceful end when all hands came tumbling down the ladder, calling and pointing. Monkeys! Monkeys! It took quick turning, but I saw them: two little black balls clinging to the top of an amate tree among the vines. One of them, as though to prove he could, let go and swung lazily by his long tail, leering at me with his funny white face. Then we rounded a bend, and that was all I saw of monkeys.

After that, as afternoon shaded into placid evening, more and more birds emerged until I longed for an ornithologist. Small darting canaries replaced the butterflies. A flight of emerald parrots went over, and a gaudy macaw flew solitary through the trees. The air was as moist and fragrant as a greenhouse. Alligators who had been sunning all day, indistinguishable against the muddy banks, manifested their hideousness as they slid into the stream. Turtles sat on logs. The water was green now, everything was green, and the river so tortuous that Victor had to attend to his steering in person. Above again, I rode smoothly head on into one bank, only to be turned aside in the nick of time by the adroit Victor and headed into the other one.

Just after sunset we docked at Panzós. The town, a mile back from the station, is reputed to be a doubtful place for food or accommodation. But Don Pablo's kindness still followed me, and the company rest-house was at my disposal. There Victor, proud to be the emissary of such efficiency, served me a well-cooked dinner. And I slept on a cool cot after a cooling shower. All this surrounded by screens and double screens. For Panzós is in a malarial swamp that never has been drained, perhaps never can be made safe for human life.

At Panzós the launch reloads and goes down the river again. My journey was by train, twenty-four miles to Pancajché, and then by bus to Cobán. The train was as scrubbed as the launch. At every station Germans were thicker, as to both numbers and girth. Brilliant posters advertised the Winter Olympics with great red cheeks and brawny arms and legs, Gargantuan and rather terrifying in contrast with the slim pale-brown Indians. Many children showed Nordic features. A modern Guatemalan is quoted as saying that German colonization is good " for putting a little milk into the coffee." All signs indicated that we were getting into Guatemala's Little Germany.

XVIII: Little Germany and the Land of True Peace

THE ALTA VERA PAZ HAS BEEN CONQUERED BY WHITE MEN
a couple of times. First in the sixteenth century by Bartolomé de las Casas as a demonstration of what could be done
peacefully; and in the nineteenth century by Germans leaving a fatherland which offered more goose-stepping than
opportunities for advancement.

Before Las Casas's attempt the Kekchi of this region had
so savagely repulsed all attempts to conquer them that their
land was known as *Tierra de Guerra*, Land of War, and
given up as hopeless. It was after the time of the earliest
conquerors, who recognized no hopelessness. The giants of
a later day were clerics, not conquerors. And the greatest
of these was Las Casas, whose theories about Indians would
have appealed to William Penn. But the Dominican lived
a century before the Quaker.

Las Casas, in his unremitting campaign to get decent
treatment for Indians, wrote a book: *De Unico Vocationis
Modo*, " The Only Way to Teach." He postulated that all
people, however faulty, inconstant, or cruel, were worthy
to receive Christian doctrine. Logically, this included the

206

natives of the Americas. He set forth a good deal about the character and customs of these natives, of their arts and learning, which would be invaluable today if his book had not been lost. The only way to inculcate the faith, he argued, was by persuasion, leading them toward understanding and goodwill, instead of using force and battle. He supported this thesis from the Old and New Testaments, the Church Fathers, and profane authors; and he condemned as fearful, unjust, perverse, and tyrannical a war to make Indians accept the Christian faith. That sixteenth-century Dominican belonged in a modern progressive school!

As Fray Bartolomé had this translated into Spanish and proclaimed it at the top of his lungs in all company and at every opportunity, plenty of opposition developed. He was made fun of as a visionary and dared to prove that he could, by pure persuasion, win Indians to the true faith and obedience to the crown. Las Casas formally accepted the challenge and undertook to demonstrate his theories by pacifying Tezulutlán, the so far unconquerable Land of War. In a written contract he agreed to see that the Indians accepted Christianity, considered themselves vassals of Spain, and rendered tribute in gold, if they had any, or in whatever they had. Fray Bartolomé stipulated only that for five years not a single Spaniard was to enter the region.

He then worked out a plan with three other Dominicans: Brothers Rodrigo, Pedro, and Luis. They wrote verses in Kekchi, relating the Christian legend from the creation to the resurrection of the Savior and concluding with the promise of the second coming. No copy of this survives either. As an author, Las Casas had bad luck. The monks set their epic to music and taught it to four Indian merchants who went regularly into the hazardous Land of War. To their usual packs they added scissors, knives, mirrors, bells, and other gewgaws to decoy the natives. In the cacique's village they spread their goods in the market place, and when the crowd was densest, they sang their song. The audience grew apace until the chief himself came to listen. He had the story repeated, again and again, for eight days and asked for further light.

The troubadours, well drilled in their roles, regretted that they could tell no more. But they knew men in the city of Saint James of the Gentlemen who would be glad to come and explain all. Men with hair cut like wreaths, they said, dressed in black and white robes, and chaste. They underscored how these men differed from the usual run of Spaniards in their plain ways, their disregard of gold, their modesty. It sounded dubious to the chief, who had met Spaniards, but he sent his brother to investigate. If the Dominicans were as represented, the young man was to invite them to come. And to speed the prince's journey and assure success, he ordered a great ceremony with human sacrifices!

Guatemala's reception of the phenomenal news can be imagined. Fray Luis was chosen to sow the first seeds in the new field. He was received under arches of flowers, and in a rustic chapel he celebrated the first mass for the Kekchi. He elucidated the five-year plan and promised that none of the tribe would ever be given to encomenderos. His meekness, the richness of his sacerdotal vestments, and the chapel's fragrant cleanliness in contrast with the old bloodsmirched shrines, all worked in the friar's favor. The priests of the old cult naturally balked, but the chief, thoroughly converted, was baptized and went out himself to preach.

So Christianity was carried to the Kekchi, and the name of their land was changed to Tierra de la Vera Paz, Land of the True Peace. It bears that pacific name today, though, as would be expected, all the monks' promises were violated in time. These natives are no freer or better placed than any others now.

Leaving the railroad at Pancajché, I found myself one of the too many wedged into a bus. There is a law in Alta Vera Paz against riding three in a seat. That applies, apparently, only to private cars. Even the Yankee owner of the Cobán bus was packing us in as tightly as he could. I sat with four where no more than two should have been. My closest neighbor had not recently bathed, but he was full of information. The roads were as crowded as in Los Altos with people carrying burdens. There were more bundles than crates, and women wore flat baskets like hats, even seeming to tilt them at a becoming angle. We met many bands of mozos on their way to the fincas or home again. It is hot country, and damp. Of Cobán they say that it rains thirteen months a year, and the rainy season is different because then it never stops. Everything was bursting with foliage and bloom; fence posts, house-tops, any abandoned piece of wood sets right about raising something. And the road, up and down hills and dipping again and again into the same stream's valley, was dustless and moist.

In a lane a fine-looking young man signaled the bus. It stopped and he spoke in German to the man on the front

seat. I could understand: talk about cash which he handed
over, what to tell the boss, wishes for a good trip home to
Germany.

Then, as the driver put the car in gear, the young German
in the car raised his hand. "*Heil Hitler!*"

The German on the ground responded: "*Heil Hitler!*"
In the wilds of Guatemala young men who have probably
not been in Germany since the appearance of the Nazis! I
learned later that in every German club in Guatemala (and
there is one in every considerable town) members salute on
entering. A Swiss who would not conform found it expedi-
ent to resign, and a young Guatemalan who laughed at the
idea has never since been invited to dances which he attended regularly before.

The demonstration in the lane gave me a thrill of pride
in my own people. God be praised, I thought, for that
pervasive Irish agin-the-government, or whatever it is that
keeps us sassily irreverent toward all pomposity in our
great men. Thank God for *The Biglow Papers* and Mr.
Dooley, and all cartoonists, and *Of Thee I Sing*, and the
Veterans of Future Wars! I tried to visualize one young
Yankee greeting another in a remote land with "Hail
Roosevelt" or even "Hail Supreme Court" or "Hail Con-
stitution." It gratifies me deeply to believe that the inevitable, spontaneous come-back would be: "Nerts!"

We passed several villages. The most interesting was
Tactic, where it was market day. There I heard the Kekchi
speech, so different from Quiché. My neighbor in the bus
explained that Germans learn the Indian tongues readily
because they sound so like German. And the Kekchi does

have a guttural quality. The market was on the ground, under the plaza trees. I wanted a huipil, a lovely example of weaving in many soft shades on dull blue. It was a vender's only upper covering and very dirty. We finally struck a bargain. I bought a new huipil, crude in the colors of aniline dyes, and the Indita, giggling and ashamed, but coveting the newer garment, put it on behind a hedge and brought me back the beauty, wadded in disdain.

Everybody in the bus assured me I had been cheated. An old huipil for a new one! The unwashed loquacious one explained to them all that the foreign Señorita was indubitably buying things for a museum. Then he went on to talk about the Indians.

" They used to be free men," he stated heatedly, " and now they work like slaves for the Germans."

The young German on the front seat turned red about the ears and offered to change seats with me. But I was doing well enough where I was.

Cobán is Little Germany because Germans own most of its coffee lands and produce three fourths of all the coffee harvested in that zone. Many came fifty or more years ago, when President Barrios, reaching out for capital, offered them practically as much land as they could use. It was waste land. Spanish Guatemala never considered the remote Land of Peace as a place to live. Those early Germans cleared the forest, planted coffee, practically made the land they own. German energy and frugality made great fortunes and, as any finquero is quick to state, created work for Indians. Only the Indians fail to appreciate the enormous blessing conferred upon them by white men who benevolently give them a chance to work for a living no better really than such prolific soil would give them for little or no work.

Germans are good colonists. They learn the language with ease and speed, make themselves liked and respected, often marry and establish families which claim the new country as their own. Their children have the advantage of a dual citizenship, or a choice of loyalties. Guatemala claims anyone born on her soil, and to Germany the child of a German father is German whatever the place of his nativity. Among Latin American women the German is spoken of as the most desirable husband and the Yankee as a distant second. Equally often, probably, German men do not marry, but simply go to bed with Indian girls until suitable time to bring a wife out from home. This putting milk into the coffee seems to make a successful cross racially; the children are often fine-looking and intelligent. But they may be very unhappy, especially if the father refuses them a good education or if they are left in the mother's class. The arrival of a wife from Germany hardly makes for harmony, though it all makes for drama. A thousand and one tales only await the teller.

There are less than three thousand Germans in the entire Republic, though they do seem so omnipresent. A third of them are coffee planters and their families; the rest are employed on their fincas or in German offices or business houses in the capital. Many of them stay only a few years. " Guatemala for earning, Germany for spending," is their explicit platform, and " *Heil Hitler* " is their slogan. Not many actually live in Cobán now, but they control the business. The hotel and lodging-houses, the drug and general stores, the garage and all the beneficios, where coffee is prepared for market, are German. They take no part in civic affairs, which are Ladino. But the thirty thousand souls of the Cobán region are dominated by about a dozen German families.

Cobán is a pretty little town, set on hills which round off into leafy valleys with clear streams full of fish and widening out here and there into pools deep enough for bathing. We entered the plaza under an arch whereon was carved the Vera Paz escutcheon: the rainbow of promise, the dove of peace, the olive branch. Below it sat the relic of an automobile which pitched over a curve the last time the President sped through. The plaza was full of soldiers, and government buildings surrounded it, most of them marked somehow with the name of Ubico. For His Excellency was once military Governor of Alta Vera Paz: Upper True Peace, as we say North Carolina.

I tried the German pension. It looked attractive enough with a wide gallery hanging over a hibiscus-bordered lane. The Señorita's Indian features did not match her German name. She wanted very much to please her foreign guest, who turned out to be most unappreciative. Unlike the fresh portal, the bedroom was noisome with greasy cooking and the pigsty, disturbed by the squalling of the cook's baby and a radio. In spite of the Señorita's kindness, when a gracious lady sent a note to say: " Will you not abide with me? " I snatched it as the lifeline it was.

Doña Lula, daughter of one of the first Germans to settle in Cobán, lives in the house where she was born. A tall magnolia tree in the patio made a home for orchids, ferns, and birds at evening. At one end of the long porch sacked coffee was piled ready to ship, and at the other a stuffed quetzal swung its green and courtly tail above easy chairs and magazines from many lands. Her children, like Doña Lula herself, learn Kekchi, Spanish, English, and German as they prepare for English schools. Her servants are the children and children's children of her parents' servitors. The middle-aged woman who worked at a quilting frame was as dear to her mistress, clearly, as a sister.

Callers came all day long. A man from a finca which the older son is managing, with news of him and a list of what he needed; especially a sack of coin to pay off the workers. An old woman sat a long time weeping as she talked, and went away with money to bury a son accidentally killed. A girl came to announce her marriage and was promised a wedding dress.

The most sympathetic was Doña Lula's comadre, bringing her daughter's youngest child. The two women chatted about babies: the cultivated lady and the barefooted Indian, fresh and clean in her blue skirt and white huipil. There was no bar between them. The Indian had suckled the white woman's child when she might have died. The Indian had known no experience she did not share with her children's godmother. They gossiped in Spanish, politely to include me, but slipping now and then into Kekchi. We must go back, in our history, before the Civil War to approximate such a situation — an upper-class woman so sure of social and racial distinctions that she can be unaffectedly her servant's friend, but conscious always of the gulf, which is as

uncritically accepted, quite without bitterness or revolt, by
the servant. Doña Lula's house, like cultivated homes in our
South before the War, exemplifies the charm of an aristocratic tradition. That it does not extend far enough, never
did, and never can, becomes apparent as soon as one leaves
the haven of such a home.

The comadre related that a quetzal came to her ranch
last week. It flew down at dawn, sat awhile on a fence, idly
turned its shining head, easy and unafraid, and flew away.
She thought that if we came for a night we might see one too.
But, so stupid is the world, there was no time. It would be
fun to travel, just once, doing no single obvious thing, but
heeding every hint of a quetzal bird on a fence at dawn.

That extraordinary bird is seen now only in the Alta Vera
Paz, they say; and its extraordinary beauty, scarcity, and
legend still give it a mystical power with the natives. Once,
on a finca near Cobán, a statue of the Virgin disappeared
from a wayside shrine. The Indians, appalled at the sac-
rilege, appealed to the planter. He was nonplussed. It was
unheard of to rob an oratory where travelers stop to rest
and pray and make occasional fiesta. The loss threw everyone into a state of perfect uselessness. Inconceivable that
anyone should work while the Mother of God was absent
from her niche! As the Indians chattered, a quetzal appeared, wheeled its iridescence slowly out of the jungle's
tangle to poise on a gate post and look. It was an omen, they
agreed. Probably the Virgin herself was warning them that
until her image was found only evil might be expected.

The finquero thought hard. Only a stranger could have
done it, one of the seasonal workers from a village in the

west. He must send there. So he did, calling upon a brujo
to search all the cabins. The Virgin was found, carried in
procession to her place, and the appeased Indians went to
work again — but only after several days of fiesta to celebrate.

Every road out of Cobán crosses the Rio Cobán, runs
through a canyon lovely as a park, past well-tended coffee
groves, and comes to a village. In every lane is such a house
as entices one to stay forever. Low-pitched roofs of rust-red
tile run out over wide porches. Magnolia and acacia trees,
ceiba and palm shade them, and musky scents drift on
breezes that are damp without the humidity of lower altitudes.

The villages are alike externally, but individual too. San
Juan has its market in the afternoon, and under cover.
Huipiles there are woven in primary colors and bold patterns. San Pedro, busiest at noon, centers its selling under
a ceiba tree, and in a long arcade where alien-looking traders from the highlands vend their wares. San Cristóbal's
Sunday market swarms with women weighted under head-
dresses of heavy scarlet wool. In Tactic I saw again those
huipiles of the subtle combinations of hue. In Cobán itself
nearly every woman wears a dark blue skirt in broken
white plaid and a huipil of open work, almost lace, falling
in graceful lines from shoulder and breast. In the whole
region the huipil hangs outside the skirt, loose and cool.

Every village has a church. And most churches made me
feel that the foreign millionaire who buys and carts away
paintings, beams, and doors is a public benefactor. At least
valuable antiques are thus saved and appreciated. As it is,

they are literally falling to pieces, and nobody cares. I saw silver altars in pieces under leaking roofs. Near Cobán many original tiled roofs have been replaced with the crudest thatches, often very airy indeed. In San Cristóbal an exquisite carved pulpit is almost gone. The steps are missing, the seams widely gaping. In another year it will be gone, probably into some wanderer's camp fire. Four carved and gilded altars are propped with poles, but their canvases are shredding surely away. Recently Cobán has been made the seat of a Bishop, a cultivated Guatemalan who wears his red robe, purple miter, and jeweled ring in a manner to indicate that he is a lover of beauty. Maybe he will exert himself to save the treasures in the village churches.

Cobaneros know what a garden of Eden they live in. Their only fear is of another invasion, the invasion of tourists. " Don't," they begged, " bring in tourists with money to raise our prices and spoil our Indians." For no Eden would be any good if prices went up, or Indians' ideas. So far nature is guarding the Alta Vera Paz quite well. A motor road from the capital is proposed, but mail is carried by a mozo on his back, four days over the trails. Two airplanes a week cover the same distance in little more than an hour. But the day I planned to leave, the ceiling was so low the plane could not land. It was March and should have been the dry season. But old-timers said that last year's wet season had not ended yet, and it looked to them like the beginning of this year's rains.

XIX: Coffee

EVERY VISITOR TO GUATEMALA MEETS HANS ROGOZINSKI, the expert in the government coffee office, who answers all questions with a cup of the perfect beverage, selected, roasted, ground, and brewed just right. It is said that from one sip Mr. Rogozinski can tell the region, if not the actual finca, that produced it. In reply to the charge he says: " Well, if I could not after twenty years with coffee I could never learn anything about it."

Coffee, like bananas, Guatemala's only other considerable export, is foreign. When Mr. Stephens saw the valley of Panchoy in 1840 it was covered with the cactus that fed the cochineal bug. Coffee was known then only as a decorative shrub in patios. Who first tried it as a commercial crop in Guatemala is not known, but President Justo Rufino Barrios encouraged its culture by offering confiscated church lands to whoever would plant them in coffee. Before long it had spread over all the favored regions, was the cause of annual Indian migration from Altos to coast and back again, and the principal topic of conversation.

Of the original discovery that coffee was a drink fit for the gods there are endless legends. My favorite refers to

Kaldi, an Arabian shepherd. Feeling sad and desolate one day, he observed that his goats were leaping and frisking in a most orgiastic manner. Even the circumspect old Billy was gamboling like a kid. Kaldi, who saw what he looked at, noticed that his flock was nibbling certain red berries. He tried them. The weight of his woes rolled off him, and he, too, began to dance with joy among the goats. This sight naturally horrified a passing monk, who thought the antics of Kaldi and his goats so infernal that he expostulated. Kaldi, laughing with exultation, gave the monk a berry, and that holy man — Well, one thing led to another, and Arabia offered the world its first cup of coffee.

Another pleasant tale tells of a group of monks who tossed a branch on their wayside fire, smelled roasting coffee, somehow got it mixed with water, and imbibed the resulting celestial nectar. *The Encyclopædia Britannica,* which always spoils everything, says these are silly stories; that coffee came from Abyssinia and not from Arabia, and that it advanced in the dullest possible way from island to island across the ocean to Central America. In Abyssinia it was used by the Mohammedans as a devotional antisoporific, though puritans said it was intoxicating and so forbidden by the Koran. So were founded the two schools: those who prefer to stay awake with coffee and those who will not have their sleep disturbed.

Guatemala now exports coffee to all countries, including China and Japan. The annual crop averages about a million quintals — a hundred million pounds — though variation may be as great as twenty-five per cent. About 22 per cent went to the United States in 1934; 40 per cent in

'35; and of the 1936 crop more than 60 per cent was intended for American dealers. This, according to Mr. Rogozinski, means that we are drinking not only more coffee, but better. Mr. Rogozinski is an ardent believer in the national slogan: " Guatemala produces the best coffee in the world." United States buyers, too, are the canniest. Both British and German merchants can be dazzled by a big bean and will pay more for it. The Yankee knows that the size of the bean has nothing to do with flavor, and buys by taste.

Guatemala, unfortunately, does not brew the best coffee, as any tourist can testify. Most hotels and restaurants offer a far from ideal beverage, muddily strong or ruined in flavor by being kept too long in the essence bottle. But what a good cook can do with Guatemala coffee is to produce marvels, no less. I asked how. Mr. Rogozinski said that, to the connoisseur who likes to see the coffee bean, roasting your own is fun.

"Many companies in the States," he said, " put out a very fine coffee in cans. If it is packed when freshly roasted it is good."

" And what else could Rogozinski say? " the old finquero from San Marcos asked, oratorically. " But I who know tell you that any coffee out of a can tastes and smells stale."

So rule number one is to roast and grind your own. The raw bean will keep indefinitely; it even improves with age. But once roasted, it should never be kept more than a day. There are small electric machines for roasting coffee to the precise shade of golden brown which gives the best flavor. Then grind and brew it at once. Use an earthenware pot, of course. Drip coffee is approved. A dessert-spoonful to the cup is the right amount. The pot must be hot and the water boiling, bubbling violently. It may be left one minute or several, depending upon how strong a brew is wanted, but the coffee must not boil at all. The perfect coffee will leave a dark stain on the cup and a memory of perfection at last achieved.

The questions of sugar or not, milk or cream, or *café solo* are for individual taste. It need not be taken one way or another to prove discrimination. Mr. Rogozinski is of the opinion, which seems sound, that we use cream in the States because we have it. It is notorious that cows south of the Rio Grande do not give cream — just milk. And milk that it is as well to boil before taking. Hence coffee with hot milk is the usual drink. Often one is served the hot milk and allowed to darken it from the bottle of essence on the table. The essence is only coffee, brewed very strong, and thoroughly approved, if fresh. Unfortunately it is generally used to save making fresh coffee and left on the table all day; a barbarous habit, as it is bound to ferment, and fermented coffee is the unpardonable sin. Fermented or sour coffee is not bad for the health, I am told; it just tastes like Rio de Janeiro. To the Guatemalan, nothing could be worse than coffee from Brazil. So it is watched, at every stage from the tree to the cup, to guard against that sad eventuality.

That progress is long and complicated, for the coffee shrub is a delicately bred aristocrat which gives its best only in return for the most unremitting care. Its infancy requires the tenderest nursing. Tiny seedlings are kept at just the right temperature and watched daily until they put out two leaves like butterfly wings. Then they are moved to open ground in a well-shaded place where they grow for two years before final transplanting to the orchard, the *cafetal*. Even full-grown plants are shaded, for coffee cannot stand sun. On the coast, banana plants are often used for shelter, especially on a new plantation and until the larger trees grow. In the west the preferred shade is the chalum, which gives fertilizer as well as shade and bears an edible bean: a very satisfactory attendant for the high-bred coffee. Around Antigua they use the gravilea, and in the Cobán region the cushin. In bloom, coffee is at its most patrician. Then the glistening green is festooned with white flowers set close along the branches, which reach out, tips up, as a Japanese dancer holds her hands. Protected by thorny hedges, shielded by the gray-stemmed guardian trees, rows of diminutive shrubs stretch away in their false twilight, exquisite as houris in an inviolable paradise.

The coffee shrub demands much judgment in its planting. It must be spaced to allow plenty of ventilation, but to give as great a yield per acre as possible. The plants are pruned to spread instead of growing tall. They can be forced to bear under three years of age, but they show their resentment of such treatment by fewer bearing years. The wise planter lets his cafetal grow slowly and assures about thirty years of good crops. Near Antigua there are many coffee trees still bearing at sixty years of age and over.

Coffee does best at an altitude of between thirty-five hundred and five thousand feet. So the cafetales rest like a wreath on the mountain slopes above the bananas, sugar-cane, and cattle and below the temperate-zone vegetables and fruits. Both Cobán and Antigua claim to produce the best coffee, but my friend from San Marcos assured me that his state produces not only the most but the best coffee in Guatemala, and so in the world. Heights of four and five thousand feet give a berry which is too acid alone, but mixed with low-grown coffee it makes the best blend. And the best is always a blend, which accounts for the Mocha and Java our grandparents valued.

In contrast to the foreign-owned banana monopoly, coffee-planting is in the hands of many owners, of whom more than sixty thousand are native Guatemalans and less than eight hundred aliens. But it is the foreigners who own the largest fincas and control the trade. Small proprietors, who cannot afford the machinery to clean and sack their crops, sell perforce to more opulent neighbors. The largest plantation in Guatemala, Osuna, has twenty-seven hundred acres in coffee. From that the fincas run down in size to little groves of one or two acres. Most fincas, of from fifty to two thousand acres, have a good deal of uncultivated land. Coffee requires rich soil, and of that wealth Guatemala has no lack. Periodic volcanic eruptions have kept it nourished for ages, and there is always the mountain-side drift: virgin soil washed down from the peaks. A tale is told of one finca that was ruined by a volcanic eruption. But when the owners returned a few years later to replant, they found that their bad luck was their fortune, so rich was the new volcanic soil.

Guatemala claims that its coffee has no enemies: no

blights nor bugs nor worms nor lice. They had one bad scare, though. Finqueros used to buy used coffee-bags in the States and ship them into Guatemala — sacks from anywhere. To their consternation, they learned that they were importing coffee's worst enemy, a worm that bores into the bean and is ruinous. Happily it was discovered in time, and Guatemala now has stringent laws, rigidly enforced, against the importation of any bean or seed or anything that might bring trouble. All coffee must be shipped in new bags, sterilized and, for all I know, prayed over and sprinkled with holy water. Guatemala is very proud of the cleanliness of her crop, but things can go wrong with it. Too heavy rains; rains that wet down the blossoms so the pollen cannot fly; wind storms which break the supple branches can all reduce the crop materially. There are good years and bad years for no known reason. Sometimes trees that have borne generously for several seasons take a vacation. Injuries may be caused in handling the crop, and fermentation is a possibility at every stage. Thus every aristocratic plant demands continuous expert care, and interest on the fincas never ceases, seldom lags.

Year-round work is necessary to keep the cafetales clean. Weeds are cleared out at least three times a year, always after the picking and just before. Pruning not only keeps the plant in shape, but lops off unnecessary new growth. This is done with a special machete wielded by an Indian who makes one quick sure stroke, so clean it leaves no scar.

Seasons, like everything else in Guatemala, depend upon

altitude. Coffee ripens in the lower altitudes from August
to December. Up to four thousand feet it is harvested
from the middle of October to January 15, and in the high
regions from the beginning of December to the end of April.
Each plant carries three crops at a time: ripe berries, unripe, and blossoms or tiny nubbins. Coffee is picked according to color, berry by berry, as never an unripe one
must be taken. Men, women, and children do this job.
Nobody is ever taught how; they just know. One man, if
his family helps, can pick about half an acre a day. In
off seasons the man alone can clean one or two acres daily.
So the family is seasonal, and children may go to school
between picking seasons. Nobody ever dreams of allow-
ing school to interfere with picking coffee. Mr. Rogozinski
offers, as a conservative estimate, that a hundred and one
per cent of the success of the crop depends upon the Indian
laborer — that laborer who is paid a few cents a day.

Wages vary a little from place to place and have been
generally reduced by the depression. There are two classes
of workers. The *colonos* live permanently on the fincas and
are given land to till and houses or materials for building
them. Most of them live in huts about as impervious as
baskets, but a few progressive owners actually house their
people in brick cottages. *Jornaleros,* day laborers, get a
ration of corn and beans, coffee and sugar. Wages were
established in 1923 at eight pesos (thirteen cents) a day.
In 1924 they soared to seventeen cents, and in 1930, that
dizzy era, a man could earn seventy-five cents a day almost anywhere. A finquero, discussing that time, said it

had meant utter ruination for the mozos, who knew nothing to do with so much cash except to get drunker, and more often. Today's sobriety is a great gain, he thought.

This gentleman was from Cobán, where the system is a little different. There the *voluntarios*, who go to the finca only for seasonal work, are paid ten cents a day. Such high pay naturally involves no perquisites. A man earning that sum supports himself and his family out of it. The *meseros*, who work by the month and are given a ration of food, are paid less: six or seven cents a day. Then there are the *colonos*, whose position is like that of permanent workers elsewhere.

The harvest is called *lluvia de oro*, rain of gold. Then the little trees are brilliant with berries, holly-red and about the size of cherries, among the lustrous leaves flecked with white blossoms. Each picker is paid by weight when he delivers his crop at the beneficio, which means that women and children, who pick faster than men, earn less because they carry lighter loads.

At the beneficio the pulp is removed by machinery, though sometimes the berries are tramped clean by bare feet in the old way. Then they ferment in huge vats. This, the only permissible fermentation in the whole process, loosens a jelly that adheres to the seed after washing. Then the beans are spread in the sunshine to dry while men stir them constantly with wooden rakes. Some up-to-date beneficios dry by machinery. The twin seeds are still covered by a parchment, the *pergamino*, and may be exported in that state. As a rule, however, they are sent on to other machines which break down the pergamino and clean it off by winnowing. Inside remains a delicate silver skin which must also be removed, by machinery again, to leave the absolutely perfect bean of commerce. It should be bluish green in color, semi-translucent, soft and smooth to the touch.

The finished coffee beans are then sorted for size and final cleaning: another job that requires individual skill and judgment. On a finca near Cobán I was shown the grading-room, a spacious airy loft where women sat before tilted wooden trays of coffee berries. Fatly spread on their benches, their faces stoic, they gave us no greeting; but their slim brown fingers flew nimbly, pushing the beans about, discarding every imperfect one or bit of foreign matter. This is piecework, nicely adjusted to pay five or six cents a day.

In the warehouse I saw piles of coffee sacked and ready for shipping. Some shipments are made from Pacific ports, but railroad rates are so manipulated that it is often cheaper to haul the crop across the country and out by Puerto Barrios. Most of it goes to San Francisco, New York, or Hamburg, where the tenderly nutured gray-green berry must meet the final test: the world market. The million quintals shipped yearly may fetch from eight and a half cents a pound, which has been the scant return in recent years, to as high as forty-six cents a pound, which exalted peak it touched once in the London market. Such fluctuations make all the difference between affluence and comparative poverty to the planter.

I asked a Guatemalan finquero what spelled wealth in the coffee business. " Well," he said, " if a coffee-planter raises a thousand quintals per year and has no debts, he would be considered well off. He would sell his coffee at six dollars and it would cost him three dollars per quintal. In Guatemala an income of three thousand dollars a year is not so bad. In the capital a man with a family needs about two hundred dollars a month to live quite well. A man spending five hundred a month would be classed as of the absolutely upper crust in these low-price times. The ideal coffee-planter should have a reserve in cash of about three thousand dollars to take care of price fluctuations, and another three thousand for expenses. Alas! — thrift is not one of our national virtues. Few finqueros practice it, and that is the reason why foreign-owned plantations are increasing."

No wonder all conversation in Guatemala gets around, sooner rather than later, to the coffee crop and the world market.

XX: Indian Dance and Ancient Rite

IT HAS BEEN REPEATEDLY STATED THAT AMONG PRIMITIVE peoples ceremonial usage is slowest to change. A Pueblo Indian may dress like a white man, drive an automobile, organize his people to buy a tractor and use it co-operatively, discuss agricultural and industrial problems with United States senators to their confounding, and then, in his kiva, make prayer sticks to invoke the ancient gods. He may even take off his tailored shirt, paint his body with colored earth, deck his head with feathers, and dance all day in the blazing sun. In Guatemala the exact opposite is true. Indians live, eat, dress, trade, and travel as their pre-Columbian ancestors did. Privately they may worship the gods of old, but their public ceremonies are so corrupted by Spain and the Church that they retain very little semblance of the aboriginal Indian.

My experience in looking for dances in Guatemala was a sad sequence of disappointments. The first Guatemalan I met as I crossed the frontier advised me to go at once to Chichicastenango, where I should see dances of consummate art and astonishing loveliness. He dwelt upon the costumes of silk and velvet, " made, most richly, by the designer of Totonicapán." It sounded discouraging; Indians have a way of turning tawdry in velvet and silk. But a people whose everyday dress is as extraordinary as the Guatemalan Indians' should contrive ceremonial attire of even more stunning color and cut. In older ceremonies, the pre-Conquest dances which must lurk in unfrequented places, I hoped to see fine native work in furs and feathers. So when my enthusiastic friend went on about jaguar skins, hand-carved masks, and feathered coronets, I decided to miss no chance to see any dance anywhere, however remote.

At the feast of Santo Tomás in Chichicastenango, to which I hastened forthwith, I suffered my first disillusionment. Instead of animal dances, inspired by primitive sympathetic magic, I found a weak and decadent performance of *El Torito*, a Spanish play. Such dramas were composed by sixteenth-century missionaries to teach their converts and to compensate, perhaps, for the old tribal dances which were forbidden. Naturally, having no roots in Indian history or psychology, *El Torito* was a spiritless performance. The quintessential Indian is lost. One does not expect to find Indian music or steps, Indian form or content in these pitiful survivals of centuries of suppression. But one hopes that the underlying Indian will modify even the most Spanish content, put some savage vibration into the thinnest tune, mark a rhythm with the vigororus stomp of the red man. None of that appeared in *El Torito* in Chichicastenango. That the Indians had wholly lost the significance of what they did was clear from the slovenly manner in which they did it. They danced and sang like children performing before hostile grown-ups, ashamed, hating it. The typical Ladino attitude is one of sneering condescension, a tone I noted wherever white people watch an Indian fiesta. The wonder is that the shamans have the dignity to stand it off in religious rites. Probably they do only because many of their observances are protected by the odor of sanctity: saints in a cofradía, candles in church, cofrades treated respectfully by Catholic priests.

The truly indigenous Indian persists, however corruptly, in a few ceremonies. Something of the ancient cult of the Plumed Serpent may lie buried under the trivial Snake Dance still presented in Los Altos. There may be faint memories of sun-worship in *El Volador*, which in Mexico ties in so closely with the Aztec calendar. Old animistic rites certainly underlie animal dances like *El Venado*, The Deer, which may feature lions and tigers, monkeys and dogs as well as deer. The dance, which dramatizes the struggle between man and beast, is a pantomime of the hunt. If the actors are good mimics and funny, the dance may be very entertaining. Much of it is impromptu. The dancers gambol up and down a tight rope or swing from a high pole as in El Volador. In these dances appear the vaunted costumes of real animal skins with well-carved realistic masks. They may have some of the significance of costumes in truly primitive dances where the killing of the animal for the pelt, the painting of the mask, and the placing of a feather are part of the ritual and must be done in an orthodox manner. Otherwise the costumes are the puffed and quilted output of the workshops in Totonicapán and

Chichicastenango, quite unrelated to anything Indian and only vaguely suggestive of the Spanish parts. The Indians, happy to dress up, wear whatever is sent and pay for it if they can. This is the catch in the Guatemalan dance program. Many times I went to places, hopeful, assured by cognoscenti that a dance was a certainty, only to find that it had been given up for lack of costumes. A fee of twenty-five or thirty dollars is prohibitive now that times are hard. And added to that, Indians must pay a tax for dancing.

Truly Indian music is, like indigenous costuming, practically lost in Guatemala. I was privileged to talk with Señor Don Jesús Castillo of Quetzaltenango, Guatemala's recognized authority on Indian music and dance. After forty years of intensive search and hopeful listening Don Jesús has found only three themes unquestionably Indian, and one of those he would not stake his reputation on. Nearly all show Spanish or Moorish influence. When he was younger, Don Jesús used to go from village to village and ask for Indian songs. Somebody always promised them for a consideration, paid in advance. Then the musician would appear with his flute and twitter some sentimental ditty from Andulusia, Valencia, or Mexico. Once, in Chichicastenango, Don Jesús spent a week and twenty-five dollars for a few tunes from Spain. Another time, in Momostenango, they brought him a lad with a home-made flute. The boy was so young, looked so inadequate, it seemed doubtful if he could play at all, but Don Jesús asked him for the oldest tunes he knew. And that unparagoned child put his reed to his lips and blew the only true music out of antiquity that Guatemala can claim.

The flute itself is ancient, and it sings a minor birdlike note which sounds very archaic indeed. This and the drum are the only pre-Conquest instruments used by modern Guatemalans. They often appear in strange company, in churches and religious processions, even in competition with a brass band.

After months of unrewarded search for " real Indian, undefiled," I was promised the Snake Dance in Momostenango. Or *Los Gracejos,* the Funny Ones. Or possibly what I saw was a degenerate combination of the two. Dr. Franz Termer, who studied Guatemalan Indian dances exhaustively and reported upon them in various scientific publications, describes this Snake Dance as sadistic, sexual, full of meaning. Herr Lang, the friend who had told me so much of the Indians' ancient beliefs, thought he could arrange for me to see it, but he hinted at gross improprieties. I was flattered to be considered broad-minded enough to stand it. Altogether it seemed that I was at the threshold of something very unusual. I planned my schedule for weeks to be there, I took stiff trips to make it, and I arrived. Only to be told that there was no dance! Last Sunday, yes, Gracejos in numbers had been out in the plaza. But now, nothing.

I suspected that Herr Lang's influence with Indians was being brought to bear. I don't doubt that officials were appealed to, shamans summoned, and cash provided. At any rate, it was announced that Los Gracejos were coming out. I saw what Dr. Termer describes. With his help, I could trace sadism, even sexuality, and my broad-mindedness was more than wide enough to encompass them both.

Twelve-year-old Fritz Lang was my squire for the day, a most competent and attentive guide. We sat on a piny hillside above the chapel of the Calvario. It was the fourth Friday in Lent, and Indians were coming from all directions with candles and flowers. Ladinas had set up tables along the roads to sell edibles and drinkables. But nothing like a dance appeared. The only hint of something not Catholic was a boy with a flute who sat piping in the arch over the church door. I wondered if he was the lad who played the only indigenous tunes for Don Jesús.

Los Gracejos, Fritz told me, are under vow to Dios Mundo to dance every year for nine years. Last year was the last, and this year they appeared only because the authorities ordered it. So I was right about Don Ernesto's kindly machinations.

From Termer's published report and from older informants I learned that the snake typifies earth and moisture, which bears out Termer's theory that the dance is descended from a prehistoric fertility rite. The dancers are trained by the leader, who plays the woman's part. After prayers against evil, especially fainting in the dance, he leads them into the country and tells them where the snakes are to be found. Always, they say, when the young men go back, they find the reptiles just where the shaman indicated. They scotch them with a stick and carry them back in a jar: gopher snake, coral snake, moccasin, and even rattlers. To avoid unpleasantness, the snake is either teased to exhaust its poison on a stick, or its mouth is sewed shut with thread. After the dance they are allowed to escape.

The dancers, when they came at last, were six young

ABOVE, *The jungle comes down to the river.*

BELOW, *The old Fort of San Felipe.*

ABOVE, *Dance of the Venado.*

BELOW, *Dance of the Snake.*

men in ragged clothes and little black masks. The shaman
makes and owns the masks and I found it quite impossible
to buy one. Termer says the costumes represent Quiché
and Cakchiquel, and their mutual beatings typify the pre-
Conquest wars. I could distinguish no difference in their
tatters except those of the woman, who wore a full blue
skirt, a huipil, and a red handkerchief hiding her face
under a gray felt hat. The marimba, played by four men,
never let up on its three persistent bars. The songs were in
an Indian tongue, so far as I could tell, and mostly im-
provised at the moment. The dance was a pointless jigging
and solo; no one paid the least attention to what any
other did, except that each one took a whirl with the
woman, making suggestive if not obscene gestures. Sadism
was more evident than obscenity. Each dancer carried a
whip with which to lash the others. It must have been pain-
ful beating, for they wore nothing under the torn and
dirty shirts, and each one invited the strokes as though
he hoped some good would come of it. Only one man
showed flashes of humor, but clown as he would, he got no
response, even when he made most daring advances to the
woman, dancing in someone else's arms.

Aware that this indifferent show had been pumped up
for me, I was troubled to know how to show my appreciation. The gentleman sitting beside me advised aguardiente,
so we sent a bottle. The dance stopped at once and all the
dancers went into the church, buying candles at the door.
When they came out, they took to the bottle, passing it
round and round until it was empty. Then they danced
again, punctiliously observing my request that no attention

be paid the donor. No snake appeared, though traditionally every dancer should handle one, putting it around his neck and letting it squirm down under his shirt and out his trouser leg.

Afterwards Don Abel León, the village folklorist, showed me the legend of Los Gracejos which he wrote as one of the shamans told it to him.

" One day God was very worried and as if something annoyed Him. Seeing Him so, those who surrounded Him sought a way to please Him. Some dressed in costumes typical of the Quiché kingdom, others like Spaniards in the time of the Conquest, to imitate before God the battles and struggles that they had in that time, and presented themselves before Him. But He looked at them with the greatest indifference.

" Then others presented themselves representing the personnel of an hacienda, including the cattle — that is, the dance of El Torito — and followed by the dances of Los Moros, of the Venado, and of San Miguelito. But none of this brought even a smile from the Great Creator, and He continued pensive and as it were suffering.

" Finally others got the idea of putting on their oldest clothes and the ugliest and funniest masks. They yelled like drunks, moved their heads so their plumes floated in the air, said whatever occurred to them. So they approached God, fearful of making Him angry with their cries and their ugly aspect, and what was their surprise and pleasure when God laughed with roars of mirth. And from this comes the Dance of Los Gracejos."

More seriously, Don Abel explained that the dance is

a representation of sinful acts which should be punished by beatings as was the custom among the Indians. He said that anyone making bold or dishonorable gestures with the woman should properly be chastised; and that sometimes dancers who have actually sinned offer themselves for this just punishment.

In Momostenango too I saw the *Guajxaquip Bats*, Eight Monkey, as one would say " Tuesday, the eighth." Its explanation I take from an article by Antonio Goubaud C., published by the Society of Geography and History of Guatemala. It is a dark rite, performed in retired places which strangers should not approach, much of it at night. It is truly Indian and so closely connected with antiquity that anyone knowing the Maya calendar can calculate the date. I saw it on January 26, 1936, that year's Eight Monkey. It is a date important as the beginning of a new cycle and as a day when prayer is especially efficacious.

Praying began in the church, Padre Carlos of San Francisco El Alto assisting his brother, and for as many hours as they could stand they were occupied with kneeling suppliants. People carrying pine boughs for the mountain shrines went first to the Catholic temple, arranged their candles and flowers, and waited their turn with the priest. The two tall Hollanders moved among them, repeating the names the Indians gave, dispensing the Church's holy words and holy water as the Indian shaman directed. I wondered aloud if the shamans might not be invoking their ancestors rather than praying for the recently dead. The padres did not know; they were only pleased that so many people came devoutly to church, that so many coppers fell into the sack.

Don Ernesto considers this church-going a sad debasement of the old faith.

" More go every year," he said, " but still twice as many worship at the shrines in the hills. It is not unusual for fifteen or twenty thousand to come here for the Guajxaquip Bats. These Indians are not Catholics. Even in the church what they do is pagan. It is the shrines in the hills that represent a living faith. They are never untended. At any time you will see pine needles there or newly burned copal, and always they are guarded. You may look respectfully without being disturbed, but touch anything and an Indian will be beside you in a moment. Maybe only a boy, but if you violate anything, he will bring a man, and quickly. Their faith is real, and the white man had better respect it, for only that faith holds them down. Not the Catholic religion, but faith in the old gods, belief in the final triumph of the old creeds; that's what keeps them tractable."

During the day I visited several shrines. The hills and valleys were dotted with them; from every one four or five others could be seen. Momostenango means " surrounded by oratories," so called by Alvarado's Mexicans, whose gift for nomenclature begins to bore. Each altar was only an earthen mound a couple of meters high and so simple as to verge on the sordid. A closer view disclosed that they were composed of broken potsherds, scattered loosely on top, merged below into solid clay. Many suppliants had brought broken pottery, and everyone a spray of evergreen; symbols among so many Indian tribes of the transitoriness of life and of its everlastingness too. Before a hollowed niche smoking with pungent copal, the shaman stood, praying while the suppliant prompted him as to what to say. Prayers were interminable. I saw liquor taken with liturgical effect, but no drunkenness. Many altars were surrounded by people waiting their turn. Probably they sought a zahorín famous for success or one regarded as the trusted family physician. The younger shamans had the fewest clients, I noticed. There was really nothing an outsider could see, no form; only credulous people standing in reverent hope before the man they believed in touch with the divine, asking his intercession in their affairs. I was ashamed to stay very long watching.

After dark it was more impressive. At midnight the year turns, a very sacred time. With Don Ernesto and Don Abel we climbed to other altars, used by the more powerful shamans, where only visitors of great confidence might go. Each oratory, lit by candle-glow, was surrounded by worshipers. A soldier stood for long minutes while a shaman knelt praying for him, making motions with the clay censer in his hands, mouthing queer words. At a small oratory where no other people were, a young woman knelt before a man standing, and strong firelight was reflected upward into their faces. Her whole attitude expressed intense devotion, and the lambent eyes in her flat face glowed with something not the altar flame. Don Ernesto thought she was a neophyte receiving instruction from a graduate shaman. The man was a commanding figure, slim and erect. He might have been of that ancient nobility they tell about.

Without understanding at all, I was conscious of a direct chain, worn very thin perhaps, but somehow, link by link, connecting these people with their antiquity. I felt what I was told many times by those closest to the Guatemalan Indians, that they know their ancient power and hold what they can of their ancestral beliefs.

XXI: Holy Week

SITTING ON A ROCK ABOVE SANTIAGO ATITLÁN, I REALIZED
that if I did not see a single dance, I should know the
pageantry of Guatemala from watching Indians. The
dances I had seen were dull — steps, music, costumes above
all — the pathetic efforts of an ignorant people to hold
onto a culture they have really lost. But going about their
affairs unobserved, they move in the rhythm of their race,
with felicity and precision. It is an unconscious ballet
which a clever choreographer, sympathetic with Indians,
knowing more of their history than they know, could trans-
form into a superb ballet. Maybe some day, before it is
all lost, Guatemala will produce the master who can do it.

From my rock I watched the first movement. For back-
drop the shining riffled lake, darkened by the shadow of the
volcano of Atitlán. Men were paddling in dugouts, lifting
dripping paddlefuls of sopping weed. Men in white
drawers and hats, with red sashes and brown arms and
legs. On the shore a wrangle was going on. Fifty more
such men formed gesticulating rings which dissolved and
came together again, shouting in their hoarse guttural.
Women, as always at Atitlán, were washing along the lake's

margin; red skirts, red laundry, and wet brown skins
against gray rocks. And when the boats came in, men staggered up the bank with piles of wet weed to add to the
mass horses were nibbling. Only the horses and the working men were not shouting. It was no riot, I learned; just
the ordinary talk that accompanies clearing out the weeds
that infest the lake, impeding the navigation of dugouts,
the washing of clothes, even fishing. Every Indian owes
one day's work in fifteen, and keeping that record straight
requires so much hubbub.

Suddenly all the hats wheeled about, disclosing brown
faces looking up. For the clack of metracas was coming
round the hill. Fourteen men passed; second movement of
the ballet. Dressed like the men on the beach, each carried
a cacaxte with a long brown tube winging out to right and
left of it. Two or three whirled the wooden rattles which
sound all the way from here to New Mexico in Holy Week.
In silence they trotted down the hill and off through one
of the lanes between stone walls.

The village of Atitlán sits on a ridge between the arms of
the lake. All the houses, except the ugly frame shacks in the
plaza and the fine old church now roofed with corrugated
iron, have peaked thatches of dried grass. Around every
house is growth: the wisteria-toned jacaranda that blooms
all over Guatemala for two spring months; bougainvillæa and hibiscus, coffee shrubs, pepper trees, and enough
of orange blossoms and roses to scent the whole village.
I did not follow the procession. I went to the plaza instead
and found market day.

They advertise Guatemala's eternal spring, but it is

spring with a March in it. Gusts of wind raised stinging puffs of dust to settle on the offerings laid out for sale. Each woman sat uninterested beside her pile of beans or coffee, sugared cakes or spices. Everyone had a turkey, it seemed, or at least a brown and golden cock. To give the final chic — *chiste* in Spanish, — I recommend a live turkey gobbler. At his quietest he lends color with his black and white stripes and his red wattles. Riding *en masse* in a basket on the head with spread tails he suggests something that Mae West would like in a hat. Borne on the back, a couple of turkey necks arch into most decorative lyre shapes. And at his pinnacle, there is the gobble. The ensemble with turkeys in scarlet wattles and women in rosy skirts would make most stage shows look pretty dull, especially as any Indian group can be trusted to get in enough yellow huipiles and green stripes to avoid any studied effect. Just how any business was done in that market I leave to the ethnologists who are studying it. I only postulate the problem. If every woman brings a fowl to market and pegs it out while she gossips with friends who have all brought fowls too, who buys? Who gains? Maybe everybody gains on account of the gossip. Matrons who had come with baskets inverted on their heads wore them home again full of yellow corn, red tomatoes, or topped with a banana leaf. In either case they must make a welcome shade from that fierce tropical sun.

I called on the Presidente Municipal. His Honor was out, but I was received by his two assistants, in formal blue jackets and the Atitlán panties adorned with woven birds and animals. They gave me paper to write my name and

assured me that nothing of interest would happen soon.
Little Rebecca Girón, my self-appointed interpreter, knew
better. They would bring the baskets now, she said. While
we waited, she helped me purchase a man's kerchief. I
suggested wearing it.

" You have, of course, the right," she agreed primly,
" but as it is for men, what a shame you would make! "

Putting a stranger right, she said it was always best to
leave Indian things alone. She could speak the language,
but her mother beat her with a strap if she played with
Indian children.

With all her snobbishness, Rebecca knew. Very soon
along came the procession, this time without their burdens
and with brand-new yellow baskets. Just as chorus girls
prance on again without changing, but twirling red para-
sols. This men's chorus brought their orchestra: a big
drum carried by one man and pounded by another, and the
chirimilla. Observing my unvarying rule of following the
band, I found myself tagging most of the children in
Atitlán. In spite of school, they wear the native dress, which
is especially attractive on little girls with their unformed
hips like tight-wrapped red buds. Rebecca had gone; doubtless anything so Indian would rouse mother to activity with
the strap. But another child walked with me. She carried
a heavy baby, her half-brother, she said. Her own father
was Ladino, Don Arturo; did I know him? But he left, just
abandoned the family. You know how Ladino men do with
Indian women. But her mother had another man now and
two more babies and he would probably stay because he
was a native, and where could he go, anyhow?

The men in the procession, when I could get my mentor off the family, were the *alguaciles* who go every Palm Sunday to the coast for the flower of the carrizo. Those long brown cases the men carried were the bud keeping the blossom fresh inside. Other men, about thirty of them, went on Wednesday for the fruit, selected in the fincas weeks before. They watch it mature so it shall not be sold to others, and then they cut it with much ceremony. She had never seen it, but she knew that the marimba played, the fruit was laid on fresh petates, censed with copal smoke, and packed with leaves and such art that every piece arrives unbruised and just ripe. Other men had brought in the cypress to make arches across the streets. Cypress grows everywhere, but changeless custom demands bringing it across the lake in canoes, at night, with drum and chirimilla and metracas.

All this she told me, they all told me, as we women leaned against the wall outside the ceremonial house, I wishing I were a man and could go in. As many men as could had gone in, and the rest jammed the doorway. Now and then one came out with an empty crate. " They are blessing the fruit." I was torn between my conviction that intruding on Indians is inexcusable and my distress at missing the party. Then a man appeared, looking. The Intendente presented his compliments, invited me to enter. So was virtue rewarded.

Coming from the bright day, I saw only a candle on a low table, throwing its glow up into the thin worn face of a young man who swung a smoking censer. Above the table hung the carrizo flower, delicate drooping tassels of faint yellow. Then the Intendente was before me, bowing and inviting me to sit beside him. As the pupils expanded I made out a wattled room with benches all around, and against one wall all the cacaxtes still unpacked. At the other end was the marimba, quivering and wailing under the assault of four players. The beams were hung with bunches of everlasting varied with ears of corn. The sharply pitched roof ran down into deep eaves, missing the top of the wall by a wide space through which light reflected upward from the ground. No windows and only one door. Cool, fresh, shaded, and with enough light for all purposes.

Two men worked down the room. One lifted the fruit tenderly from the cacaxte. The other received it, wiped it, and laid it on fresh petates at his feet. The bananas came in pairs, unblemished, huge, pale golden. He made a pattern by separating the piles of bananas with oval mahogany-colored melons, and putting cacao and pataxte down the middle. Eighteen crates were emptied, reverentially, watchfully, for a single piece of unripe fruit would mean a fine for the man who brought it; as much as five hundred pesos, about eight dollars.

When the fruit was unpacked and piled in richness on the floor, and the marimba had played and played, and the first man with the censer had wearied and handed it to another, they brought in jars of a thickish cornmeal gruel. The men drank from polished coconut shells. Then they toasted with bendings over little glasses of aguardiente and offered beer to the Ladinos. No women came in, even to serve the drink.

Without doubt it is a ceremony underlaid with meaning. It must go back to some primordial fertility rite. Fruit brought from the tropical coast to a highland village, fruit that must be perfect, bananas in pairs, the cacao, which was of great value to the ancients; it would be too easy to fake an explanation and no student has reported on the ritual.

That night I was invited by the Intendente to see the dressing of Judas. I knew the custom of rigging up a straw Judas to hang or burn on Good Friday. This was different, a rite of the Cofradía de la Cruz. It took place in a house like the other one, but with several shrouded crucifixes against the walls and a row of women on the floor, their heads circled with red halo-like head-dress. The men wore red kerchiefs with ends sticking out behind their ears and the sleeveless black ceremonial wrap. There was candle-glow instead of reflected sunlight, but the same smell of copal and scented fresh air wafted in over the walls. The headman was dressing the Judas, a larger than human straw man. They say that at the heart of it is hidden an ancient silver image; whether of saint or god nobody knows. They held blankets to conceal what they did; and the seat of honor was a bench behind a table which further screened the proceedings. But we could see piles of clean clothes, all of the style of Atitlán. Surrounded by red-coifed and sullen Indians, the image was invested with six shirts, six pairs of drawers, a mass of colored sashes, a dozen silk neckerchiefs, and two Stetson hats, one on top of the other. This Judas, I was told, also represents Don

Pedro de Alvarado. His name Maximón might be interpreted as the Great Conqueror, but I was unable to get confirmation of that theory.

All the time I was abashed to find myself one of the dominant race. I remembered reading somewhere that the only position for a civilized person is as one of a subject group. I was grateful, and I am, to the Intendente for permitting me to see what few strangers see. But we were there by force of his office; we were too noisy, talking in a room where all the Indians were silent. There was no reverence in us, no appreciation of the real though unknown meaning of what we saw. The government officials, two young men who had been duck-shooting on the lake, a finquero, and a woman from a far country. Among the things we said was that these customs should by all means be preserved. And we were, by our presence and lack of courtesy, taking the surest means to kill them: showing disrespect and snobbish scorn of the doings of the aborigines. The Intendente had forbidden the whirring of metracas, the proper accompaniment of the ceremony, so there was none except our talk. I was glad, as the old men were, when the Judas was raised for our inspection and we were shown respectfully out.

Late at night, near two o'clock, I was awakened by the muffled booming of metraces. The air was redolent of flora pundia, hanging its green-white bells over the wall; and hissing with some insect's insistent note. Soon the procession rounded the corner, passed under my window, and disappeared down the hill. I was glad they had gone on with their ceremony after the withdrawal of the noisy interlopers, and I hoped the zahorín had been able to conjure off the blight of our presence.

In the morning I was reminded of my ballet again when the alguaciles brought their fruit to the city hall. The bananas had lost their fresh yellow, but were starred all over with gold and silver paper. This time they were piled on the floor and left in charge of kneeling women. Women in ceremonial moments always seem mournful; sorrowing mothers. Men get all the fun of dressing up and frolicking. When the bell struck eleven they broke and ran like youngsters and came back again, gamboling puppy-like around their doll. Judas was as before, except that a big black cigar stuck out of the mask under the Stetson hats. His attendants carried candles, burned copal, smote the drum, and tootled the flute. The man bearing the image was the zahorín, a fellow of less than middle age and less than half Indian judging by his delicate skin and soft full mustache. He had great power, Rebecca said, to cure, and to cause harm too. They laid Judas on the floor among the fruit and the women, kneeling patiently with their dripping candles, their opaque eyes. What did it mean to them? Christ's betrayer? A saint? Pedro de Alvarado, who defeated their ancestors not far from here? Or does one look like that and spend hours on one's knees for magic that has no special drama or legend? Anyway, the women sat and the men made another dash to the church, where they were giving out maguey stalks, for what I could not learn.

Crossing the plaza, I met the brujo, supported, literally, by two of the older men who had looked such scorn of us

last night. The zahorín was affable, but reeling. He had
been serving well his god, who likes libations of liquor,
and his government, which demands that so much be drunk.
Did I like the ceremonies? And when I expressed my appreciation of the seriousness of the ceremony and of the
deep honor they had granted me, I think they were molli-
fied for last night's rudeness.

Judas was finally hung in the church porch, where his tan
buttoned shoes dangled just off the floor, and people sat
before him worshipfully. This Judas is never burnt nor
destroyed — all those good clothes! Instead he is taken
reverently back to the Cofradía of the Holy Cross. Someone
some day must learn what he means to his servers.

The temple at Atitlán attests to the Church's poverty in
Guatemala and to its neglect of fine antiques. The nave is
like a vast lumber-room with carved wood stacked in the
corners; statues of the saints have lost their paint and are
spattered with whitewash. An Indian's idea of what to do
with a working saint is to put a silk petticoat on it, and of
what to do with the rest is nothing at all. The high altar does
not exist. In its place they were erecting a rough log scaf-
folding and decorating it with cypress and maguey, flowers
and fruit. That afternoon, though no priest had come, they
made their own Maundy Thursday ceremony. Men read
from a big book, chanting the words musically. Women
carried the Sorrowing Mother on a bier, and in the procession marched little boys who would figure in the ceremony of the Washing of the Feet. Uncouth brats, clumsy
in white frocks and paper miters, with hands folded and

faces all of a grin. Everybody kissed the altar. They seemed to be doing their best, but the fundamental Indian is much stronger at Atitlán than the Church.

Outside again, I saw them make ready for the races. Arches had been built of the same cypress and maguey, but on top of every one were stuffed squirrels and badgers, and on the one nearest the church a couple of miserable living creatures. They told me about the races of San Juan, which I did not stay to see. Two teams of four young men dash from one arch to the other, carrying an image of Saint John. At one end of the course stands the Virgin, at the other Christ Crucified, and every time the runners touch an image it is moved a step forward. So the race shortens each time, but a man may run as many as a hundred lengths and end sweating, spent, stumbling with fatigue. One who actually falls is arrested and held for a fine of two quetzales. The rite is a part, they say, of the training or testing of neophyte shamans.

Rebecca was disgruntled that I should not see it. It was even worse, she said, to miss Sábado de Gloria. She and her mother were going to the lake tomorrow to bathe and wash their hair, and she had a new dress. On Sábado de Gloria there were much noise and fireworks and joy. Rebecca did not remember, but older people told me that they used to arrest the Virgin and San Juan on Holy Saturday and release them only when their cofradías paid the fines. That was because the heartless things would be discovered dancing while Jesus still lay in His tomb — a most ill-bred thing to do! But times are changing and that touch is lost.

Delightful as it would be to see Rebecca in her new dress,
I found myself thinking poignantly of the contrast between
my lodging in Atitlán, friendly but not so shiningly clean,
and the hotel at Chichicastenango. I decided that I owed it
to my reader to see how Holy Week was celebrated elsewhere. And the saints had mercifully provided a finquero's
launch bound for Tzanjuyú.

The afternoon was typical of a Guatemalan spring. A
murky sky, roiled with clouds that augured rain, muffled
everything in dusty indecision. The lake, so azure a month
ago, was dun gray; and the blue mountains had dulled
into purple spotted with smoke by day and fireglow by
night where farmers were burning off dry stubble. Every
day huge thunder-heads rolled up and went away as though
the time were not yet. Some days they lost all form and
spread a luminous colored mist over the whole sky. Infre-
quently they spattered a little rain. Nature was like a sentient thing, trying to give birth and unable to. No wonder
primitive people make magic to help it. Catholic priests had
been saying special masses for water; doubtless that urgent
need vitalizes much of the Lenten observance. In every village we saw men in cofradía hats and women in ceremonial
huipiles around the church or pine-decked houses. The
road was bumpy, for powdery dust masked the hard ruts
and hung in smothering clouds when anything passed.
Blooming jacaranda trees were everywhere. For weeks they
had carpeted the ground with dropped lavender petals
without seeming to lose a blossom from their gray boughs.
They toned with the blue sky, with the puce-gray clouds;
even the smoky air took on their tint. It was as though the

whole country veiled itself in violet as the altars are draped in purple for Lent.

Chichicastenango was behaving in a strictly Catholic manner. A churchful of people kept vigil before the shrouded altar, idly watching men prepare the setting for the drama's end. The cloister was massed with Indians and Ladinos, waiting admission to where the padre and the cofrades were washing the holy body. A few Ladinos shoved; the Indians were immobile and intent. Important men held maces with silver bells and crosses. Their black costumes and turbaned heads never seemed so fitting. A Ladina woman offered me a seat on a fallen stone pillar. Octavio came pushing through the crowd, apologetic because he had not met me sooner; he was working now.

" Working? " I whispered as his hard little fingers touched my shoulder and then my hand.

" In a weaver's." During the long wait I got the whole story. Octavio's mother had decided his schooling was over; she needed his help. From seven until noon; from one to six. He gave the money to his mother.

" Twenty-five cents," he answered me, " a week."

So the world has begun to do what I feared it would to gallant little Octavio. But only begun. The boy was still there. Crouched on his heels, he went on with the family news. Last Sunday he walked to Quiché to see his sick sister; mother wanted news. She was better now, but the trip was somewhat sad because Octavio had hoped to buy a football, number four; but it was two quetzales and he had only one. Number four, he said again, and now and then absently. Number four.

Suddenly the crowd began to surge without moving its feet. The door opened and the padre, flushed, annoyed, stalked out, a basket held high above his head.

"Now go save yourselves," said he, " if you can, but not through me. Never have I seen such ill-mannered people! Go away, I tell you, go away! "

The basket, Octavio said, held the cotton with which they had washed and anointed the body. Everyone wanted some for the cures it would make. With my permission he would go to the padre's study, where he would get a bit. At last, inching along, we entered the sacristy, where people on their knees crept the length of the crucified figure on the floor. With smacks their heavy lips kissed the painted bloody feet, the tortured knees, the wounds in the sides and hands. Even upper-class women were crawling there, fingering their rosaries, making sucking sounds with their praying lips. I was glad to get outside, where religion was not so close. From my favorite seat by the padre's little window I could see that the Calvario had turned mother-of-pearl in the sunset, and the white roadway was dramatically studded with men in black, women in brown and blue.

" The best football," said Octavio, " is number four."

XXII: Aristocratic Antigua

THE SEÑORITA DELFINITA INVITED ME TO VISIT. So I should be in Antigua not as a tourist in a hotel but as a guest in a home! The bus left me at heavy double doors a block south of the Cathedral, and I let the hand-of-Fatima knocker fall with reverberations. In a moment the Señorita herself was there.

" How it delights me to see you! " she said. " Here you have your house! " Her dainty hand touched my shoulder as she signed to a round-faced Indita to take the bags.

This house was the residence of the Rector of the University in its prime, but it has been cut into three now. We mounted the roof, one day, to see the octagonal fountain where two stone lions face each other across the basin with bowed heads and folded paws like nice old ladies at tea. The Señorita's blue-walled patio keeps the old built-up flower-beds and ponderous arches. The ceilings of incised tiles rest on the original cedar beams, and a turnstile creaks between the Rector's kitchen and dining-room. The Señorita does not use that refectory now, but a boarded part of the corredor. Other modern notes are electric lights, a cement floor, and a shining white basin for hand-washing at the dining-room door.

Pancha staggered around with the bags, trying to navigate the doors without removing her globular eyes from the weird tall person who was the Niña Pinita's friend. Guatemalan servants call the unmarried woman child, whatever her years may be. My room was half the original, but still spacious as a skating-rink, with tiled floor, ceiling fifteen feet high, and fluted arches above the doors. The old tiles in the window-sill surely date from the Rector's day, and sitting there I had an overwhelming view of the Volcán de Agua at the street's end.

" The neighbors will see that you are very friendly," said Niña Pinita. " The old Antigua custom is to sit where one cannot be seen, but others call us ill-bred. He who looks should let himself be seen."

Truly little is seen of the Antigueña ladies. Only for mass, Pinita told me, and on market days, do they go abroad. Then they emerge from their prison-like doors, and pass quietly along the shady side of the street. Black dresses and veils are still the mode in Antigua. Girls, of course, dress, and very smartly, but even they find it avoids criticism to go veiled to market and to mass. Three churches are favored by the best. The Cathedral is presided over by the scholarly Spaniard, Padre Alvarez, whom his parishioners esteem for his priestly culture and worldly charm, but do not understand very well because of his Castilian accent. He says mass, however, a bit early, and on Sundays society prefers the eleven o'clock mass at La Merced or the Escuela de Cristo. Padre Alvarez, learned in colonial history, does much to enhance the Antigueños pride in their distinguished ancestry. On a feast day he

may state from the pulpit: " You celebrate this day because in such and such a year . . ." or " It is this sacred
statue your ancestors venerated in the year of the great
earthquake." And if even the poorest offers a child for
baptism: " Do you know that your name is famous because
such and such a man centuries ago was noble or brave or
true? "

The market has a new building, but its most dramatic sec-
tion is in the ruined church of Santo Domingo, where yellow petates are piled in impressive arches, and animals
and fodder are sold under noseless saints in weather-beaten
niches. The eating-places have smoked up a covered side
aisle where slanting daylight and charcoal fires make dark
faces glow like bronze. It is busiest about noon when the
ladies are choosing their meats, looking over the piles of
fat carrots, furry güisquil, shining onions, and many-
colored leaf vegetables. They buy flowers — tall clusters
of gladioli or lilies, or bunches of short-stemmed blossoms for the church or household altar. But in Guatemala
flowers serve also as food. The maguey flower is dipped in
thin batter and fried. They use the flower of the madre de
cacao in the same way. Flor de quixtán makes a soup said
to lower high blood-pressure. Sweet-peas are boiled and
salted. And the flor de chojón's big leaves are used to cover
the pot in which the tamales boil; it enhances the flavor.
Breadfruit is sliced and toasted, and that is as close to
toast as Guatemalan cooks can get. The usual breakfast
bread is hard rolls in infinite assortment. Antigueños eat so
much fruit and vegetables that they are vulgarly — much
too vulgarly for so patrician a town — called *barrigas*

verdes, green bellies. After all the ladies have gone home, their baskets of purchases on the servants' heads, merchants who buy to resell are allowed in, but only then.

When her heavy door clangs to behind the lady, she is seen no more. Niña Pinita told me of old people who leave their houses only for mass; of people of wealth who will not travel to Mexico for fear of the Revolution — they have been told it is over, but don't believe it; to Salvador for fear of train wrecks; to the United States for fear of gangsters; to Europe for fear of shipwreck; nor to Guatemala because why should anybody want to go to Guatemala? Earthquakes and volcanoes they do not reckon as dangers. In their hushed houses ladies sit in bent-wood chairs, always reserving the sofa for the honored guest. They crochet and knit; visit and receive occasionally; read a few religious books; devote much time to their gardens; manage their servants and see that the proper dishes are prepared for holidays. Antigua is much visited at important festival seasons. Children and their children come home. People who cannot claim a place in the old capital may rent a house for the long vacation in the hottest months of March and April.

So the feasts, even the most mournful, are replete with gayety. The Day of the Dead has its specialty: *fiambre,* rather like a Russian salad, made of meat, fish, and vegetables and served with a sharp mustard and vinegar sauce. During Holy Week, the mistress alternates pious hours in church with hours in the kitchen. To spice up the Lenten fish, special *empanadas* must be made: crisp turnovers filled with chopped vegetables and fruits and served with

RIGHT, *Atitlán (Santiago) market, with San Pedro volcano.*

[PHOTO, WEBSTER M^CBRYDE, FELLOW, SOCIAL SCIENCE RESEARCH COUNCIL, 1935–6]

BELOW, *Corn-planting ceremony, San José Chacayá.*

[PHOTO, WEBSTER M^CBRYDE, CARNE-GIE INSTITUTION – CLARK UNIVERSITY PROJECT, 1932]

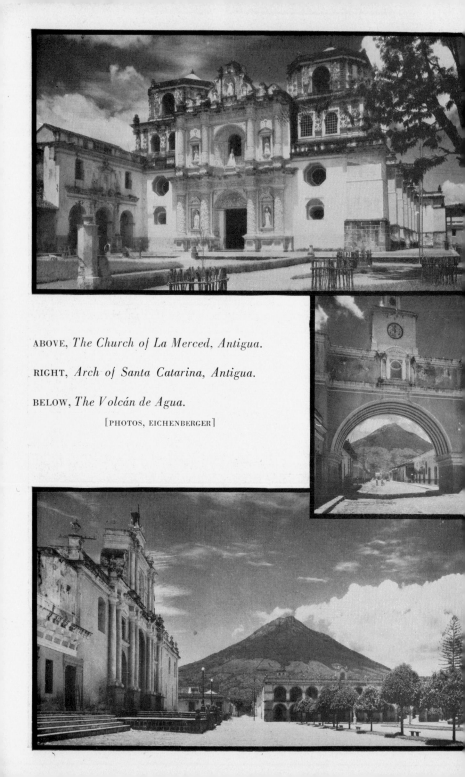

ABOVE, *The Church of La Merced, Antigua.*

RIGHT, *Arch of Santa Catarina, Antigua.*

BELOW, *The Volcán de Agua.*

[PHOTOS, EICHENBERGER]

recado frito, a mixture of tomatoes, onions, and garlic moistened with vinegar and fried in lard. Corpus Cristi is the best eating-time of all. They have stuffed chiles then; *pepián,* a complicated meat dish with a sauce reminiscent of the *mole verde* of Mexico; native cheese; and tamales stuffed with red beans and wrapped in fresh corn-husks. The Guatemalan cuisine is less piquant than the Mexican. Chile is used sparingly or served as a condiment in a separate dish.

Antigua boasts of her tamales, and with justice. They always appear for birthdays, first communions, Christmas, and often for Sunday breakfast. They used to be the thing for weddings too, but lately marriages occur so late in the day that a luncheon and champagne have replaced the breakfast of chocolate and tamales. Chocolate is still important in some families, where they take it at four in the afternoon and then dine lightly on beans, perhaps, tortillas, more chocolate, and fruit. The favorite, the most typical of Antigua, are *tamales colorados.* Made of rice flour, flavored with strange herbs and spices, filled with turkey meat, and wrapped in banana leaves, they are a delicacy never to forget.

Many of these dishes I tasted at the Señorita Delfinita's table, where we lingered over the coffee's perfection and I heard endless tales of the old city's aristocracy. Antigua is so secure in her dignity that she remains unabashed by poverty, unimpressed by official grandeur, unattracted by spurious wealth. Once, years ago, a dictator sent his photograph to every state in the Republic with the suggestion that it be given a place of honor. Every capital expressed

deep appreciation, most humble thanks, and hung the portrait in the city hall. Only in Antigua was the procedure
different. The council held a meeting, deliberated, and sent
the great man a letter. They were sensible of the honor, the
Antigua gentleman said, grateful for the gift. But in Antigua it was the custom to display in the city hall only the
likenesses of patriots of outstanding achievement. His
Excellency, in their opinion, showed promise, but as a
young man his worth was yet to be proved. In brief, the
Antigueños refused, in the most courtly Spanish periods,
but firmly, to hang the picture. Recently the descendants
of these stiff-necked councilors remained unmoved by the
blandishments of a promoter who wished to open a gam-
bling-place. His rosy promises of endless wealth had no
force whatever. Antigua will have neither bogus great men
nor false wealth.

She has her legends, though, of buried treasure. Once,
while I was there, Niña Pinita's old nurse, Mercedes, came
to beg her to dig in the kitchen patio. In the course of its
varied history the house had been an orphanage and Mercedes an orphan there. She said that once, as punishment, she
was left alone while everyone else went out. During the
lonely afternoon the little culprit saw one of the older girls
pass through the patio. She looked very tall, she moved
quietly, and she did not answer when Mercedes spoke to
her. But when the others came home that girl denied that
she had been there; she had stayed with the others all the
time. And Mercedes knows that where such a strange thing
happens there must be treasure, and every now and then she
comes to beg the Niña Pinita to search for it. She reminds

her of a family who did find wealth. They were a humble
family, almost Indians, and they lived in a small house.
The husband and wife had many quarrels, and once he beat
her and threw her out in the middle of the night. As she
sat in the patio not knowing where to go or what to do, the
poor woman saw a tiny point of light moving through the
air. Then she noticed a shadow, formless and little opaquer
than the night, but definitely a shadow. It pointed toward
a certain spot. The light meanwhile floated erratically, but
always it came to rest on the spot where the shadow pointed.
So that spirited woman, afraid neither of man nor of ghosts,
went to the door, asked her husband's pardon — this point
is not quite clear; presumably because he threw her out —
and when she mentioned ghosts and treasure he decided to
get up and dig. They found an adequate capital there,
enough to build a fine two-storied house and to educate
their children abroad. Those grown-up sons and daughters
now own fincas on the coast and often come to Antigua.

That treasure was buried is easy to believe. When there
were no banks, men kept gold in their houses. In a country
liable to be flooded, shaken by earthquakes, or torn to
pieces by volcanic eruptions, what more natural than to
bury hastily or to keep buried the family treasure? Besides
these acts of God, there were acts of men to fear, specifi-
cally the Luisillos, men from San Luis who had a way of
dropping in unannounced. No, announced by terrified citizens shouting through the streets: " The Luisillos, the Luisillos! " Then, they say, everybody left his house as it was
and retired for an indefinite stay in the mountains. The
Luisillos would move in, eat and drink what they could,

and take the rest along. The only cash that might escape them would be cash buried only a ghost knew where.

Niña Pinita planned excursions for me. On an evening after rain we drove out to San Juan Obispo, where Bishop Marroquín made his home near Ciudad Vieja and high enough on the volcano to overlook the entire valley of Panchoy. Beyond the gray-green gravilea trees the hills were misty blue, and the near-by orchards glowed in emerald green. The church is in sad disrepair, but the altars have been fine and there is one lovely statue of Saint Elizabeth with the tender brooding face of a Mother's mother. The caretaker led us across the Bishop's cloistered patio, where unpruned roses, azaleas, and violets were tangled with meanly persistent little sticker burs. Then he seated us on the terrace and stood a moment to enjoy the view before he went to bring coffee. Antigua was almost lost among the trees. Only the Cathedral towers and a few other bits showed like ivory in the green. It was dreamlike in the sunset and mysterious in the dusk when lights began to sparkle like sequins on dark velvet.

The tamales had kept warm in the basket, the native cheese was creamy, the coffee delicious. We ended with pineapple. Surely there are no pineapples in the world equal to those of Panchoy; crisp as a good apple, honey sweet, and saved from insipidity by a tart tang.

Another evening we visited San Antonio Aguas Calientes, at the bottom of a canyon with clouds tumbling down its sides. Battered Adams urns top its pink fountain, and two cedar trees and a heavy stone cross stand in front of a pale-blue church. One man was twisting tixtle fiber into rope on his bare flank, and another had his lasso pegged out along the ground and was painting it red and green and purple. We strolled between corn-stalk fences weathered gray like New England shingles, each with a door of polished wood and a knocker. Every home was bursting with plenty: coffee and bananas, pigs and chickens, vegetables and berries. And every one was gorgeously draped in bougainvillæa and hibiscus and poinsettia, fragrant with orange blossoms, Easter lilies, roses, and heliotrope. Even the clothes-lines seemed abloom with the women's huipiles — mauves and lemon yellows, tawny rose and turquoise and jade, woven in cross-stitch zigzags.

In the twin village of Santa Catalina we sat on the church steps while Pinita talked with an Indian, about Benito who learned " Bingles " years ago and went to the States to be a pharmacist. Nobody had heard from him since and all his family are dead now. The Indian was attentive as the caretaker at San Juan El Obispo, as all Guatemalans are, and as quick to disappear when he could no longer be of service. The fountain was choked and chipped, but still stately. Water gushed out of a stone crown and splashed unevenly down over a wrought stone pillar and into a flat basin shimmering with moonlight. The moon stood near the volcano, and cloud flakes scudded across them both, downy yellow and feather white.

On the way home we stopped at the Niña Pinita's tiny coffee orchard, which she does not dignify by calling a finca. Two small boys ran out to greet us, ducking their heads for the Señorita to touch in blessing. The mother held the baby for a touch too and led us to the table ready for our supper, which Pancha had carried out on her head. A sheaf of calla lilies and gladioli lay on banana leaves, a cloth as shining as satin. The woman brewed coffee over her charcoal fire, and the man brought a papaya and watercress from the stream. Then they herded the staring children away and left us with only nesting birds to hear, evening bells from the town, and insects that hiss and whisper on tropical nights.

We walked home. There was fiesta and we could see the reflection of light on the clouds. But its sound was lost in the hushed and empty streets. There was only the fairy-like rustle of paper fringes looped across the way, no louder than the cicadas in the gardens.

XXIII: Fairs and Feast Days

Fiestas, like everything else in Guatemala, are marked by sharp racial distinctions. There are Indian fiestas, often of Catholic inception, but never quite free of pagan rites and beliefs. Ladino fiestas are very Catholic and with almost no Indian participation. Fairs, city or state or national, are approved and sponsored by the government. They feature agricultural exhibits, display schoolchildren's work, and abound in athletic games and races. To the stranger they offer endless amusement and unequaled opportunities to see Guatemalans off guard at the lottery tables, the shooting-booths, and the merry-go-rounds.

Such a one was the summer fair at Antigua in February. Confident of the ancient capital's imperturbable quiet, I was wholly unprepared for a bombardment of explosions at four o'clock in the morning. Fireworks. Then the band, playing just as one would expect it to at that hour. After it passed, the silence was deep and soft. Only a few dogs bugled, far away, and cocks tested their clarions in the dark. I was just sinking into the stillness when it was rent to tatters by church bells. Clangs and clangs. First call for early mass. Another heavenly spell of quiet. Then the bugler began with the brazen insistence of buglers everywhere. Another spell of peace. The second call for mass. Then a marimba, but not too near. People began to run through the streets with the rustling sound of strong wind punctuated by sharp little whacks like tiny shutters banging. Hard Ladino heels among soft Indian feet. Then silence. The band again. It must have been all around the town and coming back. Dogs with more spirit, and cocks aware that day was here. The house across the street was exactly the color of the flat pale sky above it, with a monkey tree etched sharply in black. The first car honked. A detachment of troops marched by, officers snarling. Day now, and no one stayed in bed. Last call for mass. The upper class went by: ladies in black veils, well-dressed men.

At seven the parade began. A bright red car with a radio going full blast. Private cars decked with flowers, occupied by fair-haired maidens dressed like Gretchens. *Viva la Feria* done in pink roses against white daisies. The queen's car was a fire-truck bearing a throne draped with cotton ermine and waving bunches of pink and white artificial flowers. In a country where flowers grow like weeds, paper blossoms represent more refinement. The girls were pretty like the beauty contestants in any small city. Unfortunately here they had to stand comparison with the Indian contestants, beautiful in their glowing dresses, with well-marked features and dignified bearing.

As always when Ladinos handle Indians they were doing it in a way to indicate that unbridgeable gulf between races. No effort had been made to see that the costumes were correct. A couple of old Inditas, instead of the ceremonial scarf, had folded lace window-curtains over their heads. Huipiles from one village and skirts from another were usual. A few carried Madonna lilies and whole orchid plants with blooms. Four fine old matrons were draped in long white wraps speckled all over with a design, and each carried a tall wax taper. They were on pilgrimage, not in the beauty contest. Another group had brought the saints from their cofradías in San Pedro. Even the saints wore finely figured huipiles, as did the bearers, and heavy chains. Those women stood at ease while the beauty judging went on, and afterwards knelt with the candles and saints before the church. The judging was painfully suggestive of finca managers handling cattle. Miss Antigua and her maidens stood in a vapid row behind the judges while two men, one with a riding-crop, shoved and poked the Indian girls around. The girls were shy, they tried to do as they were told, and they seemed to like the folded skirts they received. The prize-winners were not the stunning Indian types, but the most Ladino-looking.

Most fiestas, both Indian and Ladino, are the occasion for plays. Both races present *Los Moros y los Cristianos*, that tedious dramatization of the defeat of the Moors which flourishes wherever Spain went still flushed with her chivalric success. And Indians, with their puzzling willingness to play their own downfall, like to perform *La Conquista, The Conquest*. Written by a monk, it was first given before Bishop Marroquín at his palace near the old capital. It relates the familiar encounter between the Quiché king, Tecum-Umán, and Alvarado. Versions differ. In one, Alvarado, very dashing in the costumer's interpretation of what he should have worn, capers about on a horse while the Indian faces him from the ground. In another, Alvarado's friend Portocarrero kills Tecum-Umán after he has overcome Don Pedro. No director seems to have appreciated the dramatic possibilities of the killing of the king's nahual, the quetzal. Possibly the clerical playwright repudiated such a pagan idea. In the end, of course, the Indian perishes and Spain triumphs.

El Torito, or *Los Toros,* is Spanish too, and a prime favorite at fiestas on the fincas where the Indians are graciously allowed to celebrate the master's saint's day. The cast includes the master and his overseer, a corporal, a Negro slave, and a chorus of cowboys and shepherds. Like characters in a Wagnerian opera each is recognizable by his leitmotiv. The dance is a bull-fight, which they make as convincing as they can, and which ends with the killing of the master.

In all these dramas the argument is clear enough to any patient spectator who knows beforehand what it is all about, and readily comprehensible by a linguist well grounded in sixteenth-century Spanish and the Maya-Quiché tongues, for Indians will revert to their native speech.

The Ladino plays are more pious or romantic, but with enough slapstick comedy to delight an audience largely of boys. Some date back to colonial days, but many are written as needed, by the villagers. It is a more living folk-art than anything the Indians do. One lady told me that her servant girl, as soon as she learned to write, set about making plays for the holy patron saint of her town.

Any place will do for a stage: the terrace in front of the

church, a school's patio, or one end of the plaza. The actors
are drilled for weeks until they can stalk stiffly about and
utter their speeches without mistake. The most important,
and amusing, part of the actor's art is the false tone and the
metronomic beat with which he recites — a convention that
kills what little sense the lines might originally have had.
But the moral is there, always, and the audience is entertained and proud to know people who can learn so much and
say it so fast.

Not quite drama, but very amusing burlesque is the
Christmas Eve procession in Antigua. In Guatemala, as in
all Latin America, parties every night for nine nights dram-
atize the search of Joseph and Mary for a lodging in Bethle-
hem. Children make toy stables, with animals, angels, and
stars, and the festival comes to a radiant climax at midnight
in churches banked with flowers and spangled with candles.
Only early evening is different in Antigua, when a procession in honor of La Virgen de la O winds through the streets.
The floats have little meaning for an outsider, but townsfolk
laugh at them with unrestrained glee, delighted to recognize their fellow citizens in caricature. For many generations a society of artisans and servants have amused themselves by burlesquing the town's aristocrats, making bold
but always good-humored fun. Members of the great families like it; they even lend their typical hats or canes and
are as entertained as anybody.

Ladino festivals are religious and Spanish. During Lent
I saw the two finest statues in the Cathedral carried in procession. Acolytes with silver crosses and lanterns were followed by six men in long black robes and peaked caps like

members of the Misericordia in Seville. But there were no masks, as in Spain, and under the robes instead of gentlemen's boots were Indians' sandaled feet. Their faces were roughly modeled on the Oriental lines of modern Maya: bony cheeks, flattened noses, and thick lips shaded by scraggly mustaches. Each bore an old brass lantern with a candle inside. My little squire Eugenio told me they were *Los Romanos*. But the next group more resembled Romans: a couple of burly Indians in yellow and pink togas with helmets and lances. Two little angels with wings of real feathers. The Cristo was carried by ten men, walking in such perfect step that the figure swayed in regular time. Padre Alvarez, attended by dignified gentlemen in black, walked in reverent humility behind the Christ Crucified, his scholarly face pale under the biretta, his long skirts swishing. Two long files of men and boys carried unlighted candles or old-fashioned brass carriage-lamps.

Then women. An old lady walked telling her beads, unaware of the people watching. The other file was led by a younger woman in conventional black, but smartly set off with white collar and gloves. Black-robed women carried the Sorrowing Mother, richly dressed in brocaded velvet and clasping the silver-handled sword that pierced her heart. Some of these women wore high heels, and in spite of staves to steady them, they never struck a rhythm, and the Virgin seemed to stumble along with none of the lofty smoothness of the Cristo. How strange it was to see that the flags these Guatemalans carried were the standards of royal Spain!

At half past four the procession had left the Cathedral.

At half past nine they were coming back. The bearers had changed, but the same worshipers were walking over the hard conic cobbles. Five hours of going slowly, inch by inch, from the Cathedral to the Merced, to San Francisco, and back to the center, through streets hung with red and yellow banners, windows set with flowers, grilles strung with garlands. Light from a hidden lamp swept up against the Cristo, bringing out the lines of the tortured body, and from all the candles flames floated in dark currents of air. Faces were white from the long strain, and small groups of the older women were reciting prayers in unison. They rounded the plaza, completely immersed in their religious mood, altogether unaware of the noisy hubbub of the fiesta.

Lottery criers, just as oblivious of the murmuring penitents with their figures of suffering, called their cards, took in the cash, dispensed the prizes. "The Apache of the mountains of the north," intoned the leader. And then, antiphonally, "The Apache." "The lady goes walking alone. Who wishes to accompany her?" "The lady." The merry-go-round calliope vied with the radio program from Eagle Pass, Texas, and the marimba in the kiosk.

Special police, down from the capital, kept order courteously, scornful of the boys dancing in the park. Only in Antigua, so far as I know, do boys dance without girls. It began several years ago with ragged urchins trying their steps in front of the Cathedral. They were too young for girls, and it would have been improper for girls in any case. Later they moved nearer to the music, and there they are, under the kiosk. The same pair always dance together, but neither leads and often they hold left-handed instead of right. Their bare feet slide across the harsh cement with a rasp to make one squirm, and their clothes are ordinary and worn to rags. But how they dance! Like professionals, they cross their feet, sway and glide, making the most of every cadence of the excellent music, faces and bodies plastered together, legs and feet moving in complete harmony. Most of them were from ten to fifteen years old. I saw one mustached couple, and a pair of babies clutched each other and lurched fatly, but with a sense of rhythm that portends future prizes. One or two pairs looked languishing, but altogether it seemed pure sensuous enjoyment of rhythm, dancing for sheer love of the dance. And the Antigua marimba is the best in the whole country. Occasionally, when inferior marimberos substitute, the boys are irritated and critical as only artists can be.

The marimba is not native to Guatemala, though it is Guatemala; and you can go nowhere, do nothing, without marimba accompaniment until the whole nation seems moved to its beat. Students find it like the African limba, in note as well as in name. Don Flavio Guillén, a Mexican historian of Chiapas, says that a Negro who came with Las Casas introduced it there. Now every village has one, or it is brought over from the next village on all occasions. Home-made marimbas are the rule. The frame may be anything and is often mahogany. But the twenty-one keys must be of granadillo, a tree of the ebony family, or of hornugon. Under each key is a gourd or polished fine-wood box. Graduated in size, they form the sounding device. Four men play, striking the keys with rubber-tipped sticks; but three will do, as a virtuoso can manage two sticks in each hand.

The usual repertoire consists of popular airs from Mexico or the United States, as Guatemala produces no music, not even regional folk-songs. But clever marimberos do not demand a whole tune. It is astonishing what they can do with one phrase, and at what length. Standing alert, sticks poised, the players await the leader's signal and then dash into it. And with what verve they attack it, hard on, freshly every time, a bit higher, a bit lower, hitting it squarely, making the little instrument pulsate and all but leap from the floor as it responds with good will, if a bit stringily. It is superficial, if you like, but always, under even the merriest melodies, the marimba wails a muted minor note, so expressive of the underlying sadness of Guatemala.

Once, as I watched the dancing, I was aware of a small warm brown face at my elbow. A finely-cut nose was set between cheeks that looked like a squirrel's full of nuts, and were as velvety. A curved rosy mouth and glistening jet eyes smiled at me under a hat. And such a hat! A well-brushed felt, tilted over one eyebrow with all the jauntiness of all the swells from Beau Brummel to Jimmy Walker. That his shirt was dingy, his trousers cast-offs, and his feet unshod detracted nothing from the tone of that hat. I have said that Guatemalans never wear their hats with the éclat of Mexicans, but I retract, unreservedly. A nation need produce only one like that. He was Eugenio, and at my service whenever I was in Antigua. Always ceremonious, he would approach me in the plaza, smiling, doff his hat, and resettle it at the precise angle. He could sit for the longest time, unmoving, if the conversation did not include him, and his gallantry never failed.

" But do you really go, Niña? Oh, you should stay another week. But you will soon be back? "

So devious was his approach that I hardly know how I sensed that Eugenio would like to ride on the merry-go-round but was short of funds just then. Supplied with coin, he lingered awhile in desultory chat and then, unhurried, he slipped off the bench, straightened his little figure, lifted the slantwise hat, bowed, and strolled off to the horses, a gentleman of leisure and of means.

XXIV: Finca Week-end

FROM TZANJUYÚ WE CROSSED LAKE ATITLÁN TO SAN Lucas, riding the launch with highland merchants, making the coastwise arc of their trading circle. Most of them passed directly through the village, already set in their steady jog-trot. Our host met us there, and in his car we rounded the volcano and lost it as we tunneled through a verdant lane and into the canyon beyond. It was like plunging over a waterfall, so fast did we descend. Heat increased, ears popped, vegetation grew greener, ranker, bigger-leaved. There was the humid smell of growth fertilizing itself on its own decay. Many times the car slowed down for passing mule-trains or for loaded men who stood smiling aside, resting on their staves. Everything to live on comes from the highlands, for the zone that is best for coffee is not allowed to produce anything else.

As we dropped lower, giant ceibas reared above palm frond and fern. There were patches of sugar-cane, but only where the road dipped into valleys too low for coffee. A gentleman on horseback stopped to salute us, speaking to our host in German, to me in English; one of the few Guatemalans who have kept their fincas in this region.

Much of the land belongs now to Germans living in Hamburg or Berlin and is managed by young men spending a few years in the colonies to learn the producing end of the business. Our host was such a man; highly cultivated, of good family, set adrift by the war, he commanded respect by his tolerance and humor. I was grateful for his corrective slant on what I saw.

We stopped at a roadside store where a red pump advertised Standard gas and a shaded road curved away through a stately gate. Our finquero made a brief call, and as he put the car in gear he was moved to talk.

" That man," he said, " has got his troubles. He has been a hard master; he has always overcharged in his store. The Indians hate him, and now that they cannot be held for debt, he has lost eighty per cent of his workers."

In 1934, by a law epochal in Guatemala history, planters were allowed two years in which to collect debts owed them by their Indian laborers. All uncollectable obligations were to be canceled in May 1936, a signal date in the emancipation of the Indian, whether he realizes it or not. Since the descendants of the encomenderos discovered that debt will enslave a man as effectually as chains and more cheaply, Indian labor has been held in bondage.

The method was simple. It began with an advance on wages. The finquero kept the books. The Indian could neither read nor figure. A debt would mount for a lifetime and be passed on to a man's sons and grandsons. Until it was paid the family owed labor to the planter who held the loan, and could work for no one else. The whole force of the state backed the master. Men were marched to the fincas under guard, pursued like criminals if they ran away. In 1876 President Barrios, the Reform President, issued a circular to political chiefs calling on them to supply the planters with what labor they needed. " If we abandon the farmers to their own resources," he said, " and do not give them strong and energetic aid, they will be unable to make any progress, for all their efforts will be doomed to failure owing to the deceit of the Indians." The circular ends: " Above all else see to it that any Indian who seeks to evade this duty is punished to the full extent of the law, that the farmers are fully protected, and that each Indian is forced to do a full day's work while in service."

In 1894 this system was abolished by law, but it continued to flourish. In 1906 the Congress declared null and void all agreements between planters for the exchange — virtually the sale — of mozos. But the finqueros still found a way to hold their workers, and perfectly legally. An Indian could sign a contract to work for any period of less than four years, and if he left a finca before he had worked off his debt he could be arrested and returned to his master.

Twenty years ago a twelve-year-old boy was taken for his father's debt. In the finca commissary they allowed him a blanket, a machete. He received his ration of beans and corn. He got food from the store. Doubtless he charged liquor too. Maybe he had candles for the church, tissue paper to deck his hut for fiesta. For a year he worked from dawn to night. Then he asked his reckoning. He was many additional quetzales in debt. He worked another year. Older now, maybe he bought more liquor. Certainly he made gifts of glass beads or colored combs to the girls he liked.

Possibly a hat, a petate, calico shirts. When he asked for his account again, it had more than doubled. Hundreds of quetzales of debt were his only gain for years of work from sunrise to sunset. The story has no variations. It went on so for years: man working, debt piling, life passing in flashes of joy and passion, of drunkenness and religious fervor. But this Indian had somewhere inside himself a strength to call upon. When the total was eleven years of work and a debt of twelve hundred quetzales, he walked out; dared the finquero's anger, the danger of being overtaken by the police. He went to a British finquero, a man known widely for justice and fair dealing, who paid his debts and got him free. That Indian, who learned to live in a house, to keep himself clean, to wait on table, serves now in a highland hotel. He is married to a Ladina, a clean active woman. This is a story neither of them tell; I got it from an old friend.

My host said the new law would be good. " The change will be trying, of course. Finqueros who have been hard on their Indians will be short-handed for a season or two, and at harvest-time that can mean enormous loss. Already the mozos are looking for new places. But it will do them good to work as free laborers, and it won't hurt the finqueros to have to bid for labor by decent treatment."

" But if the Indians don't come back? "

" They'll have to come back. The law not only relieves them of debt; it requires every man to show that he has worked a hundred or a hundred and fifty days a year. That's more than many of them have ever worked."

Later I looked at the Vagrancy Law. It will keep the

Indian at work, and responsible, but to the government rather than to the planter. It has teeth, too, to catch other classes. But I was interested in Indians then.

" Have you lost any workers? " I was bold enough to ask.

" Not yet." My host smiled with a hint of scorn. " But I make no boast. That these Indians have been treated well somewhere will not hold them, I think, for long. Feeling foot-loose for the first time, they will change just to prove they can. Only where they have lands in the highlands will they be inclined to stay with the owner."

" Lands in the highlands? "

" Yes. It is an old Guatemala custom, you know, to give an Indian land to till. Many finqueros own ranches in the Altos, where their workers may each have his little patch. The Indians have come to think it is their land. They may stay with the same finquero rather than lose those little fields. Anyway, I think that letting them work like free men will be better at last." That is why I admire that finquero.

As we neared the finca we passed the sunny drying-floors and the office buildings. Beyond I glimpsed the workers' huts, roofed with grass or corrugated iron, deep-eaved, picturesque under palms. At the vine-arched gate a couple of urchins trotted up for the luggage. Dirty-nosed children poked around the hedge and scampered back to their mothers. I thought how little alteration would make this a setting for *Uncle Tom's Cabin*. Only the traditional wide-mouthed Negro laughter was missing; these people seemed sullen, spiritless.

Our hostess met us with the sort of welcome that makes a guest feel truly in his own house. Inside the hibiscus hedge, dampened lawns were shaded with mango and cedar trees, and a fountain jet spired in the sunshine and splashed back on water-lilies. The house, with porches all around, was bisected by halls both ways; everything was designed to bring in the breeze and exclude the sun. Built of imported Oregon pine, the walls had suffered badly from termites, so the newer kitchen and bath were of native mahogany, not so elegant but more durable. Barefooted maids skimmed back and forth at their effortless pace. " *Qué manda Vd?* " " What does your worship order? " I yielded gratefully to the lazy heat surging up against trees and fountains, modified into half-light by hanging vines. Nothing seemed important but a clinking drink, a nap, a tingling shower. To me, as to the Indian, work was unthinkable. They can be goaded into it; I never could be.

With amazement I watched my host and his assistant. What the German drive in the system can force a man to, even in the tropics! Before seven in the morning they were in the office, laying out the day's work with native foremen, putting up the mail. Then they came in for breakfast. Luscious mangoes easy to munch from their special forks, and the flower-like strawberries we had brought from San Lucas. Our hostess had taught somebody to make German breads and to crisp bacon to the taste of kings. Dressing I had scented the aroma of roasting coffee and heard the whir of the hand-mill for grinding it. It came to the table bubbling in its machine. It poured steaming clear brown-gold. And when the cup was turned in the hands, it left an amber stain against the porcelain. Such coffee is known only on a finca where the best comes to the table, freshly roasted and ground.

The gentlemen went back to work. The children to the German governess. I heard the mistress summoning her maids from their washing, floor-polishing, or bed-making, giving orders, inspecting what was done. I watched an old crone raking dry leaves out of the paths and flower-beds. Her withered brown fingers were her only tool; her lean haunches, wrapped in a faded red skirt, creaked almost audibly as she stooped. She did not hear or her toothless mouth could not form words, but she understood a cigarette and squatted to smoke and grin awhile. My hostess rested long enough to tell me about her.

She was old Candelaria, who still wanted to work, so they let her putter about. Her old man, Estevan, was as useless and as fixed at the stables. A couple of years ago they faced tragedy. The family hoard, the amassment of years of penny-piling, was stolen. They used to count it every night, taking the sack out from under the petate where they slept. Somebody must have heard the telltale clink. Fifteen dollars it totaled and some cents more. It was capital, dignity, backing. They never spent anything. Food came from the finca stores or the kitchen. No need was ever denied. The treasure could only grow. But its loss meant desolation. The finquero thought he knew the thief, but he had no proof. So he called the headman. Every group of Indians has its leader; a clever planter knows and uses him.

" This money," was the ultimatum, " must be found. I don't know who stole it; I don't care. If you can find out you may say that nothing will be done if the money comes back by Saturday night. If not, I'll bring a brujo down from Los Altos, and if it costs me a thousand quetzales I'll have that thief caught and punished! "

So the money appeared, but not quite all of it, and Estevan and Candelaria, heedless of the quetzales that had come home, were wailingly afflicted for the missing odd pence. The finquero naturally made that up, and the old couple were again contentedly doddering about.

I commented on the excellence of the maids, soft-spoken, moving with satin tread, quick and so clean in cotton skirts and huipiles.

" As long as they stay with me," the mistress said, " they are clean because I insist upon it. But when they leave they go back at once to the filth of the cabin. With water right at the door, they won't wash themselves, their clothes, their babies! " It was a wail. " They can learn to cook too, but they never really change. When I first came I was enthusiastic to help them. But they don't care, they won't try. You shall see them, how they sit pig-dirty all day. Last year I gave up. A cook I had for seven years went home. You should see the filth she lives in! After that I decided it was no use. I go whenever they send for me, of course. Especially I try to help women in child-birth. There is no doctor near here and the midwives are deplorable. But my husband always warns me to be careful. They are so superstitious that if anything goes wrong we are always to blame, even if we have only brought a mosquito netting or sent a woman to clean. . . . Nothing can be done for them, nothing! "

A doctor in the Health Department had told me of the

government's struggle to lessen infant mortality. Families increase with the utmost regularity and babies die almost as regularly. Many who survive infant dysentery succumb to the adult diet offered them as soon as lactation ceases. But Indian mothers are apathetic; there is always another baby coming. And witchcraft is considerably more valued than science.

It was disquieting to hear these things, tempting to dawdle behind the hibiscus, as secure from the peon's misery as a millionaire isolated from a world of want by unending wealth. But honest books are not written so. Guatemala deserves the warts in her portrait. I went out to see.

The cabins, so picturesque from afar, were dirt-floored hovels. Only the corner posts were solid; smoke from charcoal fires seeped through the bamboo walls. There were no garden plots, not even flowers in tin cans. The finquero requires sweeping up before Saturday-night payment, but this was Friday and unwashed babies rolled on piles of trash. Women sat, spread-kneed, on the door-sills, fanning half-heartedly or picking nits out of each other's uncombed heads. Most of them replied sulkily to greetings. A few were fetching water from the big fountain, but nobody was washing anything. No wonder a woman fresh from scrubbed Germany, eager for social service, was defeated.

Yet these were the very people I had seen in Los Altos, where village and cofradía give them distinction and self-respect. Reduced to undifferentiated laborers on the fincas, they struck me as only distressing. Cut off from the sustaining power of their racial background, poorly paid, and

badly housed, they seem an abased and hopeless lot. De-
serving of the upper-class assumption that they are con-
genital hewers of wood and drawers of water. Doubtless
these peons are the descendants of the lower classes who
served their Maya overlords before the Conquest and their
Spanish masters in colonial days. Who can say why so
large a proportion of the population have allowed themselves to be misused through all these years? Most discouraging, from any social point of view, is that they appear
resigned if not content. Aside from too apparent ills — big
stomachs from hookworm, goitre, undernourished children
— these Indians look comfortable in their squalor. Weather
favors them, food is easy to get. Women gossip more than
they scrub; work moves at a moderate swing. If they feel
any resentment, it does not show.

The working sphere was pleasanter. We walked between
rows of shining coffee shrubs, flecked with unseasonable
white blossoms or crimson fruit. Men were pruning, cleaning debris away, clearing new ground for planting. Only
recently coffee from this region went out man- or mule-back,
but trucks travel a good government road now, and the finquero was building bridges to reach the farthest plantations.
A finquero, I found, must be engineer as well as office man
and agriculturist. As a merchant he was dickering for
women's skirts with a vender from Totonicapán. Diplomacy
is no small part of his job, what with owners in Germany,
neighboring planters, village bigwigs, and now the trying
adjustment with Indians working for the first time as free
labor. I was not surprised that Guatemalans, who know so
many beguiling things to do, have taken to Paris and motor-

cars and let the Germans have the fincas. Even after the day's official end at seven, our host was called upon to sit as judge.

A man came in great distress, and in the dark, away from the house, he told his tale. His daughter and her stepmother were always quarreling, he said. That was bad enough, but he had just learned that each had been paying a brujo to bewitch the other. His wife, first, had given the man a hen. The daughter, a suckling pig. Each, believing the sorcerer her loyal aide, watched the other for sign of illness. Both stayed hearty. So more fowls and animals disappeared. The women denied everything, even when soundly thrashed, as the man explained to show he had done his part. He demanded relief. The brujo was living on his meat while he, thrifty one, worked hard. Knowing the malefactor, it would be simple enough to scare him out of that graft, the finquero said, " but he will have another one working by next week. These Indians are so entangled in superstitions they believe nothing else."

Sunday morning I watched the market while the mistress called on a new baby to see how her instructions were being carried out. She came back worried. " She must go to town," she told her husband, " and today. She has a temperature; I don't know what to do."

The finquero was busy in the store, but he turned to order a car to get the woman to the train. The mistress summoned another who would suckle the baby meanwhile. Six men were intensely occupied in that store. Canned goods and toilet articles, yard goods and cutlery, from the States and from Germany were piled neatly on shelves. Outside, the native market revolved in its orbit around the axis of a ceiba tree. Men I had met in the launch greeted me. Business was bad, they said. A boy from Totonicapán sold me figurine whistles from his gimcracks. Women had their usual piles of garden truck. These people were nondescript in dress, a melange of whatever skirts and huipiles the store offered. Only a few kept their distinctive dress; I recognized huipiles from San Martín Jilotepeque. " They stay apart," said the finquero. " And they are good workers. I used to think they were too independent. Now I believe they will be better under the new system." He turned to confer with the government expert on eye diseases, making a circuit of the danger zone.

A lady from a neighboring finca joined me in a breezy doorway that commanded both store and market. She was eager to correct my impressions.

" They're a comic-opera crew, aren't they? Watch that woman swing her baby onto her back like a sack of wool. Might as well be wool to her. I know her. She collects her husband's wages every Saturday night and gives him what she thinks he needs. Lots of 'em do that. They're the only independent women in Guatemala.

" Oh, they're docile enough if you know how to handle 'em. Our danger now is that the government will ruin them. Things are very stable now. The President is admirable, we have to thank him a lot. If he just doesn't give the Indians too much! In his barracks now, he has them all shod. A rank extravagance. And he gives them wonderful places to sleep, and marvelous food."

" Marvelous food? "

" Yes, you should see. They get soup, rice, potatoes, even meat once or twice a week. A wonderfully rich diet, and they don't need it at all. All an Indian really needs is a handful of beans, a couple of tortillas, and chile. Chile, you know, contains a wonderful vitamin. Just see how strong they are, how they can carry their quintal a day and never feel it. Look how rosy the women and children are! They are perfectly happy and well off. Nothing to worry about. Look, they get a house. No house could be better suited to the climate. . . ."

She left at last to return to her house, so different from the admirable porous Indian hut, to a lunch that would not much resemble the Indian diet she found so marvelously sustaining.

I came away from the finca when the sky behind the volcano was suffused with morning light. The coffee country was still shadowed, weighted with the lassitude of the lowlands. Something similar pressed down my own nerves and spirit as I thought of the people I had seen there. Surely there is no way out for them in many lifetimes. Efforts of people like my hosts are futile in face of the Indian's ageless inertia and inevitably blocked by the other type of finquero, so sure that God meant the Indian to do the work and be docile about it.

But the Guatemalan Indian, like the rest of the world, can only go ahead. Though he seems at his best when least touched by white influence, the idea of returning him to a Utopian past is untenable; his past was probably not Utopian anyhow. But what will bring the change? Public health? The government has a program. Education? There are schools. But I was told that the few Indian children who attend are consistently neglected by Ladino teachers. Some leak of social ideas through the impervious ramparts of government, owners, and church, all afraid of ideas? This lifting of the peonage debt? Or the President? His Excellency is generally considered the Indian's friend. Certainly the relief from debt could not have come about without his approval.

XXV: These Indians

A STRANGER, I WAS TOLD, CAN HARDLY HOPE TO KNOW the Indian. Only one born among them can understand their curious ways or hope to handle them correctly. So I asked here and there and achieved the following portrait.

The Native Finquero:
The Indian has only one idea, thinks only along one line: to avoid work. If he has lands he will not work. With his tortillas and his frijoles, that's all he wants. If he gets any money, he drinks. He never thinks of bettering himself, of improving his house, of buying more land or better clothes. To eat, and if anything is left, to drink: that's all the Indian thinks of.

The only thing to do with him is to make him work, make him produce, make him progress, make a useful citizen out of him. . . . I don't mean with the whip — the day of the *latigo* is gone forever — but I mean by educating him to some ambition, to some needs. Now, if you do not make him work, he just stops, goes back to his place, raises a handful of corn, a few beans, and is perfectly content. That's why Guatemala has no internal trade. Our only trade is external — coffee for the rest of the world — and the greatest problem about raising coffee is how to make the Indian work. If he were not forced by debt he would not work at all.

You can't deal with the Indian, either, on any human basis. Don't get a lot of sentimental ideas about him. He is an animal, that's all. There is no decency or gratitude in him. You can take care of a man and his family for years, lend him money, get him out of jail, give him work in hard times, patch up his wife when he beats her, and the first chance he gets he walks out and leaves you. They lack the human instincts, I tell you. An Indian loves his children, yes, but for his woman he has no feeling at all. If she doesn't feed him well, he beats her; if she gets sick, he only hopes she will die in a hurry so he can get a better one.

And now this government is trying to help him — to help the Indian! Hmph! Before, the government forced the Indian to work. Now the Indian works and then is paid, so he knows nothing better to do than to drink. He will not work, you'll see, until he is actually hungry.

They are also arming the Indians. In every pueblo there is a troop of soldiers. Indians given arms and ammunition by the government and taught to use them! They are even taught Spanish, those precious soldiers, and to read and write.

Señorita, imagine Indians with education, with arms, with money! If they are learning to better themselves it is a great danger, you see, to the whites. The Indians educated, armed, could take the country away from us!

And I tell you this, I who have worked Indians for years.

The Mistress of the Hotel:

Poor little things, they are so charming! I like them very much, and I feel much pain for them. Poor things, they work so hard! And we are so ungrateful, we never treat them like human beings. Look, I never go to market; it gives me too much pain to see how they treat them. You can see a poor Indian from the coast in rags, pure rags, only a shirt that hangs, maybe, from the collar, but rags, and dirty from sweat and the dust of the road. You know how they come walking, loaded like beasts, bent so they cannot raise their head to greet you, and then we refuse a fair price for their load. Isn't that ingratitude? And they are so humble, so uncomplaining. I have many friends among them, from the richest to the poorest.

But they are ungrateful too, señorita, and they make beasts of burden of their children. A woman who brings wood here always has her children loaded too. She has two on foot: a boy maybe six years old and a girl four. She has one on her back and another here in front, about to be born. And those two older children carry each his little load of wood. But it is too much, señorita! They should not do it! I scold her every time she comes, But she is ungrateful too. Once, when I bought her wood, I did not have change, so I gave her four cents. The price was three, but one child was sick, so I gave her four. I gave her medicine too. The next time she asked four cents! Imagine! The price was three and I had helped her, but she was so ungrateful that she expected four every time. I did not buy and without doubt she sold it for three. But wasn't that ingratitude?

But see, señorita, it is really all our fault. If we educate

them! Everybody wants the Quetzaltecas for servants. They
are clean and quick and intelligent. But it is because they
are educated. They can read, nearly all those Quetzaltecas,
and so they can go anywhere for good wages. No, señorita,
if our Indians are small, if they look mis-shapen, if they
are stupid, it is we who are to blame, I say. How can children grow tall if we let them carry heavy weights from
childhood? How can their brains develop if they have that
heavy leather strap — you have seen it? It is a barbarity!
No, señorita, if they were educated, and treated kindly —

Young Guatemalan Educated in the States:

Indians, I tell you, are dangerous. They have to be kept
under with force. This is not like your country, where men
are equal. I'll tell you.

A few years ago some young men made an excursion to
climb Santa María, the volcano by Quetzaltenango, you
know. Well, they came to a place where the Indians had
been making their *brujería*. It was just a pile of stones and
broken pottery — nothing, dirty. The young men looked at
it, moved the things with their sticks and their feet, maybe.
I don't know. Then they went on. Well, the next week another party came by, different young men, and they didn't
touch the things; but the Indians, watching, thought they
were the same young men, and they just killed them. Killed
them. I tell you, they are dangerous, these Indians.

Well, the government went after them. They knew what
village it was, but not what man. But they did enough, I'll
tell you, to that village so they'll never bother white men
again. They killed about ten men, I think.

Protestant Missionary:

One man, I'm sure he was a Christian man, but these people never understand the morality of the sexes as Anglo-Saxons do. . . . Well, maybe lots of Anglo-Saxons don't either, but at least they don't pretend; they are honest about it. But this man, after his wife died, he just said he had to have a woman, and he is absolutely brazen about how he lives. We talked to him. He was an elder in the church, and we explained that he could not continue in that position, living in sin as he did. We tried to give him some sense of responsibility, of Christian shame, but he just said:

" Well, God made me, and He knows how I am. He knows I can't live alone."

City Lady:

These Indians are happy people. Just watch how they laugh and run in the roads when a car goes by. They are happy like children, and content because they want no more than they have.

Look, I want you to see our cargador. For years now he has carried things in to us from the finca. He brings his load, he is paid, and then he sits in a sunny corner of the patio, money in his pocket, his stomach full, and what more does he want? Nothing. If we were all as happy as these Indians, the world would be a fine place to live in.

German Storekeeper:

Indians have not our conception of honesty, and it is not fair to judge them by it. If you give an Indian something to carry for you, he will fulfill the charge. If you leave something in his care, he will guard it as his own. He will never fail you. But if you leave something around where he can get it, he figures that you have lost it, that you do not want it, that it is his, and he might as well take it. To the Indian, that is not stealing.

Ladino Storekeeper:

Of course these Indians get drunk. What other consolation have they, in their sad lives? But they are honest, señorita, and they have curious ways of their own.

Once I hired a hall for a fiesta. I put in a marimba and a bar, and there they danced all those days and nights. You have seen how they dance, men alone and women alone, because it is not conventional to dance together unless they are drunk, and then you should see them, how drunk they get, and helpless! They are very funny, these natives!

But you will see how responsible they are. Two young men came, traders from the coast, and they said they did not drink aguardiente, but they asked me to put aside seven cases of beer for them. I did, and in the three days of the fiesta those men drank seven cases of twenty-four bottles each. They bought aguardiente for their friends. They would say: " Four aguardientes, and another bottle from the case." They never got too drunk to know their cases of beer in the corner. Afterwards they lost their money, gambling, or maybe they had none when they came. I don't know. But they couldn't pay, and they told me they would pay on the installment plan, and they do. Only yesterday one came in and gave me four quetzales. It's four months now, and they will soon have it paid. Oh, they are good, these Indians, very honest.

Such funny things happened in that zarabanda! Two women came in, drunk, oh, very drunk. They had some pottery they had just bought, and they put it in a corner, with much care, and covered it with their shawls. Then they bought a couple of drinks and went to dance. I saw them from the bar, dancing apart, but happy, poor things. A man was dancing there, drunk too. He tried to get out, because it is, as you know, sufficiently hot in a zarabanda. As he tried to walk out, he stumbled and fell, poor thing, right on top of the pots of those women, and he broke them into a thousand pieces! Poor things! They heard the crash, and they came, swearing and clawing, and calling him bad names and insisting that he must pay for them. But he was poor, he had no money.

Well, we called a judge, an Indian. You know they have their judges among them. He said that the man, being drunk, was not responsible, so it was not his fault he broke the pottery. So the women cried, but they could do no more. What the judge said was final, and it was just too. Oh, yes, they have fine customs.

The Padre:

My snuff, it is my only vice, my friend, my comforter. And it comes from that terrible, that frightening city of Chicago. . . . Is anybody here from Chicago? . . . Well, I can say that good word for Chicago, that my precious snuff comes from there. My friends bring it to me.

I am never without my snuff. But never send it, my friends, never send it! Once someone wishing to be kind, wishing to be kind, you see, sent me snuff, imagine, and I had to pay many dollars of duty. And I have no money. How should I have money, a poor priest? My people bring me food. And they leave a few coppers in the church, poor things, but they cannot leave much, they who are so poor too.

Do you see my Indians there now? Such devotion! We, with all the wisdom we have, and of course, being from the United States, we are very wise, very superior, very learned people; but even we do not have such devotion as these people. Did you go into the church to see? When you do, go, please, by the side door and sit very still so they shall not notice you. For they are very intent, my poor people there, on their prayers, very close to God they are. For they come there in perfect faith. They have been robbed, you see, for generations, robbed and exploited, their women violated, their little children loaded like beasts. They have been beaten. It is getting different now, with the fine new President we have. But still they have much that is wrong, my poor people. And so they come to church, as you see, each one with his pitiful little candle. Maybe what they do is not quite orthodox, you see. Some people may criticize that I allow it. But that Indian, he talks straight to God, as maybe you and I dare not do, even if we do come from the States and know everything. He talks to his God, telling Him everything, asking help. I know because I understand his language. How could I help these people if I did not? Often I hear what they say.

" Lord and Master," they are saying, " this is not just, this is not right, that he should take my land I have worked so hard to till. Lord, I ask You now to help me, to help my children." And he knows, friends, that the Lord will help him. That is faith, friends, yes, that is faith.

XXVI: Modern Guatemala

GUATEMALA'S SOCIAL LIFE IS AS MUCH A MATTER OF CON-trasts as its geography and as difficult to understand without a sharp readjustment of focus. The morasses and fens of the coastal plain differ no more from the crisp and invigorating uplands than the wordless enigmatic Indian does from the white and cosmopolitan upper class. There are only Ladinos and Indians. Though of Guatemala's two million inhabitants only fifteen thousand are rated as pure white, nobody admits to mixed blood. Everybody not recognized as Indian is considered Ladino. There are people of an intermediate amount of wealth and education; there is no middle-ground state of mind.

Recently, when a young man returned from school in the States, the Indians on his father's finca came on their knees begging him to remove an overseer who beat them. It should have made an insufferable prig of the young man, but it did not. To his class it is not odd that men should come kneeling to another man for decent treatment. To understand it we must remember our Southern grandparents' attitude toward their slaves.

What the Indian really is, under this superficial subservience, I think nobody knows. His potentialities, either for development or for trouble, are little understood; they have never been tested. White Guatemalans congratulate themselves that their Indians are meek and biddable, so different from the blood-thirsty Aztecs, who indulged in human sacrifice in those days, in revolution in these. The contrast is even stronger when one compares Guatemalan Indians with those of the United States who were also conquered by Spain. There they were never really overcome. Defeated and baptized wholesale, they were perforce left largely to their own devices because Spain did not have enough men to hold them down as the tribes farther south were enslaved. The consequence is that our Southwestern Indians are reserved if not haughty, and never subservient. If they have any idea that one people is superior to the other, they would unhesitatingly put the red man above the white. The Mexican Indian, who was reduced to peonage, seems tame in comparison. The joyous uplift one feels in modern Mexico is due to the younger generation standing on its own feet, looking the world in the eye, fearless and unashamed. Even unashamed of its Indian heritage. One of the most hideous things Spain did to the people of the Americas was to make them despise their Indian blood. "*Todo blanco es caballero,*" "all white is a gentleman," is a false notion which still corrodes many people with a sense of inferiority. Mexico is getting away from that. There a man can say with pride: " I am Indian." Even: " I am mestizo." In contrast, Guatemalan Indians seem defeated, crushed. Certainly in any relation with white men they appear to be as slavish as their masters would have them.

Ladinos are of many blood-strains. Spanish predominates, but many upper-class families have a fairly recent forebear of English, German, French, or North American extraction. That, and the fact that those forebears made an effort to transmit their own culture to their children, probably account for the versatile and charming social life of the capital. These people are the dominant class, though families have their picturesque ups and downs in Guatemala, as everywhere. The Spanish custom of dividing lands among the sons made for a rapid reshaping of social classes. Weak heirs went down into the class of proletarians as surely as strong men of no family rose. Manuel Cobos Batres, in a biography of Rafael Carrera, of which unhappily only one volume is published, throws fascinating side-lights on these things. Within a few miles of the capital are villages of true descendants of the Conquerors, where the people dress and live like Indians, though their looks clearly show their pure Spanish blood. They fought in Carrera's army in 1840 when that strong youth — he was only twenty-three — took the power he held for twenty-five years. Señor Cobos Batres proves by references to church records that Carrera had less than eleven per cent of Indian blood. He had more of Negro. And he was the most Indian president they ever had! They called him the Savage of Mita, the Son of God, Chief of the Pueblos, and Miserable Swineherd, according to the point of view. He ended the long disorder following the revolt from Spain in 1821. Carrera's descendants of the Conquerors fought for liberty of the Church, abolition of anti-religious laws, and re-establishment of tithes.

This prepared the way for Justo Rufino Barrios, honored still as the nation's great liberator and reformer. He dissolved the religious societies and exiled the monks and nuns. Only the Sisters of Charity remained. They conduct many schools and hospitals and add a mediæval note as they pass through the streets in their long blue gowns and white starched wimples. President Barrios confiscated much wealth of churches and great families and weakened their power in every way. His was the age of reforms, and he sponsored many, most of which remained on paper. Some effort was made to replace the suppressed church schools with government institutions, but as late as 1921 the census showed that less than fourteen in a hundred Guatemalans could read and write.

Hating the Catholic Church, Barrios invited Protestant missionaries, even financed the first comers, and so added one of its strangest anachronisms to the Guatemalan scene. What a labor of futility, trying to force a Nordic pattern of thought onto minds molded by centuries of ritual and incense, candles and flowers, pilgrimages and confession, and images to dance before and pray to! All Maya as well as Catholic. It is too violent a wrench to a pallid " cult meeting " where a foreign gentleman in a business suit expounds John Calvin or Roger Williams. In contrast with the sixteenth-century teachers, few Protestant missionaries learn the Indian tongues. About Indian customs I found them uninformed and uninterested. By nature, missionaries must, of course, go abroad to persuade the inhabitants of whatever cultural background that the mores of the missionary's village are better and should be adopted forthwith. Nobody would deny them that right. But it would conduce to better international feeling if all evangelists bound for Latin America could be thoroughly grounded in two facts: one, that Spaniards are white; two, that Catholics are Christians.

After Barrios, who was killed in battle with Salvador in 1885, a couple of lesser men held sway, making themselves remarkable for extravagance rather than statesmanship. Then, in 1898, Manuel Estrada Cabrera took the office of President and kept it for more than twenty years, getting himself re-elected by methods shiningly exemplified today by Hitler. Sometimes his adherents were so enthusiastic that their votes outnumbered the voting population. Cabrera is described as strong, smart, unscrupulous, and of an amazing memory. It is rumored that he was found on a doorstep and that the lady who figured as his mother was not so. But he exalted her and all suitable virtues and founded an orphanage in her name. His extraordinary memory retained the fact that Minerva had to do with education, and he decreed a temple of Minerva in every town. Some are finished in handsome style, some are unfinished, with rusty wires sticking out of cement pillars. In the villages they are even made of logs, with grass roofs. It was a monument to the President's approval of education and it cost little. Schools, meanwhile, were conducted by unpaid teachers, often unalphabeted (as the picturesque Spanish says it) who worked the children on their own lands. Even today Guatemalan education has not progressed much beyond the rote and examination system. Nobody has thought of going to the Indians to teach them what they need to know.

Agricultural and craft schools are few, and the students who win scholarships are generally the sons of Ladino *politicos*. But President Cabrera was less concerned with education than with keeping himself in power.

In 1923 opposition to Cabrera was strong enough to declare the Congress indissoluble and to send a medical commission to examine the President for sanity. The doctors reported him insane without running the risk of approaching him. Cabrera took refuge in the fortress of La Palma and fired on the city. People rushed through the streets, yelling and beating on whatever would make noise. Prince William of Sweden describes this revolution very excitingly in his book *Between Two Continents*. As a guest in Grace's Hotel he took his turn at hauling sand, piling bags. He would accept no special consideration, but he asked for a Swedish flag to hang from his window. Mrs. Grace claims to be the only woman in history who stitched somebody else's flag under fire.

Foreign pressure and the concern of Cabrera's officers for their families in the city finally broke the old man down. He retired and Herrerra was elected. Then came Orellana, who put the country on a gold basis and adopted measures for education. And Chacón, who gave a wag in the capital occasion for a witticism that still brings pleased chuckles.

" Other countries," he said, " erect monuments to their Unknown Soldier. Guatemala makes hers President."

Then, after a period of some disorder, Ubico.

Guatemala has been a republic for a century and a quarter, but she has never been self-governing. Her history is that of one dictatorship after another. And it is the history of a class, not a people; for the Indian has never been considered a citizen. Thoughtful Guatemalans recognize the disadvantages of a country divided between peoples on such vastly different cultural levels. But the problem, as they see it, is to get enough work out of the Indian to build a modern state without endangering their own supremacy. They say: " If the Indian does not work, who will? " And indeed, in view of his numerical predominance, if the Indian does not work they all perish. To educate him to enough needs so he will want to work, but never to give him notions, is a ticklish undertaking.

Still, they do progress. An efficient, up-to-date health department is staffed by men educated abroad. Their tracks are discernible everywhere. Cattle are inspected before slaughter, meat before it is sold. All food-venders must wear caps and aprons and keep their wares screened. There is regular inspecting and grading of eating-places, hotels, and water-supplies. Drastic measures have eliminated yellow fever. A vigorous war against endemic diseases, especially a terrible eye affection which blinded whole communities, has attracted world-wide attention. Clinical trains tour the country, as there is a great lack of doctors and nurses. Midwives must be licensed, and there is constant effort to give them some notion of sanitation.

The most interesting work for children is done by the Casa del Niño in the capital. Founded seventeen years ago by women who actually scrubbed and cooked to carry it on, the three houses now get government aid and are second to none anywhere: so an expert from the States told me. Preschool children of working mothers spend the day there; they are bathed and fed, napped and amused. If they are sick, they receive hospital care. If they need special diet, it is provided. They are happy and cunning, and as mannerly as all Guatemalans. The mothers, who had to be begged to send their babies at first, now eagerly attend Saturday lectures to learn how to care for them.

This seems to be the only activity of social significance that is considered suitable for a Guatemalan lady. Indeed, it seems inapt to include her in a picture of modern Guatemala, so completely does she belong to the mediæval Church, the Moorish-Spanish tradition of hidden gardens and veiled women. The Indian woman comes nearer our conception of a woman's life. Aside from her household and children, of which there is no lack, she is a merchant or hired worker in her own right and handles her own money. She belongs to the cofradía and may be a shaman. The Ladinas of the lower class, too, run market stalls or shops and are financially independent. It is the lady whose life, now that times are changing, is so oddly out of step.

The grandmother may have been educated abroad and speak several languages, but she knows the literature of none. She goes only to church and to a few homes of intimate friends. Her daughters may order their clothes from Paris or New York, but she wears black and the drooping veil which symbolizes so well the shadowed dignity in which she lives. She is gracious and lovely to meet. She represents peace, a pattern of life that was fixed and beautiful in its finish. But it is finished also in the sense of being done for. Such a way of life can never come again. These ladies know that, whether they admit it or not, and are saddened by the knowledge.

Married daughters may have more outside interests than their mothers, read more, travel more. But the convention of the double standard still exists and goes to surprising lengths. I was invited to an evening of music and talk with a group of modern young intellectuals. The only other woman present was a Guatemalan who had lived in the States. The young men had left their wives at home. Many of a man's most innocent diversions are apart from his wife and family, and every Latin American novel treats of his less innocuous diversions. The wives seem content. Ten or twelve children, even with a nurse apiece, leave no time for repining. But mothers of grown children, still active and rich in experience, with no habit of usefulness outside the home, can only go into an early and sad old age.

The unmarried daughters are suffering through the period we passed thirty years ago. Many of them have to support the family or assist materially about it. They work in stores and offices, libraries and schools. But they have only the right to work, not the independence we think goes with it. They are regarded with pity, if not with apology, and their only social life is of the family, dominated by the mother. Men friends are unthinkable, a scandal.

A woman of thirty allowed a man from the States to escort her, before nine one evening, to a refreshment place on the main street. Before noon next day three agitated friends of her mother called, one by one. Each asked if she was betrothed to the gentleman. No? Then they adjured her, by the memory of her parents, who were indubitably turning in their graves, to be more heedful of her reputation. If the man had been a Guatemalan, I gather, all would have been lost.

Girls just grown are moving along into the future. They may walk out with their young men afternoons, but not evenings. It is in better taste to go to the movies in groups, where they meet, by merest chance, the right young men. They go to dinner dances at Grace Inn, even drive as far as Lake Amatitlán in parties; chaperoned, of course, but the chaperon may be a very young matron indeed. They know what their spinster aunts never divined — that the way to get out of the traditional fix is to step out.

Votes for women have been whispered about, but the murmur died. One woman from Quetzaltenango studied law, but could get no clients. One who studied art in Paris continues to paint in her father's house.

Men, as well as women, are trammeled in Guatemala. Cautious in what they do, they are even more careful of what they say or express in any art. Señor Castillo, who has made such valuable studies of indigenous music, based an opera, *Quiché Winak,* on Indian themes. Unfortunately this opus is seldom performed and I had no chance to hear it. Otherwise there is no musical composition. In painting and in sculpture there is some good work and some very bad, apparently received with equal respect. The outstanding artist is Miguel Garavito, painter of Quetzaltenango, who depicts Indians of Los Altos in their typical garb and at their most picturesque pursuits. Señor Garavito has studied in Paris and is influenced by the later Impressionists. Only in subject-matter is he Guatemalan. Rafael Yela Gunther, who as sculptor ranks alongside Garavito, has vigor and clarity, and he alone of all artists is trying to express the underlying tragedy, the hopeless strain of labor against too great a weight.

Writers are in the most difficult case. Ideas being taboo, they dally with whimsy and fancy. José Arévalo Martínez, when his death was reported several years ago, was hailed in obituaries as one of the finest poets writing in Spanish. Señor Arévalo Martínez has, happily, lived on and continues to produce exquisite poetry, both in verse and in prose. He is probably Guatemala's greatest literary figure. Others write history so remote that its consideration is perfectly safe; or torrid novels about sultry loves in the jungle or in perfumed boudoirs on the Paseo de la Reforma. Some of these tales are amusing; none of them seems to approach, even remotely, a picture of what Guatemalans really are or do. This is particularly true of Indians. The writers are city men or finqueros, educated abroad, trying to write like the French or the British. Indians figure in their books as servants, as typifying gusty tropical passion, or now and then as sad, noble heirs of the Cakchiquel or Quiché glories. If there is a writer who feels the tragic, suppressed surge of his country and tries to express it realistically, his work was not mentioned to me. In all these lines there is lack of any creative blaze. What they do may be good, even excellent; it is always imitative. A relentless censorship allows neither criticism nor free discussion. Consequently there is no national self-consciousness.

Guatemala is a little country, rich in resources, eager to get ahead. She admires anything labeled Progress and adopts or copies it as fast as she can. But she is hobbled, pitifully, by her large illiterate class and muted by fear. Guatemala, at the moment, has nothing to say for herself.

XXVII: The President

As I ROUNDED THE CORNER, A MOTORCYCLE CAVALCADE screamed to a halt in front of the President's mansion. Eight young men with ash-gray faces and red-rimmed, burnt-out eyes rested astride their machines. Then I realized that I was looking at the President's escort and that the brisk, heavy man on the first machine was His Excellency's self: General Jorge Ubico, who has been President of Guatemala for five years, with seven years still to go. In O.D, with varnished brown boots and a tropical helmet, he looked like Theodore Roosevelt. I am told that the President does not object when his admirers remark his resemblance to Napoleon, but I find him more like our athletic President. He stood for a moment in the doorway, an excellent target, and saluted with vigor but no smile before he strode off into the patio. The ash-gray young men were free to go and remove the dust.

The President's house is like any upper-class Guatemalan home with the distinction that all its windows are open, showing spacious rooms stiffly furnished and full of officers. Officers also fill the patio, which shows more cement than flowers. A new presidential mansion is just completed; ugly yellow and in the modern tradition, it has yielded to

Latin exuberance in incongruous white pillars and an ornate bronze entablature over the door.

On the fifth anniversary of his taking office President Ubico had a party. The street in front of his house was closed, strewn with pine needles, and set with chairs where the public might sit to hear the national orchestra. Diplomacy and officialdom went in at all hours. A morning reception. An evening reception. Calling, apparently, between times. Every night fireworks in the park. Typically Latin American, the function ran on for days, and typically Guatemalan, it was quiet, orderly, without spontaneity or fun. Two policemen on every corner are not conducive to unrestrained and ebullient joy.

The President loves motorcycling and often dashes over the roads at a rate that tests his escort and coats them with dust as I had seen. He likes to fish and to hunt. Tireless himself, he wears out everybody. One of his intimates refused all invitations and retired for a week's rest after a short jaunt with the President. On business, General Ubico goes by motor or in his private railroad car. Always his trips are quick, unexpected, and to the point. This President makes no speeches, shakes no hands, kisses no babies. He appears in a town unannounced or when they have ceased to expect him. Then he dashes in without warning, spends an hour examining the books — a chore he does not delegate — and is gone again. He quizzes officials, promotes or fires, demotes or jails. Sometimes he releases from prison people who had not heard why they were there. His whole way is that of a good finquero, who sees to details himself; and a good officer, who exacts obedience.

Jorge Ubico is an upper-class, well-educated Guatemalan of Spanish extraction. He was trained for the army, with special instruction in the United States, where he learned English. He distinguished himself in a border war with Salvador, and, as is the custom in his country, he has held political office as a military man. As military Governor of Alta Vera Paz, in 1907, he improved streets, roads, and bridges, always his pets. He built new schools, markets, and hospitals, insisting upon such hygienic conditions as had never before been seen. He even established a few experimental granges, which apparently got no farther than the experimental stage.

In 1911 Colonel Ubico stood out as the man best fitted to handle the situation in Retalhuleu. Coastal cattle country, that department had too many armed men on horseback with jungles to escape to, Mexico at hand for longer flight, and venal officers. The new Governor, then only about thirty years old, was a man on horseback too, and he demonstrated that malefactors could be caught and laws enforced. Neither wealth nor family position were accepted as extenuating circumstances. Only a few hidalgos had to be set to cleaning the streets to make that clear. Once, they say, the Jefe needed proof that certain coffee beneficios were evading the tax. That night he dressed like a mozo, pulled a disreputable hat over his handsome face, and lolled in a doorway near the warehouse. Before long, men came and offered him a job loading sacks of coffee at midnight. Governor Ubico moved the coffee that night, and in the morning certain honorable gentlemen found themselves under indictment. The tradition is that before the Colonel